Sparkling

THE BEST BOTTLES TO POP
FOR EVERY OCCASION

Wine

KATHERINE COLE
ILLUSTRATIONS BY MERCEDES LEON

Anytime

ABRAMS IMAGE, NEW YORK

CONTENTS

CONTENTS

Life, Bubbly, and the Pursuit of Happiness

Listen up, all you film stars, porn stars, rock stars, and hip-hop stars, collapsing at the Chateau Marmont, lounging on yachts, and chanting lyrics like, "Doses and mimosas, Champagne and cocaine."[1]

Enough already.

Yes, we know the story of Marilyn Monroe bathing in a tub filled with three hundred and fifty bottles' worth of Champagne. And we're aware that $400,000 worth of Perrier-Jouët flowed at the wedding of Kim Kardashian and Kanye West. We have been alerted to the fact that Harrods department store in London sells jewel-encrusted bottles of Champagne for £115,000 each.

Enough.

Sparkling wine's greatest asset may be its image, but sparkling wine's biggest liability is . . . its image.

That image has been, until recently, one of danger and glamour, exclusivity and impossibility. It's time to give that old cliché a rest.

---

[1] *A band called Cherub sings this catchy number.*

As we prepared to send this book out to be printed, that cliché was on its deathbed. The coronavirus outbreak had upended the economy, creating massive uncertainty overnight. As families lost jobs and loved ones, bottles of bubbs did not feel apropos for the moment. The mere notion of popping a pricey Champagne seemed absurd. As the author of a forthcoming tome on sparkling wine, I felt like a tone-deaf violinist, fiddling while Rome burned.

Months prior, of course, when I had been researching and writing this book, it had been an entirely different story. Bubbly wine was au courant. It was riding a wave of popularity, having enjoyed sales growth for more than a decade while demand for other styles remained more or less stagnant.[2]

We were drinking fizz from cans at sporting events! We were guzzling it at our book clubs! There was a Prosecco bus motoring around the UK, a 1972 Citroën H Van named "Celeste" proffering white or pink bubbly all over the US of A, and a mobile bar serving Aperol spritzes in the Hamptons. (You can't, of course, make a proper spritz without Prosecco.)

These sassy little vehicles administering liquid decadence made those of us of modest means feel fancy, much like the bubble-icious foot bath at the pedicure spa, or the creamy foam atop a $7 latte. Whether it was Prosecco from Italy, Cava from Spain, or a funky little fizz from Oregon or New York, it was festive, delicious, and within reach.

And before you declare such past pleasures to have been vapid,

---

[2]   *Razzo, "Exclusive: Sparkling Wine."*

consider the joy that bubbles can bring. One well-known sparkling wine producer I interviewed for this book told me that he attributed his marked uptick in sales over the previous few years to the legalization of gay marriage. (This one's for you, Cole Porter, in the key of F major: How delightful, how delicious, how de-lovely!)

While everyone's second cousin was gleefully guzzling bubbs at PTA meetings and poker nights, sparkling wine was simultaneously establishing a much more serious identity. The next generation of Maker Movement enthusiasts—those twenty-to-thirtysomething purists who knitted their own socks and braided their own beards—had fallen hard for the new wave of "Pét-Nats" (see Ancestral Method, page 24).

These fizzy, goofy, affordable, artisanal bubblies taste like cider and come sealed with crown caps (like beer). They can be utterly charming in their handmade imperfections, like a mismatched collection of hand-thrown pottery tableware. They are the simplest and most traditional of all sparkling wines, throwbacks to the funky juice our great-grandparents vinified in their farm cellars. So as I write this, it feels right to sip Pét-Nat during a quarantine, with

A Quick Fizzy World Tour

(Note: These numbers were collected prior to the coronavirus outbreak and resulting economic recession.)

- Globally, the wine trade is a $35.3 billion industry, with sparkling wine accounting for approximately 18 percent of that.

- The US is by far the biggest importer of sparkling wines, followed by the UK, then Japan, Germany, and Singapore.

- Italy is the top sparkling-wine exporter in volume, thanks to Prosecco, the world's most popular bubbly.

- Financially speaking, France rules. In 2017, France exported $3.5 billion of sparkling wine, Italy $1.5 billion, and Spain $518 million, with Germany and Australia rounding out the top five.[3]

---

[3] *Data courtesy of* Wine by Numbers, *an annual and quarterly report published by the Italian trade group Unione Italiana Vini.*

Occasions and Food Matches

Sparkling wine is no longer merely the realm of mimosas and special occasions. You need not be wearing a tuxedo and spooning caviar onto blinis in order to enjoy it. In fact, as Instagram will attest, bubbles make anything fried—*pommes frites* are my fave—better, and they love potato chips and popcorn.

In short, sparkling wine can and should, in fact, be drunk any day, anytime, with food or without.

If you demand pairing suggestions, however, here's a quick primer.

- For an apéritif, serve Brut Zero Champagne (see page 22 for more on this).
- Prosecco complements light, sweet-and-spicy fare like sushi or the kimchi bowl I'm inhaling as I type this (now where did that Prosecco go?).
- Crémant from the Loire goes gangbusters with goat cheese and is my go-to lunch wine.
- Lambrusco loves a salumi platter or a pasta dish. A pink Lambrusco is a late-afternoon pleasure.
- Riesling Sekt from Germany can offer a crisp counterbalance to rich foods like potatoes, sausages, or cream sauces.
- Good Champagne wants to be alongside something roasted, whether it be a bird or a vegetable.
- As for dessert, serve Moscato with cookies and fruit.

Or, forget all that and drink sparkling wine, anytime, with anything.

one's unwashed, uncolored hair in a messy bun, wearing no bra. (Figuratively speaking, of course.)

On the higher end, the image-driven Champers labels stocked in airport duty-free boutiques were losing ground as the new wave of cerebral wine aficionados expressed their earnest admiration for the Champagne "growers." These are the small-scale craftspeople of northeastern France who labor in small vineyard plots and chilly farm cellars rather than mounting bedazzled marketing blitzes. They make truly vinous wines, for contemplating, discussing, and tasting.

In short, just as the world took a serious turn, so, too, did sparkling wine. And so I feel hopeful. And not just because I've got to sell books. But because the quality and availability of sparkling wine have never been better. And because bubbly is a tangible and—yes—simple pleasure. In an era of iPad menus, Instagram food porn, Spotify playlists, virtual-reality goggles, and augmented-reality experiences, fizz delivers a full-on 3-D interactive feast for the senses, right here and right now.

Satisfying aromatics. Subtle flavors. The pop of the cork, the whisper of the pour, the sizzle of the foam, the ascent of the bubbles in the glass. The cool sweat beads around the ice bucket. The crunch of ice. Sparkling wine is real.

And no matter how technologically advanced society becomes, no human will ever tire of the incomparable thrill of thousands of tiny bubbles pricking one's palate and exploding with flavor. It's the grown-up version of catching snowflakes on one's tongue. It will never get old.

And you know what? For centuries—perhaps even millennia—sparkling wine has ridden history's high and low points, through wartime and prosperity. (More on this in Chapter 3.) At the end of the fighting and the grieving, there has always been reason to celebrate. And there always will be.

So maybe the rules have changed. Maybe richer isn't better anymore (thank goodness), and maybe sparkling wine needn't be a symbol of moral perversion any longer. Instead, maybe bubbles should be an inalienable right. Maybe everyone who can healthfully drink wine deserves to feel that pinprick precision, that refreshing acidity, that lovely lingering finish, that shot at a moment of happiness.

Maybe everyone should have access to sparkling wine—or, OK, sparkling juice, for my teetotaling friends and charming children—anytime.

So let's clink glasses. Here's to health, long life, and fizz-fueled happiness. And now, I'm going to open a bottle of bubbly.

About This Book

There are thousands upon thousands of sparkling wines in this world. I tasted hundreds upon hundreds during my nine frantic months of research and writing. I had to make some excruciating decisions to narrow down the choices to just a few.

I am, admittedly, a biased individual, possibly to the point of insufferability. I know that I have blind spots. That's why I asked a group of the experts I admire most—critics, sommeliers, journalists, importers, and retailers—to spill on some of their favorites in each chapter. Please reach out and thank these good people on social media if one of their suggestions turns out to be a winner with you and yours.

To all those excellent sparkling wines out there that *didn't* make it into these pages, I love you. I really do. But I maybe chose to recommend another wine from your region because it was more widely available, or more historically significant, or represented a price tier that needed to be included, or it garnered more group votes in a blind tasting. We're still friends, right?

And while I aimed for consistency in the manner in which the chapters were broken up,

ultimately I had to go with what made the most sense. If one nation gets two chapters, while another takes up only a fraction of one chapter, and you happen to live in an underrepresented nation, I am sorry. I don't know what to say, other than, "Make more sparkling wine! And export more sparkling wine!"

On to vintages. Unlike most other wine styles, bubbly is often not vintage-dated. The winemaker aims to achieve the same "house style" each year by blending wines from multiple harvests. I have noted next to each wine, with a V or an NV, whether it is a vintage or non-vintage wine. NV wines will taste similar year to year, but a vintage-dated wine might taste different by the time you get this book, because a new year, and thus a new growing season, will be represented on store shelves.

The alcohol percentage is provided for each wine to give you a guideline of the style. Champagnes tend to be around 12% alcohol by volume (ABV). Sparkling sweet wines are often lower in alcohol, say, in the 8% range. And bubblies from warmer wine regions might be as high as 13.5%. If, say, you find Champagne and Prosecco to be too flimsy and light-bodied for your taste, you might want to look for a bubbly from the US of A, where alcohol percentages tend to tip a bit higher.

I have tried to keep the technical terminology to a minimum. But there are some words and phrases that just come up a lot in regard to sparkling wine. Chapter 1, and the Glossary, will define those words for you (see pages 15 and 274). But in my wine recommendations in the following chapters, I purposefully steer clear of insider jargon. It is not your job to know what "reductive aromas" are. It is my job to describe those aromas in words that you understand.

Last but not least, where can you find these wines? In our world of app-driven consumerism, there are a few transactions that are best done in person. On page 280, you'll find a short list of online wine retailers, but I'd also encourage you to bring this book to your local bottle shop. If a wine that has caught your eye isn't available in your area, a good merchant can track down something similar that is. If you visit your local wine purveyor often enough, he or she will get to know your palate and let you know when something that fits your price range and tastes is available.

Now, let's pop some corks, shall we?

PRICE GUIDE

One wine can be represented by multiple importers, wholesalers, and retailers, all over the nation, each charging a different price, depending on a number of factors. In the following pages, I have calculated the average retail price of each wine and then categorized it according to the following tiers. →

$	=	$0–$15
$$	=	$15–$25
$$$	=	$25–$50
$$$$	=	$50–$75
$$$$$	=	$75+

Please note that prices may have changed between the dates of research and publication.

Instructions for Achieving Effervescence

If you bought this book just because you thought it would look good on your coffee table, that's cool. I get it. Mercedes Leon's illustrations are genius. Just flip through, enjoy the artwork, and move on with your life.

You are not required to read this chapter. It will be confusing. Terms that you may have never read or heard before will come up. (You can always refer to the Glossary, pages 274–279, for their definitions.) So proceed with caution. But if you are really, truly curious as to how sparkling wine is made, I wrote this chapter just for you. You may, in fact, be the only person who actually reads it. But if you are, like I am, awestruck by the idea that every bottle of Champagne has gone through its own miniature fermentation—a living storm, captured in glass— you'll appreciate knowing the nitty-gritty details of this miraculous process.

In the Vineyard

Let's start off in the vineyard. You like your summer strawberries to be as ripe and flavorful as possible, and likewise, most vinetenders prune back their plants with the aim of producing less fruit with more rich flavor and tannins concentrated in each grape.

Sparkling winegrowers, by contrast, allow more fruit to hang on each vine than they would for still wine. The end goals are freshness and acidity rather than sweetness.

By the same reasoning, bubblemakers harvest earlier than they would for still wine, because the longer the fruit hangs on the vine, the higher the sugar content. (Again, sweetness and ripeness are not the goals here.) A typical sparkling-wine harvest date might be early to mid-September (or March, if you're in the Southern Hemisphere), but this varies widely depending on the vineyard location and weather conditions.

Hand-harvesting predominates in sparkling-wine regions. Machine harvesters grab individual grapes rather than whole bunches, and they tend to tear the skins, thus coloring the juice with pigment. The world's top-three grape varieties for bubbly are Pinot Noir, Chardonnay, and Pinot Meunier. The two Pinots have purple skins, but they can make white sparkling wine as long as the grapes are hand-harvested, handled gently, and pressed as whole clusters.[1]

To maintain acidity levels and avoid the possibility of unintentional coloration of the juice, the fresh-picked fruit should be cold and firm rather than warm and squishy. Thus, many wineries harvest in the wee hours of the morning and refrigerate the grapes after picking them. They may also collect grape clusters in unusually small plastic bins, each about the size of two shoeboxes, to minimize the chance of the delicate fruit being crushed under its own weight.

Now we'll walk through the four primary methods for vinifying the four basic styles of sparkling wine. Every winemaker follows a different protocol, but I've outlined the most common procedures. We'll delve into the most detail with the traditional method and then discover the ways in which the other techniques differ.

Alors, allons y!

---

[1] *That said, some sparkling wines are red. Also mechanical harvesting technology is getting more and more precise each year.*

Traditional Method

This is the way sparkling wine is made in Champagne, where it's sometimes called *méthode champenoise*. In other parts of France, it's referred to as *méthode traditionnelle*, and in Italy, and Spain and Portugal, it's known as *metodo classico* and *método tradicional*. The key takeaway here is the bubbles that the second fermentation produces happen inside a sealed bottle . . . but I get ahead of myself.

PRESS HOUSES: The biggest *maisons* purchase fruit from all over Champagne. Rather than subject the delicate grapes to long, bumpy truck rides, during which skins could break and juice could be exposed to potential hazards such as—*mon dieu!*—pigment or oxygen, large Champagne houses typically press their fruit at centralized processing facilities, strategically located in numerous villages throughout the region. In most cases, these "press houses" are simply small wineries, vinifying their own wine while also pressing juice for others.

SEPARATING THE LOTS: The top-quality *maisons* keep separate the fruit of different grape varieties as well as grapes from different villages and, sometimes, different vineyards and even blocks of vines. This makes for a more precise blending process later on. In some cases, a single lot will be bottled on its own as a single-vineyard wine.

PRESSING: Ultra-gentle pressing will ensure that no color is extracted from the skins. The goal is, as the Oregon sparkling winemaker Andrew Davis[2] explains it, "to pop the berry, not squash the berry." As for equipment, there are many different styles of presses, including:

1. The traditional basket press, which looks like a barrel with loose slats. The grape bunches are gradually tamped down, and the juice spills through the slats.

2. A pneumatic press, in which a large rubber balloon-like bladder slowly inflates inside a perforated tank, smashing the grapes against the sides while the juice trickles out through the holes.

3. The lateral hydraulic press, in which two metal plates, arranged in a V shape, slowly close

---

[2] *Davis, owner of the Radiant Sparkling Wine Company in the Willamette Valley, was my technical consultant for this chapter.*

together. It's so sensitive that it can squeeze ripe grapes while leaving the unripe berries intact.

STAGES OF PRESSING:

While pressing, the winemaker captures the juice in chronological stages, or "cuts." The first 80 percent of the liquid that streams from the press comes from the softest, purest part of the pulp. Highest in both sugar and acidity, it's called the *cuvée*.[3] It starts out as "free-run" juice, which flows from the press from the weight of the fruit alone, and finishes with very gentle pressing. Some producers believe that the midpoint of this stage elicits the most flavorful juice—in essence, this is the pure pulp part—so they vinify this separately. It's called the *cœur*, or the "heart." The last push of pressure squeezes the firmest, innermost pulp, closest to the seeds and skins. This last 20 percent, called the *taille* (or "tail"), is tannic, and can be useful for winemakers looking to bring texture to a blend. It's not as age-worthy as the *cœur* due to its lower acidity, so it tends to crop up more in non-vintage wines.

SETTLING AND RACKING:

Overnight, the juice rests in a tank and an initial layer of sediment settles to the bottom. To clarify the wine, the vintner opens a spigot and siphons the clear juice at the top into another tank or barrel, leaving the gunk at the bottom. This procedure is called *racking*.

PRIMARY FERMENTATION:

Thanks to the magical properties of yeast, the sugar in the juice will now convert into alcohol. If the winemaker adds commercial yeast to speed this step along and control the resulting aromatics, fermentation takes approximately ten days or fewer. If the winemaker prefers to allow indigenous or native[4] yeasts to do the work, it could take much longer. The resulting *vin clair*, or the *base wine* in English, should not be more than about 10 to 11% alcohol by volume (ABV),[5] since too much alcohol is toxic to yeast, and the secondary fermentation still needs to happen. The base wine should be bracingly high in acid, but still pleasant to taste.

SETTLING, PART DEUX:

The *vin clair* sits for a couple of weeks so that the spent yeast cells,

---

[3] *Confusingly, the word* cuvée *also means "blend." This is part of the worldwide conspiracy to make wine incomprehensible to all but the most insufferable human beings.*

[4] *That is, naturally occurring yeasts that can be found floating around vineyards and wineries.*

[5] *A typical table wine these days is 12 to 15% alcohol by volume.*

About Fermentation 1.5

Bubbly is generally said to be the result of a "secondary fermentation." But this isn't quite the full story, because there's an optional mini-ferment—called malolactic, ML, or simply malo—after the first fermentation. By converting prickly malic acid (think lemons) into smooth lactic acid (think milk),[6] malolactic fermentation can stabilize the wine and give it a soft, creamy mouthfeel. Bubblemakers going for a fresh, fruity style, however, might choose to suppress this step by chilling their tanks down.

A few decades ago in Champagne, when excessive conventional fertilizer use peaked, grape production was so high as to make for lean fruit with through-the-roof acidity levels. Some big houses started promoting malolactic fermentation to soften up their spiky wines.

These days, farming methods are less intrusive, and more winemakers are letting nature take its course. "If it happens, it happens," many small growers in Champagne told me with a shrug. "Some barrels go through it spontaneously, but most barrels don't."

There are two reasons for this. First, malolactic bacteria don't like high-acid environments, and one of the basic tenets of sparkling winemaking is: Start with high-acid grapes. Second, malo can't happen in a cold tank, and sparkling winemakers tend to be working either with refrigerated tanks or in just dang cold places: The average temperature of a cellar in Champagne is between 48 and 54 degrees Fahrenheit (9 and 12 degrees Celsius). Brrr!

Sounds simple enough to let the fates decide whether to malo or not to malo, but wine insiders continue to debate the issue. If I had to pick a side, I'd say it's best to let the growing region dictate the decision. The wine importer Kermit Lynch tells me that he believes ML to be essential in taming the lean, mean grapes of Champagne, for example, saying, "That malic acid is mean stuff, the enemy of swallowability, the enemy of finesse." Meanwhile, cult winemaker Michael Cruse, working with much more opulent fruit in California, tells me, "We don't block malo, but we ask it really nicely to stop." Who's right? I have a hunch they both are.

---

[6] *If you're lactose intolerant, worry not: Lactose and lactic acid are two different things. So yes, you can keep drinking wine.*

THE TRADITIONAL METHOD,
STEP BY STEP

aka Méthode Champenoise; Metodo Classico; Méthode Cap Classique; Traditional Method. Makes Cava; Champagne; Crémant; Franciacorta.

 → → 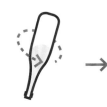 →

BASE WINE

Initial complete fermentation makes a flat wine. Often, multiple vintages are blended to make the final base wine.

LIQUEUR DE TIRAGE + BOTTLE AGING

Wine is bottled, and sugar and yeast are added. Wine ages for many months (or years).

AGING + RIDDLING

A second fermentation traps CO_2 in the liquid. The bottle is slowly rotated, to capture the spent yeast cells in the neck.

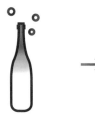 →  →

ABV 11–13%

DISORGEMENT

The neck of the bottle is frozen. The bottle is uncorked and the yeast pops out.

DOSAGE

Sugar solution may be added to make a bone-dry wine more approachable.

CORKING + LABELING

A strong bottle and cork are required to contain the high pressure exerted by the CO_2. The bubbles are small but intense and forceful.

or *lees*, fall to the bottom of the tank or barrel again. Now comes the second racking. In French, this step is called *soutirage*.

BLENDING: It's time to blend the finished base wines together to achieve the desired flavor profile. And often in sparkling winemaking, this is a blend from more than one vintage year. A non-vintage (NV) cuvée utilizes the barrel's relative ripeness or raciness of reserve wines from previous years to achieve a balanced finished product that's consistent with the house style of the winery. Even for single-vintage wines, blending typically still happens, as the various blocks of vines, vinified separately in an array of casks and/or tanks, will have made wines with differing aromatics and flavor profiles.

CLARIFYING: Filtering to remove any remaining yeast cells and bacteria renders the base wine a true *vin clair* at this point. It's also customary to *fine* the wine—that is, add, and then remove, a coagulating agent like gelatin that acts like a magnet, attracting loose particles. Next, the winemaker adds a stabilizing agent or else chills the liquid to approximately 23°F (5°C) for a week until the tartrate crystals fall to the bottom of the tank. (Not only are tartrate crystals distracting, but they also can cause a sparkling wine to erupt in a foam explosion, drenching you and everyone else in your vicinity when you pop the cork.)

BOTTLING: The wine is now bottled for the second fermentation.

LIQUEUR DE TIRAGE: The winemaker dissolves sugar in a small amount of liquid (typically a bit of *vin clair*), adds yeast to this slurry and encourages it to start growing, then dilutes it with more base wine to confirm that the fermentation is hearty. A bit of this sweet, semi-fermenting *liqueur de tirage*, added to each bottle, will send the rest of the *vin clair* over the edge into full-blown fermentation Part Deux.

CAPPING OR CORKING: Each individual bottle is now sealed, typically with a crown cap, like you'd find on a bottle of beer or an old-fashioned soda.[7] Bubblemakers tasked with turning out gazillions of bottles can make life a little easier for themselves by altering their *liqueur de tirage* a bit and popping little encapsulated

---

[7] *I could geek out here about the permeability of various crown cap rubber gaskets, which may or may not let microscopic amounts of oxygen seep into the wine, but I won't.*

yeast-and-alginate[8] pills into a polyethylene crown-cap insert, called a *bidule*, that will be easy-peasy to remove later. On the other end of the spectrum, more artisanal producers might swear by the advantages of a natural cork over a crown cap. If the cork is used, it is held in place by a giant staple called an *agrafe*.

SECONDARY FERMENTATION: The *liqueur de tirage* gets fermentation going again, with the yeast metabolizing the sugar. There's nowhere for the byproduct of fermentation—carbon dioxide—to go in the stopped-up bottle, so like a child suppressing his emotions in kindergarten class (only to have a temper tantrum when he gets home), it is absorbed. When you open the bottle, out comes the CO_2 tantrum, in the foamy form of tiny, angry bubbles.

BOTTLE AGING: Non-vintage Champagne must now rest in the bottle *en tirage*, or *sur lie*—that is, with the spent yeast, or lees—for a minimum of fifteen months. Vintage Champagne must bottle-age for a minimum of three years. *Crémants* (traditional-method sparkling wines from French regions other than Champagne) must sit for nine months. This downtime is key, because the death and decomposition (sounds so morbid!)

of the spent yeast cells, called *autolysis*, bring savory flavors and silky mouthfeel to the wine.

RIDDLING: No one wants a bunch of white gunk floating around in their wine, but lees are as impossible to wrangle as the flakes in a snow globe. *Remuage*, or "riddling," is the most effective way to settle and capture them. Each bottle is stored tilting downward, at an angle, and twisted a fraction of a turn each day until all the lees have settled into the neck. Very traditional houses have a master riddler (*remueur*) on staff, who spends his days in a dark cellar, carefully turning thousands of bottles, bit by bit. (In his spare time, he moonlights as a flamboyant, puzzle-obsessed supervillain.) There are also automated riddling machines—generally referred to by the brand name of the best-known producer, Gyropalette—that look like big metal cages set at a really odd angle.

NECK FREEZING: In preparation for disgorgement, the bottles are placed neck-down in a disk-shaped tray that looks like a giant pie crust that some mischievous person has poked a pencil eraser into 240 times. Underneath this tray is a cistern filled with glycol (a liquid substance that can chill to low temperatures without freezing) or a salt-brine solution at approximately −4 to −16 degrees Fahrenheit (−20 to −27 degrees Celsius). The bottles turn in this slurry for approximately ten minutes, transforming the yeast in the neck of each bottle into a solid chunk of ice.

DISGORGEMENT: Now it's time to pop the top off each bottle and get rid of that yeast blob. If the neck was frozen, a machine yanks the cap off each bottle, and along with the cap comes the *bidule*, which now holds the chunk of frozen yeast. Hand disgorgement is far more exciting. It's most commonly practiced on oversize bottles that don't fit in the winery's machinery or on limited-edition wines. The cellar master uses a tool that looks a bit like a bent metal barbecue fork with a wooden handle to pop the cap off, and the yeast comes flying out—*à la volée*, as the French say—in a rush of foam.

DOSAGE: Champagnes can be incredibly acidic without a *dosage* of sugar solution, otherwise known as the *liqueur de expédition*.

---

[8] *Alginate is, basically, seaweed, but it doesn't actually end up in your wine! It's a coagulating agent that's just there temporarily to get the lees to glom together and behave. This process is called fining. It already happened once, in the tank, during the Clarifying step (see page 19).*

Storing and Aging Sparkling Wine

Should you age your sparkling wine, and if so, for how long? A good rule of thumb is: The more expensive the bubbly, the longer it can probably age. A very fine vintage Champagne might be best after a couple of decades in your cellar, while a cheap Prosecco should be drunk the moment you get it home from the grocery store.

Some pundits claim that bubbly should be stored vertically, but from personal experience I can assure you that Champagne will do just fine stored sideways. That said, Champagne bottles tend to be too fat for some wooden racks, and might require a rearranging of the shelves in your wine cooler.

As with any other wine, sparkling wine will age best if it's kept cool and still in a fairly humid, dark spot. As long as it isn't next to a heating vent, a storage room in a basement and the bottom of a closet are both appropriate. A trampoline in a Phoenix, Arizona, backyard is not a good option. But you knew that.

The Bubble Standard (of Sweetness)

The addition of the *liqueur de dosage* is the final, quick step in a long, complicated winemaking process, but it can make a major difference in the flavor and mouthfeel of the finished sparkling wine, depending on how much sugar is in the *dosage*. Thus, it's helpful to learn the lingo of sweetness-to-dryness that you'll see on sparkling-wine labels.

Confusingly, a dry *still* wine contains little to no sugar, while a dry *sparkling* wine is semisweet. And while most consumers believe that the term "Brut" connotes dryness, Brut bubblies actually get a decent *dosage* to counterbalance the high acidity in the wine.

Today, Brut Zero, aka Brut Nature, wines are increasing in popularity. Because these no-*dosage* wines stand alone—bare and naked, not propped up by a sugar addition—they are thought to be a testament to the quality of the farming and the fruit. But be warned, people: Austere Brut Zeros can be tough to match with food and are typically best served as an apéritif.

Also worthy of note is the fairly new "Ice" category of Champagne. This gets about forty-five to sixty grams of sugar per liter, putting it in the Demi-Sec to Doux category. The bottles are inevitably opaque and printed with bold metallic patterns, looking like Christmas presents. They're popular in nightclubs, where they are served over ice.

In my personal tasting adventures, I have found that my Champagne happy place is Extra-Brut. It's a minimalist style that allows one to taste the true flavor of the base wine (and in fact, some Extra-Bruts have no *dosage* at all—they're just labeled as such because they have a certain intrinsic richness), but it's not so dry as to feel like ascetic self-denial.

Here's a quick rundown of the various *dosage* sugar levels and their corresponding terms:

Brut Zero/Brut Nature:	0–3 G/L
Extra-Brut:	3–6 G/L
Brut:	6–12 G/L
Extra-Dry/Extra-Sec:	12–17 G/L
Dry/Sec:	17–32 G/L
Demi-Sec:	32–50 G/L
Doux (Sweet):	50+ G/L

Most consumers prefer their bubbles "Brut," with a *dosage* that comes out to about 1 to 2 grams of sugar per glass (which isn't all that much). For more on levels of sweetness, see the opposite page.

JETTING: Just prior to corking, some producers shoot CO_2-rich wine foam into the neck space of the bottle as a preservative measure, to deter oxygen from sneaking in. The wine will look like any other, but the neck space will be filled with CO_2 rather than oxygen.

CORKING: Now a machine crams ultrawide corks into the narrow bottle necks, where they are corseted to the point that they mushroom out over the top, making for an über-tight seal. This ensures that the liquid inside the bottle will stay where it's supposed to instead of erupting spontaneously like a volcano. A *muselet*, or wire cage, is popped on top and twisted in place. Finally, the bottle gets a quick turn, to mix the *dosage* in with the wine.

Now, let's look at a more old-fashioned way to make wine.

Bubble Agents: Bubblemakers for Hire

In wine regions where the conditions are right, it's a no-brainer for a winery to offer a sparkling option as part of its lineup. Bubbly can bring variety to wine-club box shipments and tasting-room offerings. Wineries are also popular wedding venues, and can make nice little margins on direct-to-consumer sales of festive fizz.[9]

But few family wineries can afford to purchase a gyroscopic riddling machine, or a specially equipped bottling machine, or the sorts of pressurized tanks that are used for making Prosecco.

Thankfully, a new trend has taken hold in American wine country: centralized "custom-crush" sparkling winemaking facilities. These businesses invest in all the necessary equipment, and their specialized winemakers riddle and bottle bubbly all year round for multiple labels.

A sparkling wine finished at a custom-crush facility isn't necessarily any less compelling than one that was entirely home-grown. The base wine is everything. Start with delicious grapes, and you'll end up with delicious bubbly.

---

[9] *Wineries otherwise have fairly low margins, due to the cuts taken by wholesalers and retailers.*

Ancestral Method

Trend alert: *Méthode ancestrale* aka *Pétillant Naturel*, or *Pétillant Originel*, is the *très chic* wine style du jour. But it's actually a very old, time-honored method.

As you'll learn in the next chapter, not until the seventeenth century did anyone add sugar and recork a bottle to induce a secondary fermentation. Before then, sparkling wine was made by—knowingly or unknowingly—simply sealing wine in a container before its primary fermentation had finished.

The resulting beverage tends to be lower in alcohol, and often sweeter, than *méthode traditionnelle* bubbly, since in many cases it's still partly juice. Unless, that is, the vintner has managed to coax the wine into completely finishing its fermentation in its new airtight quarters.

So: no *liqueur de tirage*, no secondary fermentation, no *dosage*. Here are some other ways in which the process is a little different.

CHILLING OR FILTRATION: The earliest sparkling wines were made by happenstance when cold temperatures naturally halted

Why Wines Bubble

Your sparkling wine doesn't, in fact, sparkle until you've opened it. Until then, the carbon dioxide is dissolved in the liquid and held under intense pressure. When the cork is removed, the pressure equalizes with that of the air, and the CO_2 rushes up in the form of bubbles. Even more surprising is the fact that bubbles only express themselves because they have something to stick to, and what they stick to is, to oversimplify, microscopic dust molecules. According to Gérard Liger-Belair, a professor of chemical physics at the University of Reims Champagne-Ardenne, a glass that has been scrubbed clean by an acid bath will exhibit no bubbles at all, and the carbon dioxide will invisibly escape through the smooth surface of the wine.[10] So if your glasses are dusty from sitting in your cupboards for too long, don't rinse them off—pour Champagne instead!

---

[10] *Liger-Belair, Uncorked, 44.*

THE ANCESTRAL METHOD,
STEP BY STEP

aka Méthode ancestrale. Makes Pétillant Naturel; goes by the nickname Pét-Nat," Pétillant Originel

BASE WINE

The base wine is often a murky gold or pink color as winemakers tend to use ultra-traditional methods and equipment, with no filtering.

DISRUPTING FERMENTATION

Fermentation halts in response to chilling. The partially fermented wine is bottled and corked.

ABV
6–12%

SIMPLE BOTTLE FERMENTATION

Fermentation completes inside the sealed bottle. There is no second fermentation.

CLEAR OR CLOUDY

Disgorgement is optional. Many Pét-Nats are cloudy because the yeast was never removed.

MINIMALIST BOTTLE + CAP

The resulting wine is low-pressure, with large, soft bubbles. As with beer, a thin-walled bottle and crown cap suffice.

fermentation, and the wines were bottled before the job could finish. To make this happen on command, the winemaker can chill the still-fermenting wine to 50°F (10°C) or below in a refrigerated tank.

(NON)DISGORGEMENT: The disgorgement stage is optional with Pét-Nats, because many consumers like these old-fashioned wines to have a rustic look and texture. So the more naturally inclined winemakers send their Pét-Nats to market without removing the lees. The resulting wines are cloudy, cidery, and borderline chewy—not, in short, everyone's cup of tea.

Tank Method

This is also called the Charmat method, *Metodo Italiano* (Italian method), Martinotti method, or bulk method, depending on whom you think deserves credit for inventing it. It's how most Prosecco[11] is made, and while it does involve a secondary fermentation, said fermentation does not happen in a bottle.

HEAVY (ON) METAL: Where traditional- and ancestral-method bubblemakers might opt to ferment their base wines in wooden casks, concrete tanks, barrels, steel tanks, or a combination thereof, mainstream Prosecco pretty much always does both fermentations in steel tanks, making it a full-throttle "submarine" wine (see page 28).

FILTRATION AND/OR CLARIFICATION: These steps might be optional in other sparkling winemaking regimes, but mainstream Prosecco is all about clarity and, as such, is almost always filtered and/or clarified.

TIRAGE: The *liqueur de tirage* is dumped en masse right into a tank called an *autoclave* (see below).

AUTOCLAVE: The secondary fermentation happens in a hermetically sealed tank called an autoclave or *cuve close*.

TIME IN TANK: The longer a wine lies on its lees after the second fermentation, the finer and firmer the bubbles will be as they rise to the top of your glass. Low-pressure *frizzante* wines, like Moscato d'Asti, spend only about twenty days on the lees in tank, while more complex, fully sparkling *spumante* Proseccos spend three to six months there. A Champagne, by contrast, can spend years bottle-aging on the lees, during which it develops an elegant *mousse* (the French term for the foam).

FINAL CLARIFICATION: In order to remove the spent yeast from the second fermentation, the winemaker needn't go to the trouble of riddling and disgorging thousands of individual bottles since the wine is in one big tank. Still, Prosecco is a fresh, clean style of wine, so multiple steps are taken, including isobarometric (pressurized) filtration at bottling, to ensure clarity.

RELEASE: Many of the better Prosecco producers bottle on

THE TANK METHOD, STEP BY STEP

aka Charmat Method; Cuve Close; Metodo Italiano.
Makes most Lambrusco; Mousseux; Prosecco.

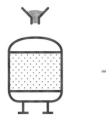

BASE WINE

The first fermentation makes a flat wine. Settling, racking, fining, and filtering are all steps taken to ensure clarity. Wines from various vineyard and harvest dates are blended to make the base wine.

ADDITIONS + 2ND FERMENTATION

Sugar and yeast are added to the finished wine, which is sealed in a pressurized tank for the second fermentation.

ABV
10–12%

CLARIFICATION

Of all the sparkling wine styles, consumers expect Prosecco to be the clearest and cleanest to look at. Multiple filtration processes ensure translucency, with no tartrate crystals.

SUGAR ADDITION

Even when it's labeled "Brut," Prosecco tends to be slightly sweeter than other sparkling wines. A bit more sugar is added during the *dosage* stage.

MEDIUM-WEIGHT BOTTLE + CAP

A medium-weight bottle and standard wine cork or crown cap are sufficient for the medium-pressure finished wine, although a wire cage and Champagne-style cork are often used.

demand to ensure that their wine is as fresh as possible when it hits store shelves. The release date is often printed on the label.

[11] *An obvious exception being* col fondo, *Prosecco country's take on Pét-Nat, which is made via a secondary bottle fermentation, with no filtration or disgorgement.*

Submarines vs. Galleons

Are you a naval officer or a pirate when it comes to sparkling wine? If you love Prosecco, you travel by submarine. If you are drawn to a Cava that's big and brassy, you roll in galleons.

Allow me to elaborate: Sparkling winemaking can (arguably) be broken into two paths: *reductive* and *oxidative*. Reductive winemaking takes place in airtight steel tanks and makes for fresh, crisp, fruity wines. Oxidative winemaking happens in oak fermenters and barrels and makes for round, soft, mellow wines.

(Disclaimer: I'm painting with a broad brush here. There are plenty of wineries that utilize a combination of reductive and oxidative techniques.)

Prosecco is a classic reductive wine, because it's made in pressurized steel tanks that are essentially the Instant Pots of winemaking. The resulting wines can be deliciously fresh, crisp, and fruity, and precise, as clean-cut as a naval officer.

Oxidative wines, on the other hand, are character-rich, peg-legged pirates. They might show signs of oak-barrel aging, and they might be a little wild and flamboyant. The winemaker might prefer to use a basket press and a wooden fermenter because these expose the juice to more oxygen during vinification.

I go back and forth, myself. I like brassy, oaky, oxidative sparkling wine when I'm feeling indulgent, and a crisp and precise bubbly when I'm feeling focused. It's hard not to root for hunky hero Denzel Washington in *Crimson Tide*—"Captain, I cannot concur!"—but one has to admit, there would never be a dull moment in the company of Captain Jack Sparrow.

For more on this concept, as well as Champagnes of each type, see page 71.

Transfer Method

This is a variation on the traditional method, also called *transversage*, in which all the hoo-ha with riddling and disgorgement gets skipped because the bottles are oversized—1.5-liter magnums, for example—and thus too big for the standard riddling and disgorgement equipment. Instead, the cellar workers open all the bottles and dump the frothy wine into a tank, where they rack and filter it, add the *dosage*, and then re-bottle it.

Carbonation

Yes, friends: It *is* possible to shoot CO_2 into a tank of wine, bottle it, and sell it for a song. It is soda pop with an elevated alcohol level, and it's often sold in cans (see page 43). There may be one or two examples of it in this book, but I can't say I'm a fan.

How to Serve Your Bubbs

TEMPERATURE: The best way to judge the quality of a nice cold sparkling wine is to allow it to reach room temperature. There's pleasure in following the progression of a fine Champagne as it warms and its aromatics unfurl, even if the bubbles dissipate and flatten with the exposure to warmth and oxygen. Not-so-good bubbly, on the other hand, starts to stick out awkwardly above about 60°F (15.5°C), increasingly tasting like a giraffe wrapped in tin foil. (You know: gawky, awkward, tinny, and maybe a little feral, furry, and

fleshy.) So keep cheap fizz in an ice bucket when you're not pouring. And speaking of ice buckets, to most efficiently chill down a bottle, plunge it into a bucket that's filled partially with ice and partially with water. After about fifteen minutes, you'll be good to go. And if you are setting your wine fridge temperature for optimum sparkling enjoyment, the CIVC, or the official Champagne board, recommends 47–50°F (8–10°C)

THE ART OF CORK REMOVAL: A sparkling-wine cork is a projectile, as unpredictable as one of Kim Jong-un's long-range missiles. Step one is grabbing a towel, and step two is turning away from fragile light fixtures, your Hummel figurine collection, and people you like, if even just nominally. Start by peeling the foil off to reveal the cork. Then, with one hand over the top, use your other hand to twist the wire and remove the cage. Now, *slowly* turn the bottle one direction while *gently* twisting the cork the other way, rocking it back and forth a bit if it feels stuck. In the trade, we aim to open sparkling wines "as quietly as a nun passing gas," but we don't always succeed. Whether the cork comes out with a dry hiss or a sudsy pop (in which case the towel will be needed), call it a win if it doesn't go flying across the room and knock your dog senseless.

GLASSWARE: No clunky medieval chalices, please; thin-walled crystal stemware offers the best visual and aromatic experience. And there's no need to purchase a specially shaped wineglass just for bubbly. Tall, narrow flutes are elegant and sized for portion control, and their troughs are sometimes engraved with circles that cause the bubbles to rise to the surface in perfect rings. But you can't fully appreciate a sparkling wine's aroma and flavor from such a small opening. At the opposite end of the spectrum, the saucer-shaped coupe, said to be modeled after one of Marie Antoinette's breasts,[12] is decadent and fun, but its wide, flat top is prone to spillage, unsuited for dishwashers, and does nothing to channel aromatics to your proboscis. Serious connoisseurs prefer the glasses used to serve still Chardonnay or Pinot Noir in upscale restaurants, in either a rounded balloon shape or an oversize tulip shape. But a standard wineglass works just fine.

---

[12]   *In more recent times, supermodels Claudia Schiffer and Kate Moss have both bravely bared their breasts for the cause of glassware design.*

Frothing Plot Points in History

If we look closely enough, sparkling wine permeates human history, from modern society's Neolithic beginnings to the Second World War era. The story of sparkling wine is one of innovation and adaptation.

The First Fizz

Imagine—god forbid—being spirited back nine thousand years to a time before iPhones, showers, Ubers, and avocado toast. The thought of it is enough to drive a person to drink, which is why I'd want my animal-skin-draped self in the village of Jiahu, in Henan Province, China.

Because those Jiahus did Neolithic living *right*. They dined lavishly on rice and millet, wild boar and venison, fish and eggs, pears and apricots, acorns and water chestnuts. They wrote in proto characters, much superior to your standard petroglyphs, and played catchy tunes on bone flutes.

Most important of all, they drank the world's earliest known alcoholic tipple, a wine-beer hybrid composed of grapes, hawthorn-fruit, honey, and rice that had a "Champagne-like effervescence with extremely fine

....

RECIPE **Champagne Cocktail**

....

SERVES 1

Cocktail historian David Wondrich dates this back to 1850 San Francisco,[1] but the appeal of this refreshing sparkler shouldn't be ignored today.

1 sugar cube
2 to 3 dashes
  Angostura bitters
5 ounces Brut
  Champagne
Lemon twist

Place the sugar cube in a chilled Champagne flute. Dash the bitters over it. Top off the glass with the Champagne. Pinch the lemon twist to release its aromatics before floating it on top to garnish. Don't stir, because the sugar cube's role is to create bubbles rather than to sweeten the Champagne.

[1] *Wondrich,* Imbibe!, *302–5.*

....

bubbles,"[2] according to archaeologist and anthropologist Patrick McGovern,[3] aka "the Indiana Jones of alcoholic beverages."[4]

That's right: The world's first booze bubbled. McGovern, who has also described ancient Sumerian beer as "Champagne-like,"[5] tells me that stone-age imbibers consumed their wines, beers, and meads mid-ferment to avoid spoilage. Better to guzzle a fresh fizzy beverage too soon than a sour, vinegared one too late.

Plus, there was the metaphysical factor: "The process of fermentation itself, with CO_2 churning the beverage, would have seemed otherworldly to our ancestors (lacking any knowledge of the actual process)," McGovern says. "Combined with the mind-altering effect of the alcohol, carbonation was probably viewed as a desirable property of any fermented beverage."

[2] *McGovern,* Uncorking the Past, *63–64.*
[3] *McGovern is the scientific director of the Biomolecular Archaeology Project at the University of Pennsylvania Museum of Archaeology and Anthropology.*

[4] *Columbus, "Meet the Indiana Jones of Ancient Ales and Extreme Beverages."*

[5] *Ibid., 87.*

Ante Bubblum

Our words "effervescence" and "fermentation" are both derived from the Latin *fervere*, meaning "to boil." In describing a well-designed villa, Marcus Terentius Varro (116– 27 BCE) advises that all winemaking operations should take place in a cool cellar, well away from the rest of the house. "For, where the new wine was laid, the jars often burst by the fermentation of the must."[6]

If wine jars were bursting, we can only conclude that their tops were being stoppered before fermentation was complete. Indeed, Pliny the Elder informs us that the Greeks knew how to halt a fermentation and contain a fresh wine in an airtight terra-cotta vessel[7] sealed with pine resin, a tradition that's honored today in the form of retsina, that piney beverage that's poured at Greek restaurants.

The ancients also used various plugs—plaster, wax, natural cork—to tightly close amphorae. These would have kept wine fresh, but also could have captured the natural effervescence of an incomplete fermentation. According to McGovern, some ancient Egyptian amphorae were punched with holes that could be stopped up or not, depending upon whether the winemaker wished to make a bubbly beverage.

Scholars have suggested that the Roman habit of burying amphorae underground wasn't merely for the sake of temperature control, but also to withstand the outward force that a second fermentation exerts upon a sealed container, the end goal being sparkling sweet wines.[8] Some sources even theorize that Roman winemakers chilled amphorae in cold water, then purposefully warmed them up to force a finished fermentation within a sealed vessel.[9]

In the *Aeneid*, Virgil describes the goddess Dido passing around a chalice filled with "still bubbling" and "gold" wine.[10] And the short-lived Roman poet Lucan (39–65 CE) tells us that Julius Caesar and Cleopatra drank a "noble Falernian" wine, "fermented too quickly, which made it foam," from "huge jeweled cups,"[11] because *of course* Queen Cleo's cups were bedazzled.

---

[6] *Varro*, The Three Books of M. Terentius Varro Concerning Agriculture, *62.*

[7] *Pliny the Elder*, Delphi Classics Complete Works of Pliny the Elder, *534.*

[8] *Osservatorio Economico Vinai, "Caesar and Cleopatra."*

[9] *Vinitaly Wine Club, "Guide to Lambrusco."*

[10] *Virgil*, Aeneid, *Book I, lines 735–40.*

[11] *Lucan*, Civil War, *Book 10, lines 168–70.*

Peter Liem on Prestige Cuvées

There's no better book on the world's most fabulous wine region than the beautiful double volume *Champagne: The Essential Guide to the Wines, Producers and Terroirs of the Iconic Region*. This magnum opus, by cerebral *journaliste du vin* Peter Liem—an American who planted himself in Champagne and has pretty much gone native—is a work of art to behold, and encyclopedic in its comprehensive survey of the region, *maisons*, and *vignerons*.

Liem is also the mastermind behind champagneguide.net and cofounder of La Fête du Champagne, the largest Champagne event in the United States, held in New York City. This three-day tasting extravaganza includes some of the finest bubbles in the world, so I asked Liem to fill us in on the crème de la crème, so to speak, of the category: Prestige Cuvées.[12]

Also called Têtes de Cuvées, these bottlings from the larger, better-known *maisons* "are intended to represent the pinnacle of a house's craft," explains Liem. "At their best, they offer an unparalleled combination of refinement and complexity, and demonstrate why Champagne is the most sophisticated sparkling wine in the world." I asked Liem to describe a couple of classic Prestige Cuvées; here are his picks:

Louis Roederer "Cristal" (V; 12% ABV; $$$$$)

Before the unfortunate day of his assassination, Tsar Alexander II sipped this special cuvée, custom-made for him by Louis Roederer himself. Sourced mostly from Grand Cru vineyard plots on poor (that is, character-building) chalky soils, it "really needs twenty to twenty-five years of aging to show its best," says Liem. "But with time, it's capable of tremendous complexity and finesse." Likewise, the house of Roederer, run by the same family for two centuries, has grown more and more intriguing over time. Today, it's "at the forefront of the progressive movement in Champagne," according to Liem, as the largest organic and biodynamic vineyard holder in the region.[13]

Philipponnat Clos des Goisses (V; 12.5% ABV; $$$$$)

"The 5.5-hectare [13.5-acre] Clos des Goisses has been bottled as a single-vineyard, vintage-dated Champagne since 1935," says Liem, making this the O.G. vineyard-designate Champers. "I've tasted vintages back to the 1950s that are still vibrant and fresh," he adds. "It's become one of the most collectible wines in Champagne, and as great as the old vintages are, one could argue that the house of Philipponnat is making better wines today than ever before." Liem describes this partially barrel-fermented, Extra-Brut blend of Pinot Noir and Chardonnay as a wine of "great richness and complexity," with "vivid structure and pronounced minerality."

Incidentally, if you are dining out on a well-padded expense account and are looking for more of these pricey-but-spectacular wines to try, I also asked Champagne expert Essi Avellan, a Finnish Master of Wine, author, and journalist, to name some of her fave Têtes de Cuvées. She recommended Moët & Chandon's famed Dom Pérignon, Piper-Heidsieck's Cuvée Rare, Taittinger's Comtes de Champagne, and Charles Heidsieck's Blanc des Millénaires. To this list, I would add Bollinger's Vieille Vignes Françaises, Salon's Cuvée S, and Pol Roger's Sir Winston Churchill.

And now, please excuse me while I run out and invest in a few lottery tickets so that I can afford to drink Têtes de Cuvées for the rest of my days.

---

[12] *Liem is often thought of as a champion of the growers, but he warns that grower status should not be equated with quality. "In Champagne, the real distinction is between high-quality, forward-thinking producers and those who are underachieving in quality or ambition, and I am an ardent supporter of the former, no matter whether they are grower estates or négociant houses," he tells me.*

[13] *Roederer had nearly achieved 100 percent biodynamic certification as I was writing this book.*

Proto Pétillant

On to Europe and the Little Ice Age, which cooled temperatures so much between about 1300 and 1850 that everyone's fermentations got stuck.[14] Winemakers, seeing their barrels no longer burbling, sealed them up for the winter and walked away. And then spring came, and fermentation restarted, with nowhere to go. Wine fizzed, and people liked it.

The French monks of the Abbey of Saint-Hilaire in Limoux, Languedoc, were the first to document their sparkling winemaking techniques, as far back as 1531. (A century and a half later, one Dom Pérignon, on a pilgrimage to

Santiago de Compostela, visited the humble monks of Saint-Hilaire[15] and poked his nose into the cellar to see what they were up to.)[16] The town of Limoux proudly proclaims itself to be ground zero for modern bubbly, as official city documents dating back to 1544 imply a glass-bottle-enclosed fermentation, in "flacons." Whether this was an ancestral method or true second fermentation (kick-started by a sugar addition) is unknown, but as we'll learn on page 40, sparkling wine wasn't fully realized until it was encased in glass.

The poet Auger Galhard,[17] writing in the Occitane language in 1569, artfully describes a *méthode Gaillaçoise* Muscat as "bubbly" and "jump(ing) in the glass."[18] A year later, a Brescian doctor named Girolamo Conforti, in his "Treatise on Biting Wine" (*Libellus de Vino Mordaci*), praises its "gassy, light and pungent surface," which "does not dry out the palate," nor "make the tongue soft."[19]

As is the case with so many since-disproven medical reports filled with unwarranted fear-mongering (wherefore art thou, MSG?), Italian physician Francesco Scacchi describes fizzy wine as though it is a scourge upon society in his 1622 *De salubri potu dissertatio*, or, *A Thesis on Healthy Drinking*.[20] "It must be asserted that 'biting' or (so-called) piquant wine does not promote good health, because that sting (or pricking) arises from no other source than an excess of gaseous spirit," he thunders.[21]

In 1633, we find the first mention of Blanquette, today's best-known style of Limoux bubbly. Historian and politician Guillaume de Catel describes it as a semi-sweet, festive drink for holidays and, in particular, the New Year. It's so beloved by Germans, he claims, that they've been vacationing in the area just to have access to the local fizz[22]—one wonders what the Airbnb rates were like in the South of France back then.

---

[14]   *Fermentation halts at temperatures of 40°F (4.4°C) or colder.*

[15]   *Phillips,* French Wine: A History, *85.*

[16]   *Since Pérignon didn't want his wines to sparkle, the reconnaissance mission may have actually been a lesson in what* not *to do.*

[17]   *Also spelled "Augièr" and "Gaillard."*

[18]   *Boucoiran,* Dictionnaire Analogique et Étymologique des Idiomes Méridionaux, *951.*

[19]   *Franciacorta, "Origins and History."*

[20]   *We know this thanks to British sparkling-wine expert Tom Stevenson, who published a translation of the chapter in question.*

[21]   *Stevenson,* Did the Italians Invent Sparkling Wine?, *Kindle, location 198.*

[22]   *de Catel,* Memoires de L'histoire du Languedoc: Curieusement et Fidelement Recueillis, *43.*

CHAPTER 2

A Glass Half-Full

Glassmaking began in early Mesopotamia, but didn't evolve much past pretty stained-glass windows and Venetian perfume bottles for millennia. The world's oldest bottle of wine dates back to 325 CE, but for more than a thousand years, no glassblower could fashion a bottle strong enough to withhold the explosive gaseous force of fermentation.

(Even today's superstrong Champagne bottles explode and hurt people. In January 2018, a Danish man ended up in intensive care after a shard of glass from an exploding Champagne bottle sliced through an artery in his leg. But, as I tell my kids, Champagne is still safer than vaping.)

Glassmaking technology picked up in 1612, when Antonio Neri published the first comprehensive manual to the craft, entitled *L'Arte Vetraria*. The groundbreaking work was translated into German, Latin, French, and English, and distributed throughout Europe.[23]

But it was the Brits who invented the Champagne bottle, which is why they like to call themselves the "True Inventors of Champagne . . . More or Less by Accident, But We Will Take Credit, Thank You Very Much."

In the late sixteenth century, English merchants were importing northern French wine by the cask. It was pink, because the grape juice of chilly Champagne never soaked up much pigment from the skins, something like the effect of dunking a tea bag in ice-cold water.

Another effect of the cold was *vinum interruptum*: After starting to ferment, the pink wines went into hibernation mode when cellar temperatures dipped below 40°F (4.4°C). The Brits bought these barrels over the winter and bottled the wines, topping them with modern, oxygen-stopping corks. Come springtime, and boom! Pink Champagne bottles exploded in English taverns and shops. Except, when they didn't, the wine was delightfully fizzy.

How to capture this delightful *frisson*? With better glass bottles, which England was uniquely poised to develop.

Thanks to advances in naval engineering and oceanic exploration in the fifteenth century, England was pretty much at war, all the time, with everyone, for much of the sixteenth and seventeenth centuries. More wars called for more shipbuilding, which called for more wood. But the timber supply in England was

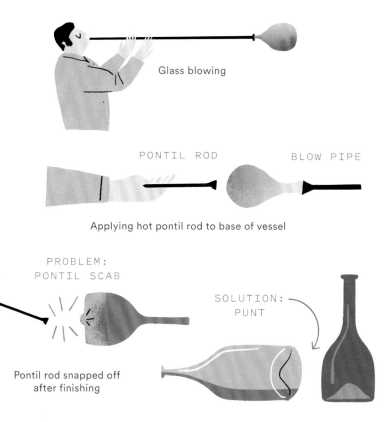

Glass blowing

PONTIL ROD   BLOW PIPE

Applying hot pontil rod to base of vessel

PROBLEM:
PONTIL SCAB

SOLUTION:
PUNT

Pontil rod snapped off
after finishing

thinning. And so, in 1615, King James I issued a proclamation banning the use of charcoal for non-naval purposes such as smelting iron or blowing glass.

Egging on this act was one Sir Robert Mansell, vice-admiral of the English Royal Navy, who, it turned out, had a side gig harvesting coal in Newcastle. And mined coal, it turned out, burned hotter than charcoal, making for stronger, clearer glass. Business-savvy Mansell patented coal-fired glassmaking, and "numerous small glassmaking operations sprung up, paying Mansell for the coal and the right to make glass," notes historian Henry H. Work.[24]

Mansell went on to take credit for the invention of modern bottle glass, which the French would call *verre Anglais*.[25] Over the following century, glassblowers used this to form sturdy, straight, tall cylindrical vessels that could be packed tightly into wooden cases and held in one hand—a vast improvement

---

[23] *Whitehouse*, Glass: A Short History, 66.

[24] *Work*, The Shape of Wine, *106*.

[25] *Stevenson and Avellan*, Christie's World Encyclopedia of Champagne and Sparkling Wine, *10*.

on the old onion-shaped bottles with their fragile, bulbous bottoms.

And so the first technical description of *méthode traditionnelle* sparkling winemaking came from an English scientist, Christopher Merret, who in 1662 wrote that vintners of the era added "sugar and molasses to all sorts of wines to make the drink brisk and sparkling."[26]

Another key development in Champagne bottle design arose from the problem of the pontil scar. In glassblowing, once a bottle has been blown into shape, a red-hot pontil rod is stuck to the base of the bottle so that the artisan can remove the blowpipe from the neck. As the glass is cooling, the trick is to remove the pontil so that it leaves a dimple at the

bottom of the bottle. If instead the pontil scab is a convex pimple, the bottle is liable to wobble, spin, and scratch the varnish on your tabletop. Eighteenth-century glassmakers hit upon the solution of indenting the entire base of the bottle so that the scar would never stick out. Thus was born the punt.

This punt, it turned out, was quite a useful innovation. Connoisseurs soon found to their delight that the moat around the punt caught sediment, while merchants noted that the indent made the bottle appear larger and fuller than it really was. It also allowed for wine bottles to be stored horizontally more efficiently, with necks fitting into bases. And there's that wonderful thing that sommeliers do, when they insert a thumb in the base of a Champagne bottle and pour, giving all of us carpal-tunnel-afflicted authors wrist-strength envy.

Most relevant to the history of sparkling wine, however, is the fact that an arched or vaulted structure is stronger than a flat one, as the Romans of antiquity taught us with their architecture. In the case of a punted bottle, the increased ratio of glass—vaulted glass, no less—to wine made for a much stronger vessel, able to withstand more atmospheric pressure than its flat-bottomed, pimply friends.

Postscript: Today, the mighty Champagne bottle is undoubtedly strong, but its thick glass walls and deep punt make it weighty and ungainly. And the heavier the glass, the stronger the consumer perception that whatever is inside it must be precious, so wineries have been slow to embrace modern advances in lightweight bottle design.

But shipping a bottle with the body-mass index of a buffalo is costly and needlessly resource-intensive, requiring excess storage space and fuel. The Comité Champagne (Comité Interprofessionnel du vin de Champagne, or CIVC) has been chipping away at this sustainability issue over the past couple of decades. Since 2000, the Champagne bottle's carbon footprint has been reduced by 20 percent.

---

[26] *Stevenson and Avellan*, Christie's World Encyclopedia of Champagne and Sparkling Wine, *10*.

No, We Can't Talk About Cans

Canned sparkling wine is a boon for those of us non–beer drinkers who like to accompany our friends to sporting events and ski lodges. However, at present, it's the vinous equivalent of Budweiser: It's there when you need it, but you never actually *want* it.

Canned fizz tends to be carbonated, and carbonated wines just don't inspire me. Imagine[27] putting flat wine in your Soda-Stream. It just wouldn't have the fresh flavor and pinprick bubbles of a classically made effervescent wine.

---

[27] *Imagine it, but don't do it unless you're prepared to mop down your walls and ceiling. There are some pretty entertaining YouTube videos of SodaStream kitchen catastrophes.*

Beverage of Bluebloods

Champagne has always had a royal following. Coronations were staged at Reims Cathedral starting in 496, when Clovis, King of the Franks, converted to Catholicism, and the accompanying celebrations perennially entailed plenty of local wine. In addition, the Comtes de Champagne always were tight with the French monarchs, while regions like Burgundy and Bordeaux at times had closer political alliances with the kings of England. Finally, the Marne River conveniently connected Épernay with Paris, making it a snap for rich and fabulous urbanites to order Champenoise wine shipments.

Champagne cemented its reputation as the soda pop of the fashionable set as early as the late 1600s, thanks to an exiled French essayist, critic, epicure, and dilettante named Charles de Saint-Évremond,[28] who served as English King William III's wingman at dinner parties. He always showed up with a bottle of Champers, and even designed a special glass for it: the tall, slender flute.[29]

At the time, Champagne's fame was more due to the novelty of a white wine made from black grapes than the fact that it (accidentally) bubbled. Dom Pierre Pérignon had mastered the art of blending and perfected the science of pressing clear juice from purple-skinned grapes, but contrary to popular opinion and legend, did *not* utter the poetic phrase "I am tasting the stars!"

Indeed, upon hearing about Saint-Évremond's decadent ways, the cellar master at the Champenoise monastery of Hautvillers became convinced that bubbles in wine weren't merely an accident of climate, but a pox upon society, and devoted much of his cellar time in a quixotic quest to rid the world of effervescence.

The Benedictine monk died the same year as King Louis XIV, and thus thankfully was not subjected to the regency of French party boy Philippe II, Duc d'Orléans, who, while ruling on behalf of his young cousin, Prince Louis XV, lived a wine-soaked lifestyle of louche decadence. Philippe was "an unabashed hedonist whose debauchery became legendary," writes wine historian Paul Lukacs. "He drank copious amounts of

---

[28] *Read about Champagne Taittinger's English winery, named after Évremond, on page 254.*

[29] *Simon*, History of the Champagne Trade in England, *10.*

Masters of Marketing

The savvy nineteenth-century Champenoise were early adopters of product-placement deals. In a particularly dramatic example, Moët's American importer provoked an international scandal by bribing the builder of Kaiser Wilhelm's new yacht to have It Girl Alice Roosevelt christen the schooner with Moët Champagne rather than German sparkling wine.

They also vied for the chance to declare royal appointments on their gold-foil labels. Crowned leaders from Spain, Egypt, and Russia endorsed the Champagne houses that courted them most flatteringly.[30]

Champagne, it turned out, had its own royalty of sorts, as well. In 1811, twenty-one-year-old Charles-Henri Heidsieck made Russia mad for Champers when he rode a white stallion a full two thousand miles, accompanied by a servant and a packhorse loaded down with Champagne, from Reims to Moscow.

It was a brilliant marketing ploy, and his son Charles Camille Heidsieck followed in his footsteps, making swashbuckling buffalo-hunting trips to the United States, bearing elegant firearms crafted by Paris's top gunsmith. The gentleman-adventurer schtick fit right in with American popular culture, and Charles Camille became known by the tabloid name of "Champagne Charlie."[31]

---

[30] *Guy,* When Champagne Became French, *18.*

[31] *Kladstrup,* Champagne, *81, 85.*

Alas, Dom Pierre Pérignon never got the chance to give French party boy Philippe II a good scolding.

fizzy Champagne, often at great banquets that he dubbed his 'orgies' . . . Philippe's court at the Palais Royale is where the ongoing association of sparkling Champagne with luxury and sensual pleasure was first established."[32]

This was fortunate timing, since the Methuen Treaty of 1703 tripled the duties on French wines coming into the UK (at least, in comparison with the duties on Portuguese wines), immediately resulting in an English preference for Port and Madeira over Champagne. With that market dwindling, the Champenoise needed to sell more wine at home, and the Duc d'Orléans did his part to promote it.

At the age of forty-nine, Philippe died in true libertine style, in bed with a mistress. By this time, his nephew Louis XV had come of age and also became an advocate for Champagne. Declaring its bubbles to be curative, he allowed the *maisons* to ship their products in glass bottles rather than wooden casks, set official standards for bottle size and fill levels, and even ruled that Champagne corks must be held in place by the string precursors to today's wire cages.

For the rest of the eighteenth century, the upper crust lapped up Champagne. Peter the Great and Catherine the Great of Russia, Frederick the Great of Prussia, George II of Great Britain, and the prolific writer Voltaire all sung its praises, as did the ill-fated Louis XVI and Marie Antoinette. Even the French Revolution didn't harm the market much, since Napoléon Bonaparte turned out to be a Champagne-ophile . . . as did the leaders of Austria, Prussia, and Russia who eventually defeated him.

---

[32] *Lukacs*, Inventing Wine, *113–14.*

Century of Change

English scientist and theologian Joseph Priestley wrote a paper suggestively entitled *Impregnating Water with Fixed Air* in 1772 that inspired Johann Jacob Schweppe to commercialize production of seltzer water in Geneva in 1783. Thus was born the technique that would go on to make the cheapest and least-interesting sparkling wines: forced carbonation.

Meanwhile, *méthode Champenoise* techniques continued to improve. In 1816, the widow Barbe-Nicole Clicquot hit upon the idea of drilling slanted holes into her kitchen tabletop and propping the table on its side. In each hole, she inserted a sediment-filled bottle, and "began slowly turning and tapping the bottles each day, coaxing the sediment onto the cork," writes historian Tilar Mazzeo. "After only six weeks, Barbe-Nicole was amazed—and gratified—to discover that with a quick flick of the cork, all the residue came shooting out, without any harm to the wine and without all the tedious work."[33]

---

[33]   *Mazzeo*, The Widow Clicquot, *126.*

The Birth of Brut

Like the famous Madame Barbe-Nicole Clicquot (1777–1866), Jeanne Alexandrine Louise Pommery (1819–1890) was a widow who took charge of her husband's winery and radically altered the history of Champagne. Not only did she convert an unprecedented 12 miles (19 km) of Roman-dug tunnels into a vast, naturally cooled cave system that served as a model for the rest of the region, but she also released the superb 1874 vintage without *dosage*, introducing the concept of bone-dry Champagne to the world. Through these accomplishments as well as many others, Madame Pommery achieved such iconic status that her funeral attracted a crowd of twenty thousand; French president François Sadi Carnot officially renamed her hometown of Chigny "Chigny-les-Roses," in honor of Madame's fondness for the flower. For more on sweetness standards in sparkling wine, see page 22.

The wines of Champagne were still a work in progress. Writing in 1851, the British journalist Cyrus Redding described them as white, gray,[34] "rose-colored," and red, many of them filling half a glass with foam. "The best are those which froth slightly. They are improved in the drinking by ice, which tends to repress the effervescence," Redding commented.[35]

Nineteenth-century engineers automated tiresome processes that had previously used up hours of manual labor. The invention of machines that performed riddling, disgorgement, *dosage*, and bottling allowed for production on a large scale. Meanwhile, scientists[36] were tinkering in the lab, continuously improving techniques.

Among these was Jean-Antoine Chaptal, who perfected the addition of sugar (chaptalization) in winemaking, and Louis Pasteur, who led winemakers to understand *why* the addition of sugar caused a second fermentation in the bottle. It took until the 1880s for vintners to weave together Chaptal's and Pasteur's work and hit upon the right sugar-yeast formula of a successful *liqueur de tirage*.

In 1884, one of Pasteur's acolytes, microbiologist Charles Chamberland, developed a revolutionary pressure chamber, which would be used to sterilize medical equipment and vulcanize rubber.[37] In 1895, Federico Martinotti hit upon the idea of carrying out one big secondary fermentation in Chamberland's autoclave, and in 1907, Frenchman Eugène Charmat fine-tuned and patented the process. Finally, Italian professor Tullio De Rosa perfected Charmat-style winemaking in the Prosecco capital of Conegliano.

And thus, Prosecco as we know it was born.

---

[34] *The term "gray" was traditionally used to describe rosé wines.*

[35] *Redding,* A History and Description of Modern Wines, *96–98.*

[36] *"The Making of Sparkling Wine,"* maisons-champagne.com.

[37] *Having read how it works, I am fairly certain that my Instant Pot is basically a small autoclave, as well.*

Seeing Stars in the United States

Meanwhile, inspired by their own royalty of sorts—Champagne-enthusiast presidents like Thomas Jefferson and Andrew Jackson—nineteenth-century Americans thirsted for fizz. But a long trans-oceanic voyage in the hot hull of a ship does pressurized sparkling wine no favors. A domestic producer was needed—someone with a bottomless bank account and an irrational sense of optimism.

Both appeared in the form of Cincinnati lawyer and real estate tycoon Nicholas Longworth, an avid horticulturist who became obsessed with wine grapes in 1830. After years of trying to coax the classic European *vitis vinifera* varieties in the inhospitable climate and soils of Ohio, he settled upon Catawba, an American hybrid variety that is described as having a "foxy" aromatic profile.

(Sadly, a "foxy" wine is not "sexy," but rather, smells like a fox den. Or, perhaps, a dog crate that

has had the same old blanket in it for the past five years. To fight the foxiness, Longworth's winemakers pressed the juice off the skins—a good first step for sparkling winemaking.)

Longworth's first French winemaker drowned in the Ohio River. His second failed to read the memo about *verre Anglais*, and 42,000 of Longworth's 50,000 first bottles of bubbly exploded. But the third Frenchman proved to be the charm. "Sparkling Catawba has increased beyond all calculations," Longworth wrote in 1855, having finally found success. "[It] can scarcely be prepared fast enough to meet the market."

The Urbana Wine Company of New York's Finger Lakes region followed Longworth's lead in 1865, hiring its winemaker away from Louis Roederer. By 1870, another Finger Lakes producer, Pleasant Valley, was making the bestselling "Great Western" brand of bubbly. (The winery is still in business, but I don't recommend its sweet red "Great Western Sparkling Burgundy.") But despite all the money and momentum in Ohio and New York, Catawba was no Chardonnay.

The Scourge of California Champagne

The best soil and climate for growing *vitis vinifera* were on the West Coast, as Spanish missionaries had demonstrated as far back as the seventeenth century. Unfortunately, those missionaries had left California planted with the eponymous Mission grape, which was high in sugar and low in acid—the worst possible combination for sparkling-wine production. In the 1840s and '50s, an intrepid fur trapper named Benjamin Davis Wilson, and then the Sainsevain family (the Gallos of the nineteenth century), made a brief go of sparkling Mission, but both ventures failed.

When the noble Hungarian Haraszthy family arrived in 1857, they improved the California winescape considerably. Agoston Haraszthy, known today as the "Father of California Viticulture," planted the still-extant Buena Vista Vineyard in Sonoma's Mayacamas Mountains and brought myriad noble vine variety cuttings back with him from his frequent travels to Europe.

Agoston's son, Arpad, went off to Épernay to work as an apprentice, sent three volumes of detailed notes and illustrations back to California, and, upon his return home, commenced winemaking à la *méthode traditionnelle* in 1862. After many years of broken bottles, dashed hopes, and false starts, Arpad struck gold in 1875 with "Eclipse," an elegant blend of whatever he could get his hands on—Zinfandel, three clones of Riesling, Chasselas, Burger, White Colombard, and more—that *wasn't* Mission. For the next quarter century, Eclipse was the toast of the United States.

Meanwhile, the American vine-root louse known as phylloxera had made its way to France, debilitated *vitis vinifera* vineyards, and crippled the French wine industry, resulting in a mass exodus of talent. One of these expats was Paul Masson, a Burgundian, who, like Agoston Haraszthy, brought key vine cuttings to the United States from France, including the Mount Eden clone, a strain of Pinot Noir that continues to be prized today.

Masson made his first bubbly in 1892, and by the time of Arpad Haraszthy's death, in 1900, had—yes—eclipsed his rival as the "Champagne King of California." His most famed cuvée was a sparkling blush-colored wine, named

"Oeil de Perdrix" after the pink eye of a partridge—a European term that sounded wonderfully mysterious to American ears.

But while Masson did much for the American wine industry,[38] he did inestimable damage to a French wine trade that was already reeling from the scourge of phylloxera. Because Masson labeled his sparkling wine "California Champagne." American-born wine producers were doing the same—Great Western even went so far as to claim its bubbly was made in the fictional city of Rheims,[39] New York—but Masson, being French, should have known better.

As the title of a specific geographic region, "Champagne" is a proper name. Yet many early California winemakers felt no qualms about using this term on their labels as a generic trademark, in the same way we might bring our coffee to work in a Thermos, go make a Xerox of a document, put a Band-Aid on a paper cut, or throw a bag of trash in a Dumpster, regardless of whether or not we are actually using the brands we are naming.

Unfortunately, some California wineries—the highest-volume, lowest-quality houses—even today use "Champagne" as a catch-all term, despite an international outcry against the practice. And these wineries tend to be the highest-volume, lowest-quality producers.

---

[38] *Although he died in 1940, Masson's name was so legendary that his brand lived on for decades; readers of a certain age may remember the tagline, "We will sell no wine before its time."*

[39] *Suggesting Reims in Champagne.*

War Boils Over

Back in Europe, false advertising wasn't the only worry of the Champenoise in the early twentieth century. Because the age-old rivalry between the French and Germans was bubbling up again, and Champagne was inconveniently located between Paris and Frankfurt.

When the Triple Entente between the Russian Empire, the UK, and France squared up against the Triple Alliance between Germany, Austria-Hungary, and Italy, in 1914, the fortified trenches of the Western Front were dug less than a mile (1.6 km) from Reims. In September,

the Germans bombed the Reims Cathedral, destroying its lacy Gothic towers and the priceless artwork inside, dealing a symbolic blow to the region.

The human costs were even greater. While the cathedral burned, children harvested grapes on behalf of their conscripted fathers. At least twenty were killed bringing in what may have been the greatest vintage of the century.[40] And the first and second Battles of the Marne were fought on Champagne's doorstep. In total, Reims was bombed for 1,051 days, and more than 80 per-cent of the city reduced to rubble.

But Champagne had a secret: Gallo-Roman and medieval laborers had burrowed into the chalk substratum as early as the fourth century BCE, leaving deep cavities hidden underground. In 1769, Nicolas Ruinart was the first wine producer to formally[41] renovate these former quarries, called *crayères*, into a naturally temperature-controlled wine-storage facility 125 feet (38 m) under Épernay. The dark, spacious *crayères* were ideal for thousands upon thousands of bottle-aging wines, and the other *maisons* soon followed Ruinart's lead.

In 1914, with the region under siege, the French military dug connecting tunnels between the vast network of underground caves, creating a system of roads hundreds of miles long. And the citizens of Reims moved in. Normal life began again, by candlelight: "Everything on the surface was suddenly underneath: schools, churches, clinics, and cafés. City Hall was moved underground, as were the police and fire departments," write historians Don and Petie Kladstrup.[42]

Just twenty-one years later, Champagne was again a pawn of war. The leaders of the Third Reich requisitioned millions of bottles for their own enjoyment, as well as selling their spoils on the international market. Already in dire financial straits due to the Great Depression, the Champagne houses quietly walled off sections of their caves, hiding bottles and barrels.

A *weinführer* posted to the region by the Third Reich punished producers if they weren't able to meet Nazi demand. With sugar rationed, the workforce decimated, all horses seized, and many of their leaders in prisons and concentration camps, the *maisons* banded together to negotiate with the *weinführer* and his commanders, forming the Comité Interprofessionel du vin de Champagne, or CIVC, which continues as the region's trade group today.

Meanwhile, the secret corners of the *crayères* became a headquarters for the Resistance, where fugitives could hide and arms and supplies could be stashed. From here, studying the *weinführer*'s Champagne orders, Resistance leaders were able to foresee where the troops were headed and relay this information to the Allies.

Champagne could also be credited with saving the city of Paris, both in the streets and in the halls of diplomacy. In the streets, Marie Curie's son-in-law, the future Nobel Prize–winning physicist Frédéric Joliot-Curie, used his scientific knowhow to make Molotov cocktails, using Taittinger bottles as his bomb casings. At a higher level, Pierre Taittinger served as the Vichy-appointed mayor of the city during the war—a position he used to talk the Nazis out of destroying the City of Lights, even after they had planted explosives. And thus, in its own way, Champagne won the war.[43]

---

[40] Kladstrup, Champagne, *173.*

[41] *Of course, people had been using the* crayères *to store food, wine, and other perishables for personal use for centuries, if not millennia.*

[42] Kladstrup, Champagne, *177–80.*

[43] Kladstrup, Wine & War, *178.*

Germany, Champagne, and Sektual Healing

Sekt is the German term for sparkling wine, and if you think the above pun was bad, just wait until you get to Chapter 7! But all joking aside, it's ironic that Champagne suffered so much from German aggression in wartime, given the key roles Germans played in creating the Champagne industry as we know it.

It started with the French Revolution, when the corrupt Catholic Church's vineyards were confiscated and put up for sale. With the French moneyed aristocracy gone and the economy in tatters, wealthy German investors crossed the border to buy them.

Then, just a few decades later, Napoleon swept through the Teutonic states, leaving chaos in his wake. This time, poorer working folks—such as Rhinelandish winemakers—came to Champagne looking for opportunity.

Both influxes left a profound German influence in Champagne and led to the establishment of a Sekt-making tradition in Germany. And today, Champagne and Sekt are both wines of diplomacy, toasted with by world leaders who come together in peace.[44]

A TIMELINE OF FRANCO-GERMAN SPARKLING RELATIONS

(A guide to the Germans who played a role in forming some of Champagne's best-known houses)

1785: Florens-Louis Heidsieck, from Westphalia, founds the Piper-Heidsieck *maison*. In 1851, his grand-nephew will establish the Charles Heidsieck Champagne brand.

1818: The German-born *chef de cave* at Veuve Clicquot, Antoine-Aloys de Müller, coinvents riddling, aka *remuage*, then later marries into the Ruinart family.

1826: Georg Christian von Kessler leaves Veuve Clicquot, starts up the first German Sekt house.

1827: The Mumm family, bankers and German winegrowers, launch the Mumm Champagne house.

1828: Hessian-born Eduard Werle becomes a partner in Veuve Clicquot, then, later, mayor of Reims.

1829: Württemberg-born Jacques Bollinger founds his namesake house.

1830S: In the United States, German immigrants with vinetending chops assist Nicholas Longworth in his quest to make bubbly.[45]

1834–42: Robert Alwin Schlumberger of Stuttgart is *chef de cave* of Ruinart.

1838: William Deutz and Peter Geldermann, from Aachen, start up the Champagne brand now known as Deutz.

1843: Joseph Krug, from the Rhine, founds Krug Champagne.

1902: Scandal erupts when Alice Roosevelt christens Kaiser Wilhelm's new yacht with Moët.[46]

1922: The Mumm family is kicked out of France in the aftermath of the First World War. They establish the G.H. von Mumm sparkling wine house in Frankfurt; this will eventually become Germany's largest sparkling-wine conglomerate.

1945: French forces discover hundreds of cases of 1928 Salon Champagne in the Eagle's Nest, Hitler's secret mountaintop retreat.

---

[44]   Among the many sources consulted for this timeline: Anne Krebiehl, MW; Romana Echensperger, MW; Grandes Marques et Maisons de Champagne (maisons-champagne.com); kulturland-rheingau.de; the Theodore Roosevelt Center at Dickinson University (theodorerooseveltcenter.org); the American Menu blog (theamericanmenu.com); Schiller Wine (schiller-wine.blogspot.com); and the books of Petie and Don Kladstrup, cited throughout this chapter.

[45]   Pinney, The Makers of American Wine, 27–28. And for more on Longworth, see page 49.

[46]   For more on this, see page 45.

Globalization and Localization

As winemaking grew increasingly industrialized in the latter half of the twentieth century, sparkling wine was churned out in hitherto undreamed-of quantities from gleaming steel fermentation tanks the size of small buildings. The nation of Portugal came out of World War II the victor of the fizzy pink category. Just in time for the Armistice, the supermarket-priced *frizzante*-style Lancers and Mateus became two of the first wine brands to go global.

At the same time, fine-wine brokers took advantage of post-war advances in refrigerated shipping technology, introducing American audiences to the big Champagne brands. By the late 1960s, shipping containers were solid steel, air-conditioned, and standardized in size, allowing smaller businesses to rent a single container or a fraction of a "reefer," as these cooled units are called.

A host of boutique importers subsequently set up shop, including the Champagne champions Martine Saunier, Kermit Lynch, Terry Theise, and Robert Chadderdon. These curators hunted down small, family-owned *maisons* focusing on site-specific, handcrafted sparkling wines, from Champagne as well as other European regions. In 1997, Theise upped the game by releasing a catalog consisting entirely of what he called "farmer fizz," "microbrew Champagnes," and, famously, "grower Champagne."

Thanks to the efforts of small importers like those mentioned above—in America as well as other markets—the past few decades have been marked by a deepening of appreciation for artisan sparkling winemaking as well as the mass production of surprisingly high-quality frothy wine, notably very quaffable Cavas and Proseccos priced at $10 to $15 per bottle.

As the Champenoise demonstrated through the worst of wartime, it's possible to epitomize elegance while pushing against power. And it's possible for sparkling wine to bring brightness to people's lives when darkness threatens to swallow them up. Because there are always small reasons to celebrate.

The Art of Sabrage

There is the normal way to open a bottle of sparkling wine (see page 31). And then there is the pirate way.

It's a party trick that could result in you living the rest of your life with nine fingers. So please, before attempting the following, draft and sign a document releasing me of any liability if you screw this up.

STEP 1: Fully chill a bottle of fully sparkling wine in a sturdy bottle. No low-pressure *frizzante* or *pétillant* fizz in flimsy thin glass will do. Traditional-method, bottle-fermented Cava works well, because it tends to be affordable, so you won't be too upset if half of it ends up on the ground.

STEP 2: Carry your saber and your bottle outside, and face away from living creatures and fragile objects. Remove the foil and wire cage.

STEP 3: Turn the bottle until you see a faint seam running vertically down the side from top to base. Now, find the spot where this seam hits the band of glass encircling the lip of the bottle. This point is where you'll want your saber to make contact.

STEP 4: Now, holding it from the punt in your non-dominant hand, tilt the bottle at a 45-degree angle, away from you and anyone else.

STEP 5: In one firm move, slide the flat edge of your saber along the side of the bottle until the blade hits your sweet spot. The top rim of the bottle should break at the seam and fly off. Ta-da!

STEP 6: Pour the wine and enjoy, taking care not to touch the jagged top edge of the bottle.

NOTE: *While a curved sword sure does underscore the ceremony of the event, a saber is not mandatory. In fact, a blade is not mandatory. Google the phrase "saber Champagne bottle" with just about any object you can think of ("spoon," "credit card," "boot," "wineglass") and you'll see what I mean.*

Champagne

Most consumers don't realize that vinetenders and winemakers aren't one and the same. In Champagne, this holds particularly true: Ninety percent of the vines are owned by farmers who don't bottle their own wine. That is, there are nearly 16,000 families growing grapes, and only 320 wineries.

The big houses, aka *négociants manipulants* (NM), make 70 percent of the wine. Their facilities look like either large office buildings or small palaces, and many are located in the centers of the cities of Reims or Épernay. Thus, the structure of this chapter is somewhat artificial in that it's broken into geographic regions even though the Grande Marque winery locations don't necessarily reflect the wide array of locales that they source their fruit from.

RECIPE

KIR ROYALE

SERVES 1

Legend has it that Canon Félix Kir, resistance hero and mayor of Dijon, invented the Kir cocktail during World War II to keep Burgundian spirits up during a red-wine shortage. The original drink was inexpensive flat white Aligoté wine colored red with cassis. Postwar, the livelier sparkling version became a symbol of celebration.

½ to 1 ounce crème de cassis (black-currant liqueur)
4 ounces Champagne

Add the crème de cassis to a flute and slowly pour the Champagne over it. You can adjust the amount of cassis depending on how deeply colored you want your drink and how good the bubbly is.

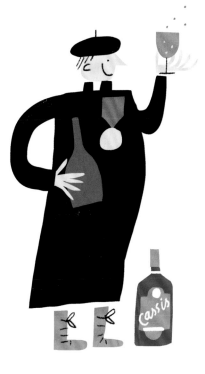

But over the past four decades or so, an increasing number of small family producers have been vinifying and bottling their own wines. These "growers," aka *récoltants manipulants* (RM), are shaking up the industry by bringing a renewed focus on the *matière première*—the source material—forcing the big houses into a bit more accountability as to where, exactly, they are getting their grapes from and how those sites are being farmed.

Which is not to say there's anything wrong with a *grande marque*—"big brand"—Champagne. It's just a different product. The luxury conglomerate

REIMS

MONTAGNE DE
REIMS

ÉPERNAY

VALLÉE DE
LA MARNE

CÔTE DES
BLANCS

CÔTE DE
SÉZANNE

TROYES

CÔTE
DES BAR

FRANCE

LVMH (Louis Vuitton Moët Hennessy), for example, owns a number of familiar fashion, cosmetics, and watch brands. It also owns Champagne houses Krug, Ruinart, Moët & Chandon, Veuve Clicquot, and Mercier, *maisons* that turn out tens of millions of bottles a year.

Is Moët's Dom Pérignon an outstanding wine? Of course it is, but like Louis Vuitton handbags, it manages to be simultaneously ubiquitous and overpriced. On the flip side, calling a small producer a "grower" doesn't guarantee that the wine will be good.

And regardless of the size of the *maison*, there is no such thing as cheap Champagne. Many of the wines recommended in this chapter sell for upward of $100 a bottle, and it's impossible to find quality for less than $35. So if you're seeking value, flip ahead to the next chapters.

Climate change has hit Champagne hard. Harvest used to be in October; now, it's in August or September. Spring is coming earlier and earlier, increasing the chances that frost, hail, or hard rain will damage or destroy the vines' nascent buds and flowers. Meanwhile, summers are rainier and warmer, creating the ideal environment for the double threat of downy mildew and predatory insects. (For this reason, in every vineyard in the region, capsules hanging on trellis wires emit a pheromone scent that discourages butterflies and moths from mating. And you thought Champagne was the wine of love.)[1]

On a more positive note, while other sparkling winemaking

---

[1] *The answers aren't coming as easily when it comes to the downy mildew. Viticulturists feel like they're stuck between a rock and a hard place, because the organic fungicide that works best on mildew, copper, is imprecise and toxic to the soil. Thus, the generally accepted practice among conscientious farmers is to employ highly effective conventional fungicide, in as small amounts as possible.*

What We're Drinking from Champagne

According to the Comité Interprofessionnel du Vin de Champagne (CIVC), Champagne exports fall into the following categories by value:

65.8% NV Brut	3.2% High Dosage
16.2% Préstige Cuvées	1.5% Vintage
11.8% Rosé	1.5% Zero Dosage

regions are struggling with over-ripe fruit, Champagne—which always struggled in the past to achieve ripeness—has hit a temporary sweet spot. While nighttime temperatures have remained cool enough to ensure appropriate acidity levels in the big three grape varieties (Pinot Noir, Chardonnay, and Pinot Meunier) the fruit gets riper these days thanks to warmer daytime temperatures and more "hang time" on the vine. This allows winemakers to dial down the *dosage* sugar, in many cases making for a more harmonious, integrated wine.

Equally if not more important than climate is geology. Back when dinosaurs roamed the planet, a large part of northern France was a depression, known as the Paris Basin, that was covered in saltwater. Over time, the floor of this sea was littered with the calcite shells of microscopic marine creatures, called coccoliths. As more and more sediment settled over these little buggers, the shells were compressed to become white, powdery, hard chalk. Fast-forward to the era of the saber-toothed cat. The African and European tectonic plates smashed against each other, the Alps were formed, the Paris Basin popped up, and those layers of chalky seafloor became the substrata of the earth.

While there are multiple soil types in Champagne, the white chalk that underlies much of the region exerts the most influence on the vineyards. Experts at the CIVC (Le Comité Interprofessionnel du vin de Champagne) can identify a fraudulent Champagne by looking at the wine's molecular structure under a microscope, and a seasoned taster can merely take a sniff and a sip and just *know*. There's that hint of seafoam, that saline note to the finish, that chalky minerality, that transports you to a primordial place where the seafloor sparkled white with billions upon billions of tiny shells.

The remainder of this chapter is broken up into the unofficial wine-growing subzones of Champagne, each representing a different geographic area with its own soil types and microclimates. Note that these designations—such as "Montagne de Reims"—are used solely as points of reference. Everyone *talks* about subzones, but you never actually see them on labels.[2] Instead, the most prominent word you'll see is, simply, "Champagne."

That said, there is something of a geographic hierarchy on some labels. In Champagne, villages that are considered to have the best vineyards are designated as "Grand Cru" or "Premier Cru," which roughly translate as "da bomb" and "so dope." Then again, Champagne is unlike any other region in the world in that the most expensive and sought-after bottles are often blends. (As you'll recall, Têtes de Cuvées/Prestige Cuvées are typically blends from more than one vineyard.)

Even though individual Champagne vineyards don't receive official Grand or Premier Cru designations—as they might in another French region—some parcels are recognized by name on wine labels. These are called *lieux-dits* ("named places"). Since so much Champagne is made from a blend of grapes from a number of different locations, it can be exciting to taste one of these single-vineyard wines.

The bottom line is this: More than any other French region (OK, other than Bordeaux), aficionados select Champagnes based on the producer name first, and the village or vineyard name second—an approach to wine that Americans can understand.

---

2   *In comparison, many other wine regions display the name of the subzone more prominently than the overall region. For example, a consumer could look at a label and not even realize that a wine labeled "Chablis" is from Burgundy or a "Pomerol" is from Bordeaux.*

Montagne de Reims

In the deepest caves under Domaine Pommery—a sprawling walled estate with a Lego castle look—is a series of massive bas-relief tableaux, carved into the chalk, as big as 50 feet (15 m) wide. The stunning works depict themes of antiquity, such as the Festivals of Bacchus, and seem to move and dance in the chiaroscuro light of the deep cellars. Likewise, the Montagne de Reims is where you'll find most of the Grandes Marques *maisons*, with all of their pomp and ceremony. But dig deep and you'll find significant treasures under the glamorous surface.

The region encompasses the city of Reims as well as ninety-three villages and boasts the most Grand Crus of any of the subregions: Ambonnay, Beaumont-sur-Vesle, Bouzy, Louvois, Mailly, Puisieulx,[3] Sillery, Mailly, Verzenay, and Verzy. It's planted in nearly equal proportions to Pinot Noir, Pinot Meunier, and Chardonnay, and thus produces textbook Champagnes, with a hint of raspberry, aromas of fresh-baked brioche, and maybe a whiff of earthiness.[4]

The vineyards lie on the lower slopes of the Montagne de Reims. The Pinot Noir and Pinot Meunier vines face north, and Chardonnay face east.

A. Margaine Rosé de Saignée
(V; 12% ABV; $$$$$)

I'm not always a fan of the *saignée* Champagne method, which calls for macerating red grapes until a red-winey intensity is achieved. Arnaud Margaine and his daughter, Mathilde, however, macerate their Pinot Noir for only a day, and they blend in Chardonnay, to mellow the punch of Pinot. This bottling manages to have the restraint of a paler rosé along with rhubarb, clove, and roasted red-pepper notes that make it a match for hearty foods. The Margaines are the top winemakers in the village of Villers-Marmery, farming vines dating back to 1927.

Alexandre Filaine "Spéciale" Brut (NV; 12% ABV; $$$$)

Former Bollinger cellar master Fabrice Gass farms organically and uses very old Bollinger casks for his fermentations. Buy this rich, compelling wine—with its grassy notes and a sour plum essence that lingers on the palate—before it becomes a cult phenom.

Bérêche & Fils "Les Beaux Regards" Ludes Premier Cru (V; 12% ABV; $$$$$)

Father and son Raphaël and Vincent Bérêche translate four different Champagne *terroirs* in their limited-edition releases. "Les Beaux Regards" ("beautiful looks") exemplifies the Bérêche style: pure, driven flavor floating on a galaxy of bubbles, a liquid snapshot of the family's home village of Ludes. One can truly taste the base wine, in the best way, in the fresh notes of citrus, sea salt, almond, and herbs, with a satisfying aftertaste of chalk, from vines averaging five decades of age. An emphasis on cask fermentation, base-wine aging on the lees, and bottle aging under cork all contribute to the silkiness of the Bérêche lineup.

Chartogne-Taillet "Les Barres" Merfy Extra-Brut (V; 12% ABV; $$$$$)

Alexandre Chartogne considers the grape varieties in his wines to be irrelevant. He farms his sixty-year-old ungrafted vines with horses and sheep (rather than a tractor) to avoid soil compaction, and believes that oak and oxygen should be used to balance out fruitiness, so much so that he doesn't fill his barrels of Pinot Meunier to the top, allowing for some headspace, and—*quel horreur!*—even a veil of *flor*[5] to grow, if it wants to. The result is a wine that doesn't say "Pinot Meunier" so much as it says "the village of Merfy," with a dry, salty, spicy flavor and a slightly chalky texture.

La Closerie "Les Béguines"[6] Extra-Brut (NV; 12.5% ABV; $$$$$)

Jérôme Prévost's grandmother's old massal selection[7] vines in the village of Gueux were a *closerie*—a plot of land rented out to tenant farmers—until he took

---

[3]   *Yes, I did spell that correctly.*

[4]   *The grape varieties Arbanne, Petit Meslier, Pinot Blanc, and Pinot Gris are also allowed in Champagne, but as they account for less than 0.3 percent of total vineyard plantings, I'll leave them out of the discussions about the subzones.*

[5]   *A thin layer of yeast, commonly used in Sherry making but far less common in other styles of wine.*

[6]   *Les béguines is a term for a bunch of vine shoots. It is apparently unrelated to the medieval term for a type of nunnery, which morphed into French slang for a bonnet, which somehow supplied the name of a sultry dance from the French West Indies that inspired that great Cole Porter song, "Begin the Beguines."*

[7]   *The old-school method of replacing dying vines or planting new rows. Rather than purchasing new vines from nurseries, traditional farmers graft cuttings from the best individual plants in their existing vineyard.*

What's Trashy About Champagne

In the late nineteenth century, the French wine industry was brought to its knees by the vine-eating aphid, phylloxera, that wiped out a full 40 percent of the nation's vineyards. The only solution to the problem was to replant, this time grafting delicate European vine varieties onto hardy American roots.

Unfortunately, the American rootstock wasn't well-suited to the alkaline soils of Champagne, and by the early twentieth century, the vines were withering due to a nutrient deficiency called chlorosis. Chemical fertilizers having not yet been invented, the Champenoise had to act fast to amend their soils and revive their plants. The solution was found in the overflowing dumps of Paris.

Back then, trash was mostly composed of organic materials that, over time, would break down and become a nice, rich compost. So the Champenoise solved Paris's garbage problem, and Parisian trash, spread between the vine rows, revived the struggling vines.

But the composition of garbage changed over the years. Champagne's vineyards were soon littered with cigarette butts and bits of plastic. Even worse was what wasn't visible: Struggling to maintain high yields in a warming, wet climate, the region developed a reputation as an excessive user of pesticides and herbicides.

By the mid-1990s, the trash had drawn the attention and outrage of environmentally aware journalists, consumers, and activists, who also turned the spotlight on the overuse of chemicals in the region. Vine-tenders began to adopt sustainable and organic farming techniques.

The practice of composting trash in Champagne was finally banned in 1997, and since 2001, the region has reduced its use of chemicals by 50 percent. All winery wastewater in Champagne is now treated for reuse, and all winery waste is now recycled. In addition, in 2003, Champagne was the first wine region in the world to conduct a comprehensive carbon-footprint assessment.

You can still see colorful pieces of plastic poking up out of the dirt in many highly regarded vineyards today. But, in some ways, it's a positive thing. Because that trash caused people to ask questions, and those questions spurred the *vignerons* to clean up their acts.

over. Having learned his trade in the cellar of Anselme Selosse (see page 74 for more on this guy), Prévost allows for spontaneous fermentations in a variety of large wooden casks. "Les Béguines" has the nutty aromatics and Sherry-like texture to suggest that there may be *flor* here, too. Mostly sourced from a single vintage, and nearly all Pinot Meunier, it's a layered, chewy, lightly smoky, and totally engrossing wine.

Cossy "Cuvée Éclat" Premier Cru Brut
(NV; 12% ABV; $$$)

Sophie Cossy's family has been growing grapes since 1764 and making wine since the 1950s. The "Cuvée Éclat" fruit is subtle, with a fine and delicate *mousse*. There are lavender pastille-candy aromatics, and notes of ginger on the palate. This blend of the big three grapes is composed entirely of the *cuvée* (first pressing), aged for an average of eight or so years prior to release.

Krug Grande Cuvée
(NV; 12% ABV; $$$$$)

The self-proclaimed *haute couture maison* of Champagne used to be an extremely secretive place, but its acquisition by the LVMH empire has let the daylight in. These days, you can google an ID number on your Krug bottle and learn everything you could possibly want to know about it. A team of six winemakers works with 400 different wines every year—250 from the current harvest plus 150 from the reserves—and thus the blending process for the vintage wines and Grand Cuvée is mind-bogglingly complex. The base wines are fermented in small, often very old barrels, and the bottles are all hand-riddled. While the *truly* couture wines are the single-vineyard, single-vintage "Clos" bottlings, at $1,000 and up a bottle, the "Grand Cuvée" has dignified, sappy, Cognac-like notes that might call to mind, oh, the polished wood interior of a Rolls-Royce—which is the appropriate setting for a glass of Krug.

Egly-Ouriet Grand Cru "V.P." Extra-Brut (NV; 12.5% ABV; $$$$$)

This bottling, having enjoyed *vieillissement prolongé* (extended

The Art of Ruinart

The Oyster Lunch, painted by Jean François de Troy in 1735, depicts a deliriously festive group at Versailles—corks flying, wine foaming—gathered around a table laden with oysters and Champagne on ice (before the invention of freezers!). These bottles are the distinctive pear shape[8] of the house of Ruinart, Champagne's first *maison*, and also, apparently, the favorite of the court.[9]

The Oyster Lunch was just the first of Ruinart's many iconic art moments, including an 1896 collaboration with Czech designer and painter Alphonse Mucha that epitomized the Belle Époque style and inspired superstar actress Sarah Bernhardt to commission her own series of now-famous Mucha posters.

Today, the house continues to work with cutting-edge contemporary artists, and offers to those who can afford it an augmented reality tasting experience, in which 3-D moving images are projected onto the table and the walls as music plays.

Ruinart Blanc de Blancs Brut Champagne
(NV; 12.5% ABV; $$$$–$$$$$)

Ruinart follows a stainless-steel winemaking protocol, so the flavors here are fresh and bright, with notes of lemongrass and tropical fruit; the texture is light and creamy. The "Dom Ruinart" Prestige Cuvée Blanc de Blancs (V; $$$$$), which spends a full decade sitting on the lees, is the deluxe version of this delicious bottling, oozing with brioche and lemon chiffon.

---

[8]   *The shape, with its wide base and narrow neck, captured any sediment that hadn't been removed by the imperfect disgorgement process of the time.*

[9]   *Take a closer look at the painting and you'll note some palace intrigue: The shoes of the aristocrats have red heels, indicating their positions of privilege as members of the royal court. Also, the figures pour their own wine, then place their glasses upside down in ice bowls when empty . . . not just to chill the glass, but to discourage aspiring poisoners.*

aging) of a full seven years on the lees, is masterful and generous, with a sunflower tint and a mouth-filling ginger-tinged spiciness that releases layers of allure as it warms in the glass.

Marguet "Shaman" Brut Nature (NV; 12.5% ABV; $$$$)

After his young daughter contracted leukemia, Benoît Marguet-Bonnerave began farming bio-dynamically—with horses instead of tractors—and using crystals and essential oils in the winery and vineyard. A number on the "Shaman" label indicates the vintage year of the majority of the base wine. It has a fresh-spring-flower-bud quality and is remarkably delicate for a wine sourced from Ambonnay and Bouzy.

Eric Rodez "Les Beurys Macération" Ambonnay Grand Cru Rosé (V; 12% ABV; $$$$$)

Working alongside his son Mickael, former Krug cellar master Eric Rodez farms organically and turns out exquisite juice, presented in evocative twisted-glass bottles. As with the A. Margaine (see page 64), this *saignée* is only partially composed of macerated juice, making for a toned-down, nuanced wine, with balanced notes of red fruit and white pepper.

Savart "L'Accomplie" Premier Cru Extra-Brut (NV; 12% ABV; $$$$)

I'm a particular fan of Extra-Brut Champagnes, which are to me the most honest expressions of the base wines. Accordingly, master blender Frédéric Savart's "L'Accomplie" is neither pumped up on *dosage* nor bone-dry, with soothing aromas of flowers and vanilla bean, and crisp green apple on the palate.

Vilmart & Cie "Cœur de Cuvée" Premier Cru (V; 12% ABV; $$$$$)

Vilmart has been a modestly sized family winery since 1890. The "Cœur de Cuvée" is composed entirely of the juice pressed at the midpoint of the cuvée known as the *cœur*: that soft, juicy pulp that's all flavor, no astringency. This blend of 80 percent Chardonnay and 20 percent Pinot Noir, from sixty-year-old vines, spends a full seventy months mellowing on the lees before disgorgement.

Vallée de la Marne

West of the Montagne de Reims region and the town of Épernay, the Vallée de la Marne is scenic, quiet, and low-key, with just two Grand Cru villages: Tours-sur-Marne and Aÿ.[10] Pinot Meunier thrives in the clay-rich soil here. The flavors in these wines tend toward joyous, approachable red fruit, without the ponderous earthiness that comes with Pinot Noir, so if you like your Champagne a little sassy, look toward the V de la M.

Gaston Chiquet "Cuvée de Réserve" Premier Cru Brut (NV; 12.5% ABV; $$$$)

The Chiquets are a prominent Champagne family—part of the Jacquesson clan—who were among the founding members of the Special Club (Club Trésors). The house's rosé is a pure decadent pleasure with its notes of papaya and red cherry. And the "Cuvée de Réserve" spends a minimum of five years on the lees, during which the structural foundation of this three-grape wine takes on almonds, hazelnuts, and vanilla—reflective of the family's focus on Chardonnay.

Henri Giraud "Füt de Chêne" Aÿ Grand Cru Brut Rosé (NV; 12.5% ABV; $$$$$)

From very old vines, the "Fut de Chêne" (oak barrel) rosé has aged in barrels made from specific local trees that twelfth-generation proprietor Claude Giraud's son-in-law, winemaker Sébastien Le Golvet, has selected to complement the fruit. While all the Giraud releases are sumptuous and buttery, this sunset-orange wine continues to open in the glass as it warms up, unfurling layer upon layer of Moroccan spice bazaar aromatics such as curry and saffron. Henri Giraud's signature bottle is shaped like an elegant vase and topped with a gold-plated *agrafe*,[11] its inside embossed with the name of the *maison*.

---

[10] *The double dot, known in French as the "trema" accent, signifies that the letter should be pronounced as its own syllable. So Aÿ is pronounced "eye-EE."*

[11] *This historic metal staple is beautiful to look at, but so difficult to remove that the Giraud team developed its own special knife to get under the arms. They call it a "degrafer."*

Team Submarine vs. Team Galleon

It can be difficult to discern what you're tasting when you've got sparkling wine in your mouth because the bubbles can be so distracting. So a good way to start picking apart the differences between different Champagne styles is to ask yourself: "Am I tasting a submarine or a galleon right now?"

In Chapter 1 (see page 28), I introduced the idea that some sparkling wines are like submarines, while others are more like galleons. The base wine for a submarine Champagne was likely made in an airtight steel tank. It's fresh and bright, its mouthfeel crisp. The base wine for a galleon Champagne, on the other hand, perhaps fermented in a wooden cask and aged in oak barrels, has a richer, mellower character.

Here are some of Champagne's top names, divided into teams depending on which style of winemaking they are associated with. This is an oversimplification, as winemakers are likely to dabble in many different techniques, but you may find it helpful to keep in mind as you taste wines from these producers.

TEAM SUBMARINE	TEAM GALLEON
· Charles Heidsieck	· Bollinger[12]
· Dom Pérignon	· Drappier
· Laurent-Perrier	· Gosset
· Mumm	· Henri Giraud
· Pierre Gimonnet	· Jaquesson
· Pierre Péters	· Krug
· Ruinart	· Lanson
· Salon	· Roederer
· Taittinger	· Savart
	· Selosse
	· Vilmart
	· Vouette & Sorbée

---

[12] *In an unusual twist on the vinification process, Bollinger stores its reserved back vintages in magnum bottles for later blending, so it's a wood-and-glass régime here. That still qualifies it as a galleon wine. Back in the day, fishing buoys, after all, used to be giant glass balls.*

Christophe Mignon Brut Nature (NV; 12% ABV; $$$)

Christophe Mignon, of Le-Mesnil-le-Huttier, has developed his own *Mignon Method*: farming guided by the moon and integrating natural practices such as biodynamics, phytotherapy, homeopathy, and geobiology. In addition to promising to improve your skin tone and spiritual health, this zero-*dosage* Meunier is a nice little wine, with a lovely golden color and a biting-into-a-grape purity. *Namaste.*

Moussé Fils "L'Or de Eugène" Perpetual[13] Blanc de Noirs (V; 12% ABV; $$$)

Twelfth-generation vigneron Cédric Moussé makes this perpetual-cuvée bottling just as his family did in the 1920s. Lively and drinkable, it's (mostly) Meunier at its best, fragrant with juicy red berries and even a touch of nectarine. His vineyards in the village of Cuisles have unusual topsoils composed of illite—the same French green clay that's used for beauty masks—which keeps vines from drowning in rainstorms, but holds moisture for summer.

[13]   *See Glossary, page 277.*

Côte Des Blancs

This is the land of Blanc de Blancs, anchored by the bustling small city of Épernay. The Grand Cru villages are Avize, Chouilly, Cramant, Les Mesnil-sur-Oger, Oger, and Oiry. Avize is noted for rendering wines of richness; Mesnil turns out flinty, minerally juice; and Cramant produces chalky, salty wines. It is also fun to say "Crémant[14] de Cramant."

But getting back to Blanc de Blancs. This region is planted 85 percent to Chardonnay, and thus it's a personal favorite of mine. Blanc de Blancs from Chardonnay are, for me, the soothing vanilla ice cream of Champagnes, mellow and satisfying. If your palate leans more toward berry sorbet, you might prefer to explore the other subregions, where the Champagne is made mostly from the red Pinot grapes. But who am I kidding? It's all delicious.

Pascal Agrapart "Complantée" Grand Cru Avize Extra-Brut
(NV; 12% ABV; $$$$)

Bonaparte, Abelard, Baudelaire . . . no one can string a bunch of syllables together in a surname like the French. This proud three-syllable family has been bottling its own wine since the nineteenth century.

The *mousse* is self-assured, and the aromatics evoke toasted almonds and certainty. The grapes are an old-fashioned field blend—the varieties grow jumbled together willy-nilly, instead of being separated by vineyard block—capturing the essence and history of the place. Arbane, Petit Meslier, and Pinot Blanc are all in the mix, in addition to the big three.

---

[14] Crémant *is a general French term for traditional-method sparkling wine. See* Champagne Lilbert-Fils, *page 75, for a description of the historic "Crémant de Cramant" style.*

**Guy Charlemagne
"Mesnillésime" Grand Cru
Extra-Brut Blanc de Blancs**
(V; 12% ABV; $$$$)

Just when I thought there could be no better French name than "Pascal Agrapart," along comes Guy Charlemagne, another producer whose roots go back to the 1800s. The name "Mesnillésime"

Selosse = The Opposite of Soulless

Anselme Selosse, Champagne's Messiah, trained in Burgundy and brought heretical ideas back to his family's winery in 1980: Farming should be natural; fruit should be cropped back for lower, more flavorful yields; and *lieux-dits* should be bottled separately, so as to explore the *terroir* of each site. Today, Anselme and his son Guillaume make wines that sell for hundreds, or even thousands, of dollars a bottle. Such is the price of art.

To get a sense of the world of Selosse, dine or stay at Les Avisés, the family's boutique hotel adjacent to its wine cave. The interior, outfitted by designer Bruno Borrione, is aristocratic country living as seen through the eyes of a pop artist. If you're lucky, you may be able to latch onto a cellar tour. Allow yourself three hours—the man does hold forth—and brush up on your French before you go.

Jacques Selosse "Substance" Avize Grand Cru Blanc de Blancs Brut (NV; 12.5% ABV; $$$$$)

Selosse's base wines ferment spontaneously, in barrels, and are sappy, nutty, and slightly oxidative. On top of this, the Substance comes from a solera (see page 278 for more on this term) of fractionally blended wines dating back to 1986, and has a Sherry-like hint of *flor*.[15] The result is a wine that's deep, sinewy, and mysterious, with peaty, earthy notes, a texture like a bow being pulled across cello strings, and a kombucha-like sweet-and-sour palate.

---

[15]   *Selosse is known to be a Sherry aficionado. And I have noted that the wines of two of his acolytes, Jérôme Prévost and Alexandre Chartogne (pages 65), both have this same subtle quality.*

is a mashup of "vintage" and the village of Mesnil. I found a fourteen-year-old bottle of this wine in my cellar, popped it, and fell into Blanc de Blancs bliss: buttery soft, with notes of honeyed graham cracker and lemon curd, and all that decadence despite its Extra-Brut *dosage*.

Larmandier-Bernier "Longitude" Premier Cru Extra-Brut Blanc de Blancs
(NV; 12% ABV; $$$$)

Minimal-intervention wine-making—indigenous yeasts, low-to-no *dosage*, biodynamic agriculture—puts the focus squarely on the fruit here. The "Latitude" bottling (taken from grape plots that are all on the same latitudinal line) has exotic notes of star fruit and melon. The "Longitude" (same idea, longitu-dinal line) crackles with lemon chiffon, lime peel, lemongrass, chervil, wildflowers, spice, smoke, and more.

Champagne Lilbert-Fils "Perle" Grand Cru Blanc de Blancs à Cramant
(NV; 12% ABV; $$$$)

The Lilbert family has farmed in Cramant since 1746, and the old-vine "Perle" is an old-fashioned "Crémant de Cramant," bottled at 4 atmospheres of pressure (rather than 6), making it indeed a relic of times past, closer to *pétillant* (see page 84 for more on this style).

Pascal Doquet "Cœur de Terroir" Vertus Premier Cru Brut Blanc de Blancs
(V; 12.5% ABV; $$$$$)

Certified organic farmers in Vertus, at the south end of Côte des Blancs proper, the Doquets allow for spontaneous fermentations in bar-rels, engage in a bit of *bâttonage* (lees stirring), and use only the first 85 percent of the pressed juice, leaving the *taille* out. Spending a decade *sur lie* before release, this wine is juicy and balanced, with some subtle caramel notes.

Champagne Pertois-Moriset "Les Quatre Terroirs" Grand Cru Brut Blanc de Blancs
(NV; 12% ABV; $$$)

"Les Quatre Terroirs" is this family winery's snapshot of the four Grand Cru villages of Mesnil, Oger, Cramant, and Chouilly. Fresh, racy, and vibrant, its aro-matics lean toward fresh herbs, like tarragon, with a seam of minerality in its youth that moves into biscuity territory with age.

....

Suenen Grand Cru Extra-Brut Blanc de Blancs à Cramant (NV; 12% ABV; $$$$)

I delighted in the fragrant green figginess of this head-turning

wine at nine years of age and can only imagine its pleasures after fifteen or twenty. Suenen practices organic farming and uses some unusual materials, such as locust-tree barrels.

Côte des Bar

Depending on your starting point, the Côte des Bar, or CdB,[16] is a couple of hours' drive south of Champagne proper. In some ways, it's a completely separate winegrowing region. Also called the Aube, after the name of the French *département* in which it is located, it accounts for a full quarter of Champagne's vineyards, and is useful to large *maisons* looking to blend diversity into their cuvées.

In recent years, there has been a renaissance here, with a new class of emerging producers catching the attention of sommeliers and Champagne geeks. The climate is a bit warmer, and the soil type is different: Composed of Kimmeridgian marl and limestone, it's similar to that of Chablis, the Burgundian region known for its crisp Chardonnays. It makes wines of profound minerality and biting

acidity, and favors one of the rarer grapes of Champagne, Pinot Blanc.

....

Marie-Courtin "Concordance" Côte des Bar Extra-Brut Blanc de Noirs (V; 12% ABV; $$$$$)

Dominique Moreau biodynam-ically farms Pinot Noir vines planted in the 1970s for the label she named after her grandmother. She only releases vintage-dated wines, with no *dosage*. The "Concordance" is made without any sulfur additions.[17] This is a fine-bubbled, raw, and honest wine, with lime juice on the palate—the Chablis of Champagne.

------

[16] *This is not to be confused with CBD (cannabidiol), which is far less salubrious, in my opinion, than Champagne.*

[17] *Sulfur acts as a preservative.*

David Speer Gets to the Bottom of the Côte des Bar

Wine & Spirits magazine has declared certified sommelier David Speer to be a "Master of Place" for his exhaustive knowledge of Champagne. I asked Speer—founder of an iconic Portland, Oregon, Champagne bar called Ambonnay—to share his recommendations from the "humble" (his word) farming region that is the Aube.

"The land in the CdB is less valuable, so there's more of a mix of agriculture and forest," Speer tells me. "Additionally, the grapes are planted in all sorts of places, such as hills and valleys with many different sun exposures. It feels less restricted and steeped in tradition relative to the north . . . much more like a New World wine region rather than one that's been around for hundreds of years."

Here are this Master of Place's go-to bottles from the Bar.

Roses de Jeanne "Côte de Val Vilaine" Brut Blanc de Noirs (V; 12.5% ABV; $$$$–$$$$$)

Cédric Bouchard's wines are all uniquely reflective of place and time, being single-vintage, single-parcel, single-grape, no-*dosage*, and vinified to 4.5 atmospheres instead of the usual 6. This bottling comes from a Pinot Noir planting, called Val Vilaine, that dates back to 1976. Speer describes Bouchard's bubblies as "the ultimate expression of what I seek in wine."

Vouette & Sorbée "Blanc d'Argile" Extra-Brut Blanc de Blancs (NV; 12% ABV; $$$$$)

"This wine can be a bit of sensory overload: big flavors, lots of acid, rich texture," Speer reflects, adding that its complexity and overall oomph can be attributed to the west-facing aspect of this parcel of Chardonnay vines, which makes for a longer ripening time. "It is a potent experience brought to you by a radical genius," the "eccentric and amazing" Bertrand Gautherot, a biodynamic farming advocate.

Pierre Gerbais "L'Originale" Extra-Brut Blanc de Blancs (NV; 12% ABV; $$$$$)

It's exciting to come across a 100 percent Pinot Blanc Champagne, from vines planted way back in 1904. Speer describes its "fruit salad of flavors" as making for an experience that's both "delicious and contemplative," offering tasters the option to savor, ponder, and discuss, or simply enjoy.

Cheryl Wakerhauser on the Special Club

Master *pâtissière* Cheryl Wakerhauser, author of the book *Modern French Pastry,* has a serious side interest in Champagne. Her Pix Pâtisserie/Bar Vivant in Portland, Oregon, has been awarded the World's Best Champagne and Sparkling Wine List prize for so many years by the swishy London-based *World of Fine Wine* that I've lost count. Wakerhauser was the first person to introduce me to the Club Trésors de Champagne, aka the "Special Club," many years ago.

"Champagne's Special Club," she explains, "is a group of grower-producers who all have the common goal of promoting the expression of *terroir* in the region. Members serve as a jury of their peers, voting for the best vintage Champagnes put forth, which are then put into a stout bottle only to be used by those that make the mark." Fine-wine retailers can procure Special Club bottles for you wherever you live, but if you visit Reims, be sure to stop in at the ab-fab Club Trésors tasting boutique, where you can try Special Club bottlings as well as other releases from Club members.

Marc Hébrart Premier Cru "Special Club" Brut
(V; 12% ABV; $$$$$)

In the village of Mareuil-sur-Aÿ in the Vallée de la Marne, Jean-Paul Hébrart (son of Marc) is making "fascinating Champagnes so full of finesse, I could drink them all day." This Pinot and Chard bottling is notable for its fresh, gossamer-like, weightless elegance. Advises Wakerhauser, "cellar it away for another ten years (if you can)."

Paul Bara Grand Cru "Special Club" Rosé
(V; 12.5% ABV; $$$$$)

Paul Bara was the first member to release a Special Club rosé, in 2004. The Bara family's village of Bouzy is noted for its expressive Pinot Noir; the *maison* also produces a highly regarded still red wine under the guidance of sixth-generation winegrower sisters Chantale Bara and Evelyne Dauvergne.

Pierre Gimonnet "Grands Terroirs de Chardonnay" "Special Club" Brut (V; 12.5% ABV; $$$$–$$$$$)

Wakerhauser describes Gimonnet's wines as "Chardonnay not to be missed!"—particularly if you can get them in magnum.[18] Gimonnet's four annual Special Club bottlings feature the output of the Grand Cru villages of Chouilly, Oger, and Cramant; the vineyard plantings date back to 1911.

---

[18] *That's twice the size of, and twice as much fun as, a regular bottle.*

* The first two wines can be found in Chapter 2, on pages 36–37.

$$$$$
Louis Roederer
Cristal*

$$$$$
Philipponnat
Clos des Goisses

$$$$$
A. Margaine
Rosé de Saignée

$$$$$
Bérêche & Fils
Les Beaux Regards

$$$$$
Chartogne-Taillet
Les Barres

$$$$$
La Closerie
Les Béguines

$$$
Cossy
Cuvée Éclat

$$$$$
Krug
Grande Cuvée

$$$$$
Egly-Ouriet
V.P.

$$$$-$$$$$
Ruinart
Blanc de Blancs

$$$$$
Eric Rodez
Les Beurys Macération

$$$$$
Vilmart & Cie
Cœur de Cuvée

CHAMPAGNE

$$$$

Gaston Chiquet

Cuvée de Réserve

$$$

Moussé Fils

L'Or de Eugène

$$$$

Pascal Agrapart

Complantée

$$$$$

Jacques Selosse

Substance

$$$$$

Pascal Doquet

Cœur de Terroir Vertus

$$$

Pertois-Moriset

Les Quatre Terroirs

$$$$

Suenen

Blanc de Blancs

$$$$-$$$$$

Roses de Jeanne

Côte de Val Vilaine

$$$$$

Vouette & Sorbée

Blanc d'Argile

$$$$$

Marc Hébrart

Special Club

$$$$$

Paul Bara

Special Club Rosé

$$$$-$$$$$

Pierre Gimonnet

Grands Terroirs de Chardonnay

The Rest of France

Sparkling wine as we know it was born in France and continues to be produced in just about every French wine region. Unlike Italy, where funky traditional village wines take every-which shape and form— as you'll learn in the next chapter—French bubblies outside of Champagne fall fairly neatly into three categories, all of which are *très bon* with *fromage*.

The first is Crémant, made via *méthode traditionnelle*. The Institut national de l'origine et de la qualité (INAO) gets to decide which regions are allowed to use the word "Crémant" on their labels, and as of now, that includes Alsace, Bordeaux, Burgundy, the Jura, the Loire, Limoux in Languedoc, the Die appellation in the Rhône, and finally, next door to France, Luxembourg.

Crémant wines must age on the lees for a minimum of nine months, as compared to Champagne's twelve-month requirement, but individual regions can adopt their own more rigorous standards. Alsace, for example, requires twelve months of aging *sur lie*. (These regions all require additional bottle aging after disgorgement, as well.)

The term *"mousseux"* is more vague, simply meaning "sparkling," but some regions have strict definitions of what sort of sparkling wine can be labeled

RECIPE

B2C2

SERVES 1

This drink, named for its four ingredients, represents the entire nation of France: the nation's finest brandy, Cognac, is from the southeast, near Bordeaux; Bénédictine herbal liqueur is from Normandy, in the northeast; Cointreau orange cordial originated in Angers, in the Loire Valley; and Crémant can be made just about anywhere in France . . . but more on that below.

½ ounce brandy
½ ounce Bénédictine
½ ounce Cointreau
(Triple Sec)
2½ ounces Crémant
(French sparkling wine)

Combine the brandy, Bénédictine, and Cointreau in a chilled cocktail glass. Top off with Crémant.

with the appellation name and this word. "*Pétillant*" also translates as "sparkling," but it suggests a wine with lower atmospheric pressure, such as a *Pétillant Naturel*.

Whereas the Champenoise don't have much choice as to what type of wine they're going to make,[1] vintners in other regions can adjust to the vintage, producing more fizz in cold years and more still wines after warm growing seasons. And if they don't mind *vin de pays*[2] designations on their labels, they can play around with different grapes and winemaking methods, as well.

And now for the regions and the wines. We'll start out in the south, because that's where French sparkling wine was born, and work our way north, eventually coming toe-to-toe with Champagne.

---

[1] *The choices are Champagne, Coteaux de Champenois red or white, or Rosé des Riceys, a dark-red rosé-style wine that can only be produced in the area around the village of Les Riceys. No Pét-Nats there.*

[2] *"Country wine"—officially IGP, or Indication géographique protégée—rather than a more specific, and respected, geographic designation.*

Southwest

The *Sud Ouest* is a low-key corner of France, known for its relaxed way of life and full-throttle traditional French food. This is the land of foie gras, Bayonne ham, duck confit, pigeon stew, piperade (a soupy showcase for espelette peppers), and Roquefort cheese. There's plenty of wine to accompany all the eating, but alas, not much of it is exported to the United States.

Southeast of Bordeaux and northwest of Languedoc, this region's two most recognizable wine subzones are Cahors and Madiran, both of which produce hulkish, tar-like reds that will put the kind of hair on your chest that can't be waxed off. And hipster wine nerds dig Irouléguy, a Basque enclave on the Spanish border that makes hearty rosés and reds and also produces well-regarded ciders. Plus, there's Armagnac. Which goes with the foie gras. Strangely, the historic sparkling wines from this region don't get much fanfare, but this book is here to change that.

GAILLAC

The Romans considered Gaillac the ne plus ultra of French wine regions. And what may have been the world's first wine brand was born here, at the end of the fourteenth century.[3] It was called Vins du Coq. (*Get your mind out of the gutter!*) Today, the locals guzzle a fizzy dry white, called Gaillac Perlé, which is the local counterpart to the spritzy Txakolí *(chah-koh-LEE)* that's produced in Spanish Basque Country. And the region is still famous for the *méthode Gallaçoise (ancestrale)* bubbly that was one of the first truly sparkling wines ever.[4]

....

Robert & Bernard Plageoles Gaillac Mauzac Nature
(V; 12% ABV; $$–$$$)

Patriarch Robert Plageoles was a scholar of the native indigenous grape varieties and clones of the Gaillac region, seeking out abandoned vineyards and wild vines and reviving more than a dozen different strains that were in danger of extinction. His son and grandsons honor his legacy, utilizing ultratraditional winemaking techniques. This is old-school *méthode Gallaçoise*: dry, cloudy, and cider-like, reminiscent of a time when everything was simpler.

BERGERAC

The tony part of the *Sud Ouest*, just east of Bordeaux, Bergerac birthed Périgord truffles, as well as the beloved seventeenth-century novelist and playwright Cyrano de Bergerac.[5] Plus there's Château de Duras, the country home of the Duchess of Duras, who wrote a woke novel aimed at ending racism. (And it worked! . . . Just kidding.) It is said that twentieth-century novelist Marguerite Duras styled her pen name after the selfsame Duchess.

But I digress. The British expat population here—lured by the horseback riding culture and the whiff of literary pretension in the air—are big fans of the local sweet wine, Monbazillac, and the hearty reds, which are Bordelaise-ish in style. And I suspect that, secretly, they have been hoarding all the Bergerac bubbly.

. . . .

Jonc Blanc "Bulle Rose" Vin de France (V; 11% AVB; $$)

Bergerac natural winemakers Franck Pascal and Isabelle Carles made this delightful Pét-Nat from the second harvest—that is, a second round of fruit that typically isn't picked for anything, arriving too late in the season—in 2017,

after their biodynamic vineyards were damaged by frost and they lost most of their initial crop. I do hope they will keep making this pale-peachy-orange delight. It's all cream soda at first sip, with a pillowy soft texture, and honey on the palate. Over time, notes of earthiness and graphite reveal its Cabernet Sauvignon core (the rest is Sémillon).

[3] Jefford, *"France's Forgotten Luxury Wine in the Hills of Gaillac."*

[4] *As opposed to the fizzy accidents of centuries past. See Chapter 2 (page 32) for more on this.*

[5] *The play and films were loosely based on this long-nosed gentleman's life.*

Languedoc

Languedoc (that's pronounced *LONG-duck*)[6] used to be something of a trainwreck, its vineyards overproducing plonk and its winemakers always loudly protesting about something. On top of this, the beach scene was meh. But Languedoc has grown up over the past couple of decades and may someday surpass its glamorous sibling, Provence, in sophistication.

For the moment, however, Languedoc offers tremendous bang for the buck. Just as savvy investors are quietly buying Languedoc country houses with ocean views, young vintners are purchasing tumbledown vineyards and reviving long-forgotten grape varieties. And wine insiders know that a good red Minervois or Corbières from Languedoc can deliver just as much pleasure as a jet-black Bandol from Provence that's twice the price.

As for Languedoc bubbly, it's one of the best deals in wine—for the moment. It's humble, self-effacing, and historically significant. Buy it now, before the party yachts ditch Cannes and Antibes, dock up at Port Camargue, and load up on the local fizz.

Mas de Daumas Gassac Languedoc "Rosé Frizant" Vin Mousseux (V; 11% ABV; $$)

The father of modern oenology, Professor Émile Peynaud, helped establish this "Grand Cru of the Midi."[7] And yet its liquid products are classified as plain ol' basic country wines due to its location and renegade grape varieties. Tucked into the hills behind Montpellier, about 25 miles (40 km) from the Mediterranean, the estate sits on a gold mine of red soil. This sparkling rosé, made from young-vine Cabernet Sauvignon and Mourvèdre, is a single-fermentation take on the Charmat method, and tastes best after it has been open a while, the peach tones mellowing out in favor of sour plum, nectarine, and maple.

LIMOUX

The wild, woolly Limoux region is recognized as the origin of the oldest sparkling wines in the world. (It's also home to the hilltop village of Rennes-le-Château, where a lot of that nonsense about the Priory of Sion, *which never existed and was a hoax*, was cooked up.) But surely the climate—just 50 miles (80 km),

as the crow flies, from the Mediterranean—is too balmy for growing the crisp high-acid fruit needed for bubbly?

Not so. This craggy landscape—furrowed by river valleys, defined by the Corbières and the Chalabrais mountain ranges, as well as the Pyrenees, and punctuated by medieval castle ruins atop natural rock plateaus—is so diverse that it supports a wide variety of grapes and styles. And the damp, cool, high-elevation growing zone known as the Terroir de la Haute-Vallée, which follows the Aude River into the Pyrenees foothills, is particularly well-suited to sparkling production.

There are three officially recognized sparkling-wine styles here. Limoux Méthode Ancestrale is made from late-ripening Mauzac, the rustic white grape we met in Gaillac. "Blanquette," in the local Occitan language, means "little white," so it's an analog to "Blanc de Blancs." Thus Blanquette de Limoux bubbly is made from at least 90 percent Mauzac, with up to 10 percent Chardonnay or Chenin Blanc. It is *méthode traditionnelle*, as is Crémant de Limoux. But the

---

[6]   No relation to the awful cliché of a Sixteen Candles *character by the same name.*

[7]   *South of France.*

Crémant grape makeup is a bit more refined, with Mauzac limited to 20 percent or less of the blend. Chardonnay and/or Chenin Blanc can be up to 90 percent of the cuvée, and Pinot Noir can be up to 40 percent.

Saint-Hilaire Brut Blanquette de Limoux
(V; 12% ABV; $–$$)

The abbey of Saint-Hilaire no longer houses winemaking monks, but it's been around since the eighth century and boasts graceful cloisters, delightful painted ceilings, and solid Romanesque architecture. This modern-day estate-bottled wine, named after the abbey, ages twelve months *sur lie* and I have seen it priced as low as $12. What's not to love?

Delmas "Cuvée Berlene" Brut Blanquette de Limoux
(V; 12% ABV; $)

Bernard Delmas was a respected chef before returning to his family estate, and he puts that highly developed palate to work, along with his wife, Marlene, and son, Baptiste. Delmas farms 80 acres (32 ha) of organic vineyards, all poised in high-elevation mountainside pockets between the

Océanique and the Terroir de la Haute-Vallée. From the aromatics and mouthfeel alone, you can tell this screaming deal of a wine gets a ton of lees time—thirty-six months to be exact.

Gérard Bertrand "Cuvée Thomas Jefferson" Crémant de Limoux Sud de France Brut (V; 12.5% ABV; $$)

Former French pro rugby player Gérard Bertrand is one of the world's largest biodynamic producers, naturally farming multiple sites around Languedoc and churning out boatloads of solid, well-made wines. (He also makes a rosé in partnership with American rock star Jon Bon Jovi. See how Languedoc is getting to be glam?) Of the many bubblies in the Bertrand lineup, I'm partial to this yeasty, brisk, classically styled bubbly, named after some guy who apparently stocked his personal cellar with a lot of Limoux.

Rhône

Following the path of its namesake river from Lyon to the Mediterranean, the Rhône Valley is a central hub of French wine regions, surrounded by Languedoc, the Southwest, the lower reaches of the Loire, Beaujolais, the Hautes-Alpes, and Provence. It's best known for its meaty, spicy reds, heady, fragrant whites, and the robust rosés of Tavel and Lirac. And yet . . . there's a secret sparkling side to this region.

rivers in winter,[9] and removing them in the spring to allow fermentation to finish, further muddying the question as to what the first sparkling wine in France really was. Alas, few of the venerable, throwback *méthode dioise*-style wines—hybrids, essentially, between *ancestrale* and *traditionnelle*—are imported to the US. But we do have access to at least a couple of traditional-method winners.

DIE

No, I don't want you to die. I want you to try sparkling wines from Die, pronounced *DEE*. The vineyards of this no-man's-land—between the dead-serious northern Rhône and the more laidback southern side—climb as high as 2,300 feet (700 m) up the breezy slopes of the Vercors Massif.[8] Clairette Blanche and Muscat, which tend toward low acidity under the usual circumstances, are more compelling up here, making for fizz that will make you—yes—want to die with happiness.

According to wine historian Elizabeth Gabay, the Gallo-Romans made sparkling Die by plunging sealed jars of wine in

Achard-Vincent Clairette de Die Mousseux Brut
(NV; 11.5% ABV; $$)

The Achard family vineyards are certified biodynamic and were early to be certified organic, back in 1968. Vinified entirely from the Clairette grape (no Muscat), this *méthode traditionnelle* tastes timeless. It's pale straw in color, with creamy aromatics that hint, delightfully, of goat's or sheep's milk. Over time, with air, the barnyard element subsides, to be replaced by fresh-picked cherries.

---

[8] *This may also be the name of a* Game of Thrones *character.*

[9] *Gabay, "Clairette de Die—The Importance of Direction."*

Cave Poulet et Fils Méthode Traditionnelle Crémant de Die (NV; 11.5% ABV; $–$$)

This super-simple quaffer goes down like Prosecco, with notes of apple peel and brisk mountain air. A blend of Clairette, Aligoté, and

Muscat, it's something to sip with lunch—*poulet*, perchance?—on a Saturday.

Hautes-Alpes

North of Provence, up on the *hautes* (high) slopes of the foothills of the Alps, a handful of brave vinetending families—just eight, last time I checked—are making and bottling wine. Farmers here have long vinified their own juice at home, but the idea of labeling and marketing the local swill is a fairly new idea. So while it's still just an IGP (*Indication géographique protégée*), this is a *haute* spot to watch.

The vineyards are between 2,000 and 3,300 feet (600 and 1000 m) in elevation, clustered around the lean Lac de Serre-Ponçon, which has a moderating effect on the surrounding hillsides, making this winegrowing region less frost-prone in the winter than its Alpine location might suggest.

Domaine Allemand Méthode Traditionnelle Brut Rosé (V; 12% ABV; $$)

After serving in the military in the Champagne region, Louis Allemand returned home to the Durance River Valley in 1954 determined to become the first professional *vigneron* in the region. Louis's son and granddaughter, Marc and Laetitia, make this appealing rosé from Mollard, an endangered local indigenous red grape variety that they saved from extinction. The name translates as "little mountain," and the wine suggests mountain meadows and honey-drizzled fresh goat cheese—I'm certain it's as good for your health as an alpine hike.

Savoie & Bugey

Looking toward Lake Geneva, on the border with Switzerland and Italy, the peak of Mont Blanc defines every breathtaking vista. This is Savoie, a place where a person can ski right up to a *chalet*, stomp the snow off one's boots, and sit down to a meal of sausage, melted *fromage*, and local ciders.

And then that person can ski to the bottom of the mountain at the end of the day, stomp the snow off one's boots, and sit down for a little apéritif of Savoie sparkling wine. *C'est bon!* Bugey, Savoie's sibling to its west, is so close and so similar that some producers make wine from both appellations.

SAVOIE

As with so many European viticultural regions, the wines of Savoie were praised as far back as antiquity. Pliny the Elder (who got *around*) wrote about them, kings enjoyed them, and nineteenth-century spa-goers visiting the town of Aix-les-Bains sipped fresh, light Savoie wines after "the thermal cure."

The Alpine grape varieties here have unusual names like Molette, Mondeuse, and Altesse; we also see the more-familiar Gamay cropping up a bit. Finally, as you might guess, the high altitude and cool climate of Savoie are ideal for bubbly production, the mountain cheeses here are *off the hook*, and the two together—prickly, zippy local fizz with gooey, savory local dairy—are pretty much perfection.

Royal Seyssel Méthode Traditionnelle Grand Cru Régional (V; 12% ABV; $$$)

The village of Seyssel is its own little subappellation of Savoie, noted for its sparkling wines since the mid-nineteenth century. Royal Seyssel was originally founded in 1901, then recently revived in 2008. This wine, equal parts organically grown Molette and Altesse, has finesse, with a floral nose, and a delicate palate that delivers a long, white-peppery lemony finish.

Eugène Carrel Méthode Traditionnelle Vin de Savoie Brut Rosé (NV; 12.5% ABV; $$)

In the village of Jongieux, near Lac du Bourget, the Carrel family has been growing grapes since 1830. The Gamay (80 percent), Pinot Noir (10 percent), and Mondeuse (10 percent) for this wine were grown on the lower slopes of Mont du Chat and Mont de la Charvaz. This pale-salmon weeknight bubbly is uncomplicatedly delicious, with peachy-rose-petal aromatics and some citrus and floral notes on the subdued palate.

André & Michel Quenard Crémant de Savoie Brut Nature (NV; 12% ABV; $$–$$$)

Jacquere, the signature Savoie white grape, is responsible for the yum factor here. The *mousse* is a touch aggressive, but you just can't go wrong with the nose and palate of stone fruit and lemon chiffon—so much fruit for a Brut Zero! This can be explained by Quenard's steep, terraced hillside vineyards above the town of Chignin, where the intensity of the mountain sunlight makes for lush ripeness.

BUGEY

Across the Rhône River, to the west, is Bugey, where the vineyards hug the foothills of the Jura Mountains. It's greener and more forested here, as opposed to the snowy, rocky peaks of Savoie—better-suited to Smurfs than a Yeti. Speaking of Smurfs, the inhabitants of Bugey are called *Bugistes* or *Bugeysiens*, and some of them speak Savorêt, a dialect of a language called Arpitan. The signature sparkling wine here, named Cerdon after the village where it's made, could be confused for the syrup you put in your backyard hummingbird feeder. It is ruby-red and silly-sweet, and it is known to make Smurfs fly.

Patrick Bottex
"La Cueille" Bugey Cerdon
(NV; 8% ABV; $$)

Raspberry-colored, *pétillant*, and lightly sugary, it's easy to see why this was traditionally a Christmastime beverage in the region. A cornucopia of ripe strawberries, cherry, and blood orange, zippy with acidity, "La Cueille" is a joyous thing to behold and savor. Serve it with cookies, or barbecue, or just guzzle it in the afternoon. It's 90 percent Gamay and 10 percent Poulsard (a red mountain grape), and is *méthode ancestrale*, fermented only partially to dryness. I dare you to not smile after taking a sip.

Tissot Extra Dry Méthode Traditionnelle Bugey Rosé
(V; 12.5% ABV; $$–$$$)

Winemaker Thierry Tissot[10] has revived a historic vineyard called Mataret in his village of Vaux-en-Bugey and is breaking with local tradition by making a traditional-method wine that doesn't fit the hummingbird-feeder mold. In the confusing terminology of sparkling wine, "Extra-Dry" is typically a touch sweeter than Brut, but this pink Gamay-Mondeuse blend is minerally and doesn't taste excessively of its *dosage*. There are notes of earthy raspberry and cherry, or, as a friend put it to me, "strawberry fluoride at the dentist's office." But the *good* fluoride.

---

[10] Not to be confused with Tissot in the Jura.

The Jura[11]

Continuing our trek through the Alps, we arrive in the Jura Mountains, where still more fairy-tale grape varieties thrive. They are the red Trousseau and Ploussard,[12] and the white Savagnin, which

---

[11] It's common parlance to use the article "the," rather than just "Jura," perhaps because the full title of the region is the "Republic and Canton of the Jura."

[12] Also spelled Poulsard.

Sure, More Jura! With Mark Gurney

Mark Gurney is the beverage director at Salon and the Wine Store in London's Brixton neighborhood and Levan in neighboring Peckham. His natural-leaning wine list at Levan is the most Jura-centric of any I've ever seen, and I love his language for describing wines.

"The Jura is a fascinating region which almost exists in its own wine bubble," Gurney tells me. "They do things in a particular style and philosophy, which hasn't been influenced by market pressures or modern farming techniques."

Domaine André & Mireille[13] Tissot "Cuvée Indigène" Crémant du Jura (V; 12.5% ABV; $$–$$$)

Gurney describes this bubbly blend of biodynamically farmed Chardonnay, Pinot Noir, Ploussard, and Trousseau as "full-blooded," as well as "rich, aromatic, and . . . woofy!"

Jean François Ganevat "La Combe Rotalier" Crémant du Jura (NV; 12.5% ABV; $$$)

This "humble" Jura producer has always pushed the envelope in natural winemaking and bottles a head-spinning number of micro-releases each year. "Not many people know he makes this 100 percent Chardonnay sparkling wine," notes Gurney. "I love it," he adds. "It's understated and nuanced, offering bright orchard fruits with a wisp of toastiness. Extremely smashable!"

Les Pieds sur Terre Valentin Morel Crémant du Jura Brut Nature (NV; 11% ABV; $$$–$$$$)

This is a "new name to watch," according to Gurney. Valentin Morel earned an international law degree before becoming enamored with biodynamic agriculture and returning to his family's domaine. "His 100 percent Chardonnay Crémant is fun, fruity, and full of life. A bona fide apéritif wine if ever there was one," says Gurney.

---

[13] *Second-generation vintners Bénédicte and Stéphane Tissot are the current proprietors, so all four names appear on the labels.*

makes a wine that's *flor*-influenced like Sherry and is called Vin Jaune because it's crazy-bright-neon yellow. By contrast, the sparkling wines tend to be nothing out of the ordinary: *méthode traditionnelle*, masterfully made from your standard Pinot Noir and Chardonnay. Since the domaines here tend to be small but the region is white-hot right now, I've included as many labels as possible to give you a lot of options.

Domaine Pignier Crémant du Jura Brut Nature
(NV; 12% ABV; $$)

Carthusian monks planted Domaine Pignier back in the thirteenth century, and there is something reverential about this blend of 80 percent Chardonnay and 20 percent Pinot Noir, biodynamically grown. Despite the Brut Nature label, it's balanced and lacy, with notes of Meyer lemon and lime peel.

Domaine de Montbourgeau Crémant du Jura Brut
(NV; 12% ABV; $$)

Nicole Deriaux manages her family's Montbourgeau vineyard—planted in 1920—in the village of Étoile ("star"), with the help of her

sons. There are plenty of *étoiles* in every glass of this precise, minimalist delight of a wine, made entirely from Chardonnay. It's understated, but there's a little *frisson* at the finish that resets your palate, making you thirst for the next sip.

Domaine des Marnes Blanches Crémant du Jura Réserve (NV; 12.5% ABV; $$–$$$)

This wine's aromatics are offbeat enough—fresh dill, baguette, vanilla wafer, cucumber—to indicate a wild primary fermentation, and I'd pair it with any food that involves fresh herbs. Winegrowers Pauline and Gérard Fromont named their organically farmed vineyard after the white marl soils here in the southern Jura.

Overnoy-Crinquand Crémant du Jura Rosé
(NV; 11.5% ABV; $$$)

If you prefer something slightly more offbeat, try this sparkling organic Ploussard. It's cantaloupe-colored and starts out with fresh raspberry notes. Leave it open for a while and you'll smell and taste dried berries and a caramelized nuttiness—no sweetness, though, as it's made in a Brut Zero style.

Beaujolais

Time to hang up the skis and snowshoes and get back to work in the lowlands, north of the Rhône and south of Burgundy. For many years, consumers only knew Beaujolais for its "Nouveau," a fruit-punchy style of wine that's released just a couple of months after harvest, with much fanfare, then promptly dies in the bottle if it isn't consumed immediately.

Starting in the 1980s, however, winemakers started getting serious about making earthy, profound, kick-ass Beaujolais Gamay—the sort of wine that demands to be sipped slowly while turning the pages of Émile Zola on a cold winter's night by a roaring fire. Since then, Beaujolais has been an industry insider beverage: Burgundy at a fraction of the price, or "the poor man's Pinot."

As I write this, Beaujolais is still fighting for its reputation. The French labeling authorities still see it as being so secondary to Burgundy that much "Crémant de Bourgogne" is in fact made from Chardonnay sourced from Beaujolais. The yields are higher down here, and the soil makes for more acidic fruit, so it's a better place to grow grapes for bubbly.

It is rumored that a bona fide "Crémant de Beaujolais" appellation is in the works. In the meantime, read on to meet a few daring winemakers who aren't afraid to make Beaujolais bubbly. They're penalized by the authorities for doing so—they're not allowed to print vintage dates on their labels, even though the following are all vintage wines—but they push bravely onward for the sake of our happiness.

....

Jean-Paul Brun "FRV100" Mousseux
(NV; 7.5% ABV; $$)

But first, a little *amuse-bouche.* Ultratraditionalist winemaker Jean-Paul Brun makes delicate, refined red wines from Gamay, relying on indigenous yeasts and age-old techniques, under his Domaine des Terres Dorées label. But I am going to tell you about his silliest wine, "FRV100," which is pronounced "effervescent," because "100" in French is *cent* (got it?). This glowing hot-pink Pét-Nat was only partially fermented, leaving a lot of juicy ripe sugar in the bottle à la Bugey Cerdon (see page 95), so drink it with dessert. At the same time, the seriousness of the Gamay grape is evident in the wine's notes of brambly blackberries and earth.

Chevonne Ball on Beaujolais

Gamay doyenne Chevonne Ball plans events like Gamay-and-jazz pairings, was working on a book about Gamay as I was writing this, and owns Dirty Radish Travel Company, leading immersive gastronomic and oenophilic tours of Beaujolais.

"Gamay is right up there with Pinot Noir," Ball says. "It has all the characteristics you need to make *méthode champenoise*. It holds its own but also—as opposed to those toast and brioche notes you find in Champagne—sparkling Beaujolais brings really good balanced fruit and acidity to this incredible palate."

In Beaujolais, Ball says, regional sparkling wine is a rarity, drunk by winemakers in small villages rather than the big city of Lyon. On the plus side, "I love the fact that it is in such small production because most of the time, the producers are hand-riddling each bottle. There is that passion-project aspect to it," she remarks. Here are a couple of bottles Ball is particularly passionate about.

Domaine Franck Besson "Dentelle" Méthode Traditionnelle Blanc de Noirs (NV; 12% ABV; $$)

"Franck Besson is a larger-than-life, gregarious man, yet this wine is so fine-*moussed* and sexy!" Ball says with a laugh. In addition to the 100 percent Gamay "Dentelle," Besson makes a rosé bubbly, called "Granit," that's a personal fave of yours truly. If you see these wines, grab them and run. "He disgorges on demand, so importers have to order the wines a couple of months in advance," Ball notes.

Nicole Chanrion "Effervescence" Méthode Traditionnelle Gamay Brut (NV; 11% ABV; $$)

After facing skepticism about her gender when she entered the business in the 1970s, Nicole Chanrion became an industry leader and was voted president of the Côte-de-Brouilly appellation in 2000; today she is known as "La Patronne de la Côte." Ball describes Chanrion's 100 percent Gamay bubbly from fifty-year-old vines as "like traditional Champagne" and "very rich" with "a sourdough brightness to it, and that high acidity is so delicious."

Burgundy

I'm a little conflicted about sparkling *Bourgogne*. On the one hand, Burgundy is set up for success, given that its top two grape varieties are Pinot Noir and Chardonnay. On the other, this world-class wine region does such a fabulous job with still Pinot and Chard, why bother with bubbly when the neighboring Loire and the Jura both make excellent, nicely priced effervescent wines?

And anyway, a fair amount of Crémant de Bourgogne is actually sourced from Beaujolais, as per the discussion on page 99. Yet, just as I was writing this, the Bourgogne Wine Board was rolling out two new quality stamps on wine labels, to designate the finest Crémants. Moving forward, the terms "Eminent" or "Grand Eminent" on labels should be helpful guides to finding the good stuff.

I'm not even including bubbly Bordeaux in this book—why would I, when nearby Gaillac, Bergerac, Limoux, and Die are so much more interesting from a sparkling perspective? So, of the two big-league red-wine regions of France, I'm including one, and that one is Burgundy. And despite all my kvetching, I will now introduce you to some very fine wines.

Parigot Blanc de Blancs Crémant de Bourgogne Brut

(NV; 12% ABV; $$$)

The south-facing vineyards of Savigny-lès-Beaune are highly regarded for still wines, many of them Premier Cru status. This Blanc de Blancs is a blend of 80 percent Chardonnay and 20 percent the traditional white grape variety Aligoté. Neutral barrel fermentation, full malolactic fermentation, and two to three years *en tirage sur lie* make for a nose that is rich and leesy and a palate that is mouthfilling and creamy, with floral notes bringing an overall sense of elegance to the glass.

Val de Mer Méthode Traditionnelle Brut Non Dosé

(NV; 12% ABV; $$)

Chardonnay-centric, chilly Chablis is only about 45 miles (72 km) south of the Champenoise town of Troyes, so it follows that great bubbly should be made here, where fossilized seashells can be found in the sedimentary soil. Val de Mer—"Valley of the Sea"—is Burgundy wunderkind Patrick Piuze's side venture, a collaboration with François Moutard of the Champagne house Moutard Père et Fils, and the sort of seafoamy notes that are markers of great Champagne are evident in this Brut Zero.

Clotilde Davenne Crémant de Bourgogne Brut Extra

(NV; 12.5% ABV; $$)

Renegade Clotilde Davenne vinifies Sauvignon Blanc from century-plus-year-old vines in Saint-Bris, a southwestern outpost of Chablis that is its own appellation. In addition, she champions Aligoté, the second-tier white grape of Burgundy. This *blanc* blend is plain ol' Pinot Noir and Chardonnay, but it brings to mind fresh-picked raspberries and wild blackberries, complete with the stray bit of leaf and bramble. There's an earthiness to it, and the acid is full-throttle. The back label suggests a pairing with escargot, which sounds just about right.

Loire

The path of the Loire River covers a large swath of central France. As such, there's no one climate, soil type, or grape that dominates; the region's official website lists fifteen different varieties. In sparkling wines, you'll find the classic Loire white grapes Chenin Blanc and Sauvignon Blanc, plus Chardonnay. And the red grapes, Cabernet Franc, Cabernet Sauvignon, Gamay, and the purple-skinned Pineau d'Aunis.

I should also mention Melon de Bourgogne, the grape of Muscadet. This winegrowing zone at the western end of the Loire, where it becomes an estuary with the Atlantic, makes zippy, salty wines that often have a "spritzy" texture. Muscadet isn't fully sparkling, or even *pétillant*, but its light, energetic style sets the tone for the Loire.

Crémant de Loire wines are classic *méthode traditionnelle*. A new "Prestige de Loire" quality stamp on labels aims to aid consumers in finding the best of these. And this region is a hot spot for *méthode ancestrale*, as well. Finally, note that some of the most interesting wines of the region are labeled as "Vin de France," because the grape varieties and/or vinification techniques don't fit the strict regulations of the Loire appellation.

Jo Landron "Atmosphères" Méthode Traditionnelle Loire (NV; 12.5% ABV; $$)

Far downriver from the heart of Crémant country, Muscadet producer Jo Landron biodynamically farms the obscure Folle Blanche, which makes a rather thin local still wine but is dynamite as the base for this exquisitely frothy blend. After a spontaneous first fermentation, Landron leaves the wine *sur lie* in bottle for two years and adds an Extra-Brut–level *dosage*.

Château de l'Eperonnière Crémant de Loire (V; 12% ABV; $$)

Moving inland, we come to savory, minerally Savennières, the subzone of the local dry white of Chenin Blanc. At the stately Château de l'Eperonnière, Mathieu Tijou makes this sparkling Chenin (with a bit of Chard and Cab Franc in the blend) that's clean and spray-starchy—Loire Chenin always makes me think of

clean sheets—with hints of citrus and mint.

Brézé Crémant de Loire Rosé (NV; 12% ABV; $$)

The central Loire is chock full of fairytale palaces like Château de Brézé, a moated, turreted Disney dream of gleaming white limestone just south of Saumur with—of *course*—two unicorns on its coat of arms. Fine wines have been produced here since the fifteenth century; today Arnaud Lambert from nearby Domaine de Saint-Just vinifies this very nice sparkling rosé of Cabernet Franc and Cabernet Sauvignon for the château's resident count. Liltingly soft and fragrant of wild roses, it will make you want to hop on a unicorn's back and trot off into the sunset.

Patrice Colin "Perles Grises" Loire Pineau d'Aunis
(NV; 11.3% ABV; $$)

Moving northeast, we arrive in the Coteaux du Vendômois, aka Pineau d'Aunis country. This grape fell out of favor in the 1960s and '70s because it didn't respond well to chemical fertilizers, which actually made it more prone to disease than it would be naturally. Farming it organically, eighth-generation

winegrower Patrice Colin brings us this yummy Pét-Nat that's like sliced nectarine on the palate, with hints of white pepper. True to its name—"gray bubbles"—it's faintly pink.[14]

Cyrille Sevin Crémant de Loire Non Dosé
(V; 12.5% ABV; $$–$$$)

When I got my hands on this bottle from Mont-Près-Chambord microwinemaker Cyrille Sevin, it was eight years past its vintage date and going strong. A field of wild herbs, Asian pear, bergamot, and coriander aromatically mark this mostly Chardonnay, with a bit of Pineau, Pinot Noir, and Cab Franc blended in. Pair it with raw oysters.

Les Têtes "Tête au Bois Dormant" Vin de France
(NV; 12% ABV; $$)

East of Chinon, near the former workshop of mobile-iste Alexander Calder, a group of natural winemaking buddies congregate at the six-hundred-year-old

---

[14] *Grapes with "Gris" or "Grigio" in their names tend to have pink-to-lavender skins that make rosé wines when macerated with the juice.*

farm of Nicolas Grosbois—whose name rhymes with "au Bois"[15]—to make Les Têtes. Their line of simple, weeknight wines from biodynamically farmed fruit includes a "Tête Nat" (hee hee) as well as the traditional-method "Tête au Bois Dormant," a bone-dry blend of Chenin and Chard. It's unfined, unfiltered, low-SO₂, and spontaneously fermented; the aromatics are citrus, toast, and fresh earth, and the finish lingers.

Le Sot de L'Ange "Sottise Bulles" Vin de France
(NV; 11–14%[16] ABV; $$)

The whimsical label of this offering from "Idiot Angel" (Le Sot de L'Ange) depicts a man in a pig suit pushing a wagon full of wine. But Angélique and Quentin Bourse, who apprenticed at Domaine Huet (see opposite), aren't kidding about biodynamically farming in the slate-riddled soil of the Touraine Azay-le-Rideau growing region near Tours. This satisfying rosé blend of Grolleau (a midnight-blue-skinned Loire grape) and Gamay has notes of wild strawberries and gravel.

VOUVRAY

Four Loire subappellations are permitted to be named on Crémants: Anjou, Saumur, Touraine, and Vouvray. You can find very nice wines from all of them, but Vouvray, which has a history of more than two centuries with sparkling winemaking, steals my heart with its gauzy, fizzy Chenin Blancs. Alas, very little bubbly Vouvray Chenin is exported. Thanks to its zippy acidity and peachy fruit notes, world-class with Loire Valley *fromage*, the locals lap most of it up.

François et Julien Pinon Vouvray Brut Non Dosé
(V; 12.5% ABV; $$–$$$)

Organic farmers, the Pinon family have been tending their vines since 1786; their bubbly lineup includes a demi-sec and a rosé Pét-Nat. This Brut Zero *méthode traditionnelle* ages *sur lattes* for two years. The aromatics range from tarragon cream sauce to canned peaches, and the bone-dry palate gets depth and richness from the minerality of the flinty clay soil. This wine will continue to evolve as it sits in the glass, so enjoy it over a couple of hours.

Alain & Christophe Le Capitaine Méthode Traditionnelle Vouvray Brut
(NV; 12.5% ABV; $–$$)

An easy-peasy, leesy bang-for-the-buck crowd-pleaser. There are notes of mochi and cream puff on the nose, and the *mousse* is pillow-soft. This is a wine not to think too hard about; just buy half a case to throw in an ice bucket the next time you have a party.

Domaine Huet Vouvray Réserve Pétillant
(V; 12.5% ABV; $$$)

Drop the name Huet to a Loire fanatic and that person is liable to put a hand on his or her heart and look heavenward. This Pétillant of Chenin is halfway between Pét-Nat and *traditionnelle*, making for soft bubbles, and it's definitely "galleon"-style, with the golden color and nutty aromatics that signal oxygen exposure in the cellar. And yet the palate is fresh, with notes of almonds, slate, citrus rind, and scallions. Geeky good fun from a biodynamically farmed, world-class vineyard.

---

[15]   Translation: "Grosbois" *means* "large woods," *and* au bois *means "in the woods." Pretty profound when one considers how many barrels Mr. Grosbois must encounter on a daily basis.*

[16]   *So that they don't have to resubmit their label to the authorities every year, some winemakers simply print the legal alcohol percentage range and stay within it.*

Alsace

Back in antiquity, a band of Germanic farmers called the Alemanni ruled Alsace, only to be conquered by the Franks in the fifth century CE. In the eons since then, the region has been repeatedly tossed back and forth between the Germans and the French. Here, alongside the river Rhine, half-timbered gingerbread houses line the streets and German shepherds roam them. Beer, pretzels, sausages, and sauerkraut are daily dietary staples. And the grapes are very German indeed: Riesling, Gewürztztraminer, and Silvaner all thrive here.

The best Alsatian vineyards sit on the sunny lower slopes of the Vosges Mountains, which protect the region from the rainstorms that curse wine regions like Champagne and Burgundy. Heat rises, so the cooler sites close to the valley floor provide the high-acid fruit for Crémant: Chardonnay, which doesn't go into any other Alsatian wines; its sibling Auxerrois, another German grape; Pinot Noir, which is the only variety allowed in rosé Crémant; and Pinot Blanc and Pinot Gris. Alsace produces a full 50 percent of all the Crémant in France, so one can afford to be picky.

....

Dopff au Moulin "Cuvée Julien" Crémant d'Alsace
(NV; 12% ABV; $$)

The Dopff family has been in the Alsatian wine business since 1574, so I must include wines from both branches (see below). This lemony blend of Pinot Blanc and Auxerrois, named after the founding father of Crémant d'Alsace, has a palate of orange creamsicle that's balanced by a refreshingly bitter acidity.

Dopff & Irion "Excellence" Cuvée Prestige Crémant d'Alsace (NV; 12% ABV; $$)

This blend of Pinot Blanc, Chardonnay, and Auxerrois from the other Dopffs offers pleasant notes of marzipan and citrus. The winery is located at Château de Riquewihr, dating back to 1549.

Château d'Orschwihr Crémant d'Alsace Brut
(V; 12.5% ABV; $$)

The crumbling Château d'Orschwihr dates back to 1049 and has been owned by Hapsburgs as well as the Bishop of Strasbourg. Since 1854, the Hartmanns have lived here. Today they farm five Grand Cru vineyards and have holdings in seven villages. This Brut is entirely Chardonnay and gets a lot of bottle age; at a decade past its vintage date, it's still sprightly, with an appealing note of mango.

Schoenheitz "S" Brut Crémant d'Alsace
(NV; 12% ABV; $$)

A thirty-minute hairpin-turn drive north through the woods from Château d'Orschwihr is the idyllic hiker's paradise that is the Munster Valley. Here, in the village of Wihr-au-Val, are Dominique and Henri Schoenheitz, whose name translates from Alsatian roughly as "a taste for beautiful things." This restrained, minerally sparkling Auxerrois (with a bit of Pinot Blanc) has a smooth *mousse* and is creamy and crisp on the palate.

Meyer-Fonné Extra-Brut Crémant d'Alsace
(NV; 12% ABV; $$)

Just northeast of Château d'Orschwihr, in the village of Katzenthal, the Meyers release a dizzying number of vineyard-designate white wines as well as this silky apéritif blended from Auxerrois, Chardonnay, Pinot Blanc, and Pinot Noir. The aromatics are fruity, with notes of ripe pear, and the palate is mineral, soft, and restrained thanks to that Extra-Brut–dryness level.

Lorraine

Winegrowing has been happening in Lorraine since 276, so it seems unfair that sparkling Lorraine should be labeled simply as Vin de France. During the phylloxera epidemic, Champenoise *maisons* full-on moved their operations here to get through the crisis, and once upon a time, Lorraine grapes went into German Sekt.

Near the convergence of the borders of Belgium, Luxembourg, and Germany, Lorraine follows the placid path of the barge-studded Moselle River, aka the Mosel. As with Alsace, there's a Teutonic love of beer and sausages here, but in place of Alsace's dark-timbered buildings, the city of Trier's are painted Easter-egg colors, and Metz looks like it was built out of buttercups, thanks to the local honey-hued limestone called *pierre de Jaumont*. The creamy-fluffy texture of the equally golden quiche Lorraine is the perfect foil for the local bubbly.

....

Maison Crochet "Les Blaissières" Vin Mousseux de Qualité (NV; 12% ABV; $$)

This organic Chardonnay and Auxerrois blend is precise and minimalist; the Crochets also release a late-disgorged rosé, called "Belena," that's a pretty cantaloupe hue, and has a wonderful heirloom apple flavor.

....

Molozay "Xb" Extra-Brut Chardonnay Vin Mousseux de Qualité (V; 12.5% ABV; $$$)

Château de Vaux can trace its architectural roots back to a Gallo-Roman foundation. Its German inhabitants crossed the border after World War I and established Schloss Vaux, "the German darling" of Sekt, which you'll meet in Chapter 7 (see page 179). Today the Molozays farm this estate organically and biodynamically. Their Chard satisfies with a yeasty nose and bready notes on the palate that are accompanied by candied lemon.

Luxembourg

I *know*! Luxembourg isn't in France. But it's allowed to use "Crémant" on its labels. And like its Moselle River neighbors Alsace and Lorraine, it historically has bounced between France and Germany, with Belgium thrown into the mix of uninvited potentates for a little extra spice. Today, it's a quiet, prosperous nation with the world's best public-transportation system, free to all. (If you are a New Yorker reading this, take a few deep breaths and pour yourself a glass of Crémant de Luxembourg.)

Smaller than Rhode Island, smaller than Yosemite National Park, and smaller than Tahiti, Luxembourg is small. Its inhabitants are Luxembourgers, as well as a bunch of tax-haven-seeking French, German, and British high-rollers, and Italians and Portuguese, whose gastronomic traditions offer a welcome break from all the sausages, sauerkraut, and whatnot.

Aromatic white wines made from Müller-Thurgau, Auxerrois, Pinot Blanc, Pinot Gris, and Elbling rule here. It's no wonder the sparkling versions are almost entirely consumed inside Luxembourg's borders, given how drop-the-mic good they are with local fried specialties like *friture de la Moselle* (fried freshwater fish) and *gromperekichelcher* (potato pancakes). The Belgians, who can't make much other than beer, but have mastered the art of *pommes frites*, drink most of the rest.

L&R Kox "Cuvée Dosage Zero" Crémant de Luxembourg (NV; 12.5% ABV; $$$)

This black matte bottle looks like it was meant for nightclub fizz. But in fact, it's for weddings, as one can scribble heartwarming sentiments on it with chalk. Cute, *non*? It's one of a panoply of sparkling releases from the Kox family, winegrowers since 1909. Today, they dabble in beekeeping, terra-cotta amphorae, and even a three-nation sparkling blend made with grapes from the Moselle/Mosel regions of France and Germany. So grab a Kox if you see it. What?

$$–$$$
Gaillac
**Domaine
Plageoles**

$$
Languedoc
Mas de Daumas

$–$$
Limoux
Saint-Hilaire

$
Limoux
Delmas

$$
Limoux
**Gérard
Bertrand**

$$
Die
**Achard-
Vincent**

$–$$
Die
Cave Poulet

$$
Hautes-Alpes
**Domaine
Allemand**

$$
Savoie
Eugène Carrel

$$–$$$
Bugey
Tissot

$$–$$$
Jura
**Domaine A & M
Tissot**

$$
Jura
**Domaine
Pignier**

$$

Beaujolais
**Domaine
Franck Besson**

$$

Bourgogne
Parigot

$$

Burgundy
Clotilde Davenne

$$

Loire
Jo Landron

$$

Loire
Brézé

$$

Loire
Les Tètes

$–$$

Vouvray
**A & C
Le Capitaine**

$$$

Vouvray
Domaine Huet

$$

Alsace
Dopff & Irion

$$

Alsace
**Château
d'Orschwihr**

$$

Alsace
Schoenheitz

$$

Alsace
Meyer-Fonné

Italy

The most popular *bollicine* (little bubbles) in the world are found floating in Prosecco. Italy's top sparkling wine has been outselling king Champagne since 2014.[1] And yet, despite all the spritzes and Bellinis, a very small portion of that Prosecco was actually served in Italy.

Italians, you see, are fiercely regionalistic. As a headline in a Sicilian newspaper vehemently declared recently, *"Prosecco in Sicilia? Ma anche no!"*[2] At the same time, Italians love to kick off an evening with a frothy glass. So what are they drinking?

Turns out that every Italian wine region, no matter how obscure, makes its own unique fizz. Many are simply sparkling versions of whatever the local quaff is, whether it's *bianco*, *rosato*, or even dry, savory, tannic *rosso*. Even Prosecco adheres to this tradition, in the reverse: Behold Prosecco Tranquillo, the still version of the world's favorite sparkling wine.

To research Italian bubblies is to dig into a boot-shaped rabbit hole. Each time you come across a style of *spumante* (fully sparkling wine) you'd never heard of before, you'll find three *frizzantes* (fizzy wines) in its wake.

And there are enough grape names to make your head spin. "The Italian wine board has documented more than 500 indigenous grape varieties, and this number easily multiplies once you begin counting the numerous synonyms," says Shelley Lindgren, a California restaurateur, author, and Italian wine expert (we'll hear more from her on page 138). "If you think about it, it was only 1861 when Italy went from many city-states and provinces to becoming a unified nation. In terms of grapes, that embodies a ton of variety," she points out.

Alas, ink and paper are limited commodities, so in this chapter, I'll breeze over some highlights.

---

[1]   *According to the OVSE (the Osservatorio Economico Vini). As I was researching this book, Prosecco sales outpaced Champagne sales by 25 percent.*

[2]   *Ragusa News, "Prosecco in Sicilia? ma anche no!"*

RECIPE

APEROL SPRITZ

SERVES 1

Formerly ubiquitous in northern Italy, home of Prosecco and Aperol (and its sibling, Campari), this cocktail is now ubiquitous all over the globe.

2 ounces Aperol
3 ounces Prosecco
Splash of club soda
Lemon or orange,
  for garnish

Combine the Aperol and Prosecco in a sturdy wineglass filled with ice. Top with the soda and gently stir. Garnish with an orange slice or lemon wheel.

Piedmont

Piedmont's world-class red wines from Barolo and Barbaresco (both made from Nebbiolo) are considered to be on par with the great reds of Burgundy and Bordeaux. And like the neighboring French, the Piemontese are accomplished gastronomes, who *do* like their Champagne. They're also increasingly making their own refined bubblies. The landscape of white truffle country certainly allows for sparkling-wine vinetending: Mountains surround all but eastern Piedmont like the letter C, with the Po River winding through the middle, providing plenty of nicely chilled slopes.

LANGHE

Langhe is a DOC that crosses borders with all sorts of other DOCs and DOCGs,[3] to the point of utter confusion. So what gives? The answer: It's a label for wines that don't qualify for any

[3] *A DOC is an officially recognized quality wine region; a DOCG is typically higher in quality. But there are many Italian wines that don't qualify for either designation. Also, the EU has tried to introduce the term DOP (Denominazione di Origine Protetta) in place of DOC (Denominazione di Origine Controllata), but Italian wineries just aren't on board.*

PIEMONTE

LOMBARDY

TRENTINO-ALTO ADIGE

VENETO

FRIULI-VENEZIA GIULIA

LIGURIA

EMILIA-ROMAGNA

MARCHE

ADRIATIC SEA

TYRRHENIAN SEA

CAMPANIA

APULIA

SICILY

IONIAN SEA

Spotlight on Offbeat Italy with Alan Tardi

A wine journalist, author, educator, former restaurateur, and sometimes resident of Italy, Alan Tardi is an expert in both Champagne and Italian wines. "Due to its cultural history and geographical position, Italy has more native grape varieties, distinct viticultural traditions, and wine appellations than any country I can think of," Tardi tells me. "The Italians have had an unbridled love affair with bubbly beverages. They love sparkling everything, from water to wines. There are countless examples of sparkling wines in all twenty regions of the country, from the foothills of the Alps to the tip of the Boot."

Here are two of Tardi's favorite offbeat Italian bubblies.

Croci Gutturnio Rosso Frizzante (V; 12.5% ABV; $$)

The Gutturnio subzone of Emilia-Romagna gets its name from a Roman term for a wine cup—winemaking happened here as early as 2000 BCE. "From the hills outside Piacenza, this dark, dry, *frizzante* red wine is similar to Lambrusco, except that it is made principally from Barbera, with another local grape called Croatina (aka Bonarda)," Tardi says. "The Barbera gives it round, ripe, fleshy fruit, while the Croatina contributes an earthy, spiky edge." Tardi describes its quirky *metodo ancestrale* aromatics as "stewed black plums, macerated cherries, wild thyme, eucalyptus, damp earth, and a hint of barnyard . . . Also, a bit of black pepper and allspice, and a touch medicinal," while the palate is "lean and tart, with green plum sour cherry and wild red currant flavors."

Cieck "San Giorgio" Erbaluce di Caluso Spumante (V; 12.5% ABV; $$$)

The name *erbaluce* (grass + light) comes from a folktale in which the daughter of colorful Dawn and glowing golden Sun—conceived during a solar eclipse—cries because she can never see her parents together; the Erbaluce vine, it is said, grows from the girl's tears. Native to the Canavese area in the northwest of Piedmont, near the border with the Val d'Aosta region, this grape is remarkably well-suited to sparkling winemaking due to its delicate aromatics and lively acidity. Tardi describes the Cieck as "buttercream frosting on a lemon-vanilla layer cake. Not that it is sweet at all, but there is a laciness to it."

other official wine appellation around here. So you'll find basic Langhe bianco and rosso as well as Langhe Chardonnay, Arneis (a very nice white), and Favorita (aka Vermentino).

....

Vietti "Vivace" Langhe Freisa
(V; 14% ABV; $$$)

Barolo star Vietti's take on the eccentric traditional grape variety Freisa starts with a base wine that is mostly from carbonic maceration, in which the grapes are not crushed in order to emphasize fruitiness. Add some Freisa grape juice to this, cork it, and you know the punchline: Bubbles ensue inside the bottle. Serve it cold,

match its blackberry-blueberry notes with salty cheeses and charcuterie, and take note that the alcohol level is high for a fizzy wine. So no Freisa for breakfast, people. Interesting aside: Like the Croci Gutturnio (see previous page), this wine looks like a garden-variety red until you open it, pour it in a glass, and see its soft foam.

ALTA LANGA

The high ("*alta*") hilltops and mountainsides of the Langhe, where the chilly nighttimes and mornings imbue fruit with brisk acidity, is a *spumante*-only DOCG, and wines must be vintage-dated and aged for a minimum of thirty months before release. As fabulous as the better-known reds and whites of the Langhe can be, this elegant fizz can surprise and delight.

....

Ettore Germano Alta Langa "Rosanna" Metodo Classico Brut Rosé (V; 12.5% ABV; $$$)

This sparkling Nebbiolo has "rose petal, wild strawberry, and subtle herbal characteristics," according to Italian wine doyenne Shelley Lindgren (see page 138). Alan Tardi is a fan as well of this wine's "rosehip, violet, cherry, and licorice profile."

Enrico Serafino Alta Langa Brut (V; 12.5% ABV; $$)

Founded in 1878, this Alta Langa stalwart produces a lineup of utterly delightful sparkling wines. The Brut, composed of Pinot Nero (aka Noir) and Chardonnay, is razor-sharp at six years of age, all fresh herbs, clean minerality, and gentle citrus at the finish. Taste it alongside Robiola Bossina, the local triple-cream sheep and cow's milk cheese.

ASTI

Forget the flabby, syrupy-sweet Moscato on the bottom shelf at the supermarket. This is the good DOCG stuff, made from the delicate Moscato Bianco grape by boutique Italian producers. It tends to be low-alcohol and peachy, although there's a new "Asti Secco" dry-wine classification. Rappers have been (pun alert) instrumental in celebrating this fresh, zippy, ambrosial juice as an after-hours sipper, but it also kills with brunch and lunch—you haven't lived until you've sipped it alongside prosciutto and melon.

De Forville® Moscato d'Asti (V; 5% ABV; $$)

In 1860, a Walloon[4] named Gioacchino De Forville became so smitten with Nebbiolo that he moved his family to the village of Castagnole delle Lanze, northeast of Barbaresco, to grow grapes. At some point along the way, the De Forvilles realized they were the only family in the vicinity with a French-sounding name, so they trademarked it. (Is that a Walloon thing?) Their totally hedonistic Moscato d'Asti tastes like liquid apricot jam, with touches of rose petals, ginger, and dripping-ripe mango. Just pour it over ice cream and call it a day.

Elio Perrone "Sourgal" Moscato d'Asti (V; 5% ABV; $–$$)

There's nothing sour about the knockout aromatics of lilies and honeydew melon, although there is a nice lemonade note on the palate. Elio Perrone also produces "Bigarò," a Moscato-Brachetto blend, and "Gi," a surprisingly successful mix of delicate Moscato and blunt Chardonnay.

---

[4] *The Walloons are the people of Wallonia, which is now part of Belgium; the language they speak is also called Walloon. Contrary to popular opinion, Philip Pullman did not invent them.*

Saracco Moscato D'Asti
(V; 6% ABV; $-$$)

Paolo Saracco is a Moscato obsessive, the sole producer in the region who doesn't also vinify any of the classic Piemonte reds. His deft, elegant, peach-pear-floral basic bottling is such a classic that it is capable of cellar-aging, a concept that is typically unheard-of in the realm of fizzy semisweet wines.[5] All the same, it's stamped with a bottling date, indicating maximum freshness.

ACQUI

Piemonte is like a 3.5-GPA student: It's all about As and Bs. Barolo and Barbaresco are the red-wine towns to know. Asti (see previous section) produces a semisweet, fizzy white. Alba is noted for its Barbera, and from Acqui Terme,[6] we get Brachetto. Think Moscato d'Asti, only red.

---

[5] Cole, *"Moscato May Be Out, But Saracco Is Still In."*

[6] Just *"Acqui"* on wine labels.

What to Drink Whilst Reading
P. G. Wodehouse and Nancy Mitford

Founded in 1867, with hand-dug caves that tunnel one hundred feet underground and have been declared a UNESCO World Heritage site, Contratto was a fashionable brand among royalty and cosmopolites at the turn of the century and released the nation's first vintage-dated *metodo classico* wine in 1919. Based in Oltrepò Pavese, Lombardy, bordering Piedmont, Contratto sources its Pinot Noir and Chardonnay from Apennine hillside vineyards ranging from 1,300 to 1,650 feet (400 to 500 m) in elevation.

Contratto "For England" Alta Langa Brut Rosé Pas Dosé (V; 12.5% ABV; $$$)

Back in 1920, Contratto's British fans liked their bubbly dry; *pas dosé* means not dosed with sugar. So for a hot minute there, back when French Champagne was being made in a semisweet style, Contratto was more popular than Champagne in England.

Braida Brachetto d'Acqui
(V; 5.5% ABV; $$)

Acqui Terme has been a spa resort since antiquity thanks to its thermal waters, and light-bodied, low-alcohol red Brachetto won't make your head spin after a day spent soaking in the heat. This is a joyous, juicy, fizzy cherry-strawberry gelato of a beverage.

Lombardy

Home to chic Milan and Lake Como, Lombardy also borders Switzerland and the swanky resort town of St. Moritz. Even the food is fancy: Risotto alla Milanese is a gorgeous mustard color thanks to the addition of precious saffron, and foie gras is popular here. Thus, Franciacorta, Italy's answer to Champagne. But there are other bubbly treasures, as well.

Bruno Verdi "Paradiso" Sangue di Giuda
(V; 8.5% ABV; $$)

Now that I've told you how posh Lombardy is, I'm going to throw in this rustic oddity from Oltrepò Pavese. It's a little bit grape Fanta, a little bit fizzy, a little bit tannic, and a little bit rock and roll. Sangue di Giuda is a style of wine named "Blood of Judas" because, according to local lore, it caused lascivious behavior among friars and nuns (who must have been total lightweights, given its 8.5% alcohol level).

FRANCIACORTA

Just as the Champagne region is an easy drive east from chic Paris, Franciacorta country is just east of *moda* Milan, ensuring a sufficient supply of bottle-fermented bubbles for the world's top supermodels. The term *"Franciacorta"* can even be translated as "little France". . . And yes, I know, that's not the proper derivation.[7] Don't rain on my parade.

Chardonnay is the prime grape of the region, accounting for more than 80 percent of plantings, and Pinot Bianco is also prominent, so there's a signature *bianco dei bianchi* here, called *Satèn*,[8] which translates as "silky," or "satiny." It's slightly lower in atmospheric pressure than Champagne for a softer mouthfeel. Ooh la la.

Triangulated by Lake Iseo, Monte Orfano, and the city of Brescia, and facing south toward the Po Valley, Franciacorta is relatively warm, making for a soft, rich, ripe wine. If you're an acid hound, fret not: An indigenous grape, called Erbamat, has joined the fray as of the 2017 harvest. Naturally high in acid and late to ripen, it's Franciacorta's answer to global warming, and it may rein in the region's languorous tendencies a bit.

Nicola Gatta "36 Lune" Spumante Nature
(NV; 12% ABV; $$$$$)

Nicola Gatta—and the two producers listed below—doesn't qualify for or care to use the fusty "Franciacorta" designation and operates more like the thought-leading growers of Champagne or the renegades of Catalonia (see pages 146–156). Gatta farms biodynamically, uses minimal intervention in the cellar, and makes this remarkably Champagne-like, fresh-yet-caramelly, sunbeam-

colored *metodo classico* using a base wine culled from a ten-year solera (see page 278). It stays thirty-six moons ("lune") on the lees; fewer than one hundred cases are produced annually, but anything by Gatta is worth seeking out.

Divella "Clo Clo" Dosaggio Zero Rosé
(V; 12%ABV; $$$–$$$$)

Alessandra Divella, part of the crew of natural *metodo classico* producers in the town of Gussago, farms organically and vinifies this elegant, golden-pink, zero-dosage rosé with minimal intervention and spontaneous fermentation. It's bone-dry, with a bready midpalate and salty finish that stimulate the appetite. Divella's style is too

---

7   Alas, the name does not derive from "little France," but rather corti franche, or "short courts." It's a medieval term that was used to refer to villages that were exempt from taxes.

8   I should add that the term "Satèn" is trademarked—a wise move, given how often European wine terms are appropriated by New World also-rans.

acidic for Franciacorta labeling standards, which leads me to seek out more non-"Franciacorta" bubblies from this region.

．．．．．．．．．．．．．．．．．．．．．．．．．．．．．．

Cà del Vént "Sogno" Blanc de Blancs Pas Operé
(V; 12% ABV; $$$)

"Pas operè," meaning "not manipulated," refers to the fact that just the base-wine juice (with no additional sugars) is added to stimulate secondary fermentation in this sappy, satisfying metodo classico. Located a few minutes east of Gussago, "Cà del Vént" translates as the "home of the wind." Again, this wine isn't labeled "Franciacorta," making it all the more interesting to this author.

Faboo Franciacorta with Rashmi Primlani

I asked Rashmi Primlani, certified sommelier, food blogger, and Italian wine ambassador, to recommend some of her favorite standard-bearers for the Franciacorta region.

．．

Bellavista Vendemmia Franciacorta Satèn (V; 12% ABV; $$$$)

Mattia Vezzola—"part philosopher, part poet, full-time winemaker"—masterminded the Satèn style in Franciacorta. This sparkling Chardonnay, aged in white oak barrels, "dances in the glass with extremely fine bubbles, creamy *mousse*, ripe peaches, citrus zest, roasted hazelnuts, and a lingering, juicy finish," says Primlani. Bellavista is owned by construction kingpin Vittorio Moretti, who dedicates a sparkling wine to every premiere at La Scala.

．．．．．．．．．．．．．．．．．．．．．．．．．．．．．．

Berlucchi "'61 Nature" Franciacorta Rosé (V; 12.5% ABV; $$$)

In 1955, young winemaker Franco Ziliani was so inspired by the elegance of Guido Berlucchi's sixteenth-century home, Palazzo Lana, that he convinced the *Signore* to make a fine sparkling wine worthy of such a setting. Today, Ziliani's three children run the winery. Entirely made from estate-grown Pinot Nero (Noir), the "'61 Nature" is "vinously complete," after a full sixty months bottle age and zero *dosage*.

Trentino-Alto Adige

The northern state border-ing Austria and Switzerland is Teutonic in its ways, *ja*. It also goes by the name Südtirol (south-ern Tyrol), and some street signs are in German as well as Italian. Thus, you'll see Germanic grape varieties among the wines, and the *weingüter* are often perched on steep alpine slopes, where they soak up gobs of sunlight by day and shiver by night. This region is tiny in terms of production, accounting for less than 1 percent of all the wines coming out of Italy, but what's available tends to be high in quality.

....

Pojer e Sandri "Zero Infinito" Trentino Frizzante
(NV; 12% ABV; $–$$)

This certified organic wine is made in the *col fondo* (see page 128) style, so it's cloudy, like cider, and topped with a crown cap, like beer. More interestingly, it's made from Solaris, a grape variety developed by German viticultur-ists to thrive without fertilizers, pesticides, or fungicides. Pear cider, caramelized onions, bone marrow, chamomile, coconut—it's all there in spades and will scratch your kooky-wine itch.

TRENTO

Around the ridiculously charming city of Trento, capital of Trentino,[9] the classic grapes of Champagne grow on the dramatic, high-elevation rocky slopes of the Dolomites, overlooking the river Adige.

The Trentodoc[10] appellation is devoted to *metodo classico* wines made from Chardonnay, Pinot Nero (Noir), and Pinot Meunier, and insiders claim that it outper-forms Franciacorta in quality even while it undercuts it in price.

....

Cantina Furlani "Macerato" Sui Lieviti Vino Frizzante
(NV; 11.5% ABV; $$–$$$)

To start with, here's a crazy funhouse of a natural wine for the kids. My assistant, Zoe, describes the Furlani's blue-toned cotton-candy color as "gender-reveal-party pink." (This odd hue is the result of the Pinot Grigio grape

---

[9] *Which is confusing. If a* gattino *is a kitten and a* gatto *is a cat, shouldn't the overall region be called Trento and the town be called Trentino?*

[10] *It is the Trento DOC, but the members of the appellation spell it this way, as one word.*

skins sitting around in the juice—
macerato—imparting the pigment
of their "gray" skins.) Popcorn
jelly beans, strawberry milkshake,
and watermelon drinking vinegar

dominate the nose, pink grapefruit
soda rules the palate, and a sense
of entering an alternate universe
takes hold of one's psyche.

Ferrari Revs It Up

No, Giulio Ferrari did not start an auto company.[11] Instead, he
studied viticulture and oenology in France, learned bottle fermentation in Champagne, and did post-grad work in yeast in Germany
before introducing the Chardonnay grape to Italy. He was the first
to cultivate Chardonnay and Pinot Noir in Trentino-Alto Adige,
and he started making sparkling wine in 1902. Today, Ferrari is
Italy's top *metodo classico* producer, accounting for 20 percent of
the market, with nationwide name recognition. The Lunelli family,
which has been running the company since 1952, is based at Villa
Margon, a nearly five-hundred-year-old estate built to celebrate
the Council of Trent[12] and adorned with intricate sixteenth-century
frescoes. Ferrari's top-flight releases have the toasty autolytic
qualities of high-end Champagne, while its everyday bottling may
represent the best deal in sparkling wine anywhere.

Ferrari Trentodoc Brut (NV; 12.5% ABV; $$)

Ferrari's 100 percent Chardonnay basic brut offers salinity and
minerality, notes of tropical fruit and citrus, a brisk and vigorous
acidity, and a persistent finish. It's much less expensive than its
riper competitors from Franciacorta, and on par, price-wise, with
a lot of crappy Proseccos. Quality-wise, it knocks this competition
out of the park.

[11] *Ferrari is the third-most-common surname in Italy and there's no relation.
That said, Ferrari bubbly has been poured over the head of more than a few
Ferrari drivers on the racing circuit.*

[12] *A series of meetings in Trento between 1545 and 1563 that established the
Counter-Reformation.*

Veneto

The name conjures up watery images of the Venetian lagoon, the banks of the Adige River in Verona, and the shores of Lago di Garda. And yet the region is one-third mountains—a topographical detail that makes it an outstanding winegrowing region. Here, in 1876, only a decade after the Veneto became part of the Kingdom of Italy, Antonio Carpenè founded the nation's first School of Viticulture and Oenology in what is now the heart of Prosecco country. (His namesake winery, Carpenè Malvolti, was the first to label a bottle as "Prosecco.")[13]

Here, the hills of Conegliano and Valdobbiadene are lush, green, and diorama-perfect. The delicate *bollicine* that arise from this fairytale wonderland are dreamy alongside the risotto, seafood, white asparagus, and radicchio on the *ristorante* menus of the Veneto.

PROSECCO

Prosecco can be *so* much more than that inexpensive, somewhat nondescript sparkler that's stocked at the grocery store. At its simplest "DOC" or "DOP" level, it is sourced from a vast area covering much of the Veneto as well as all of Friuli-Venezia Giulia—a whopping 556 *comunes*, or villages, in all. These wines are best in their youth, showcasing the fruity, floral pleasures of the Glera grape, and bottled on demand to ensure freshness. The labels

[13] International Wine Review, "*Prosecco, Prosecco Superiore, & Cartizze: Incredible Values from the Best Producers.*"

Don't Be Confounded by *Col Fondo*

The vast majority of Prosecco is made via the Charmat method, but occasionally you'll find a super-old-school *col fondo*, which roughly translates as "with the lees." This is the traditional farmhouse Prosecco, made in the way the winemaker's *nonno e nonna* used to do it. *Col fondo* goes through two fermentations, the second one in bottle, with no disgorgement, so the floating lees bring yeasty aromatics to the wine and give it a cloudy, rustic look and texture.[14] The phrase "*rifermentato in bottiglia*" is helpfully printed on some labels.

Cá dei Zago Valdobbiadene Prosecco Col Fondo
(V; 12% ABV; $$)

Alan Tardi (see page 118) loves this *col fondo*'s "salinity and minerality," which he attributes to "the shallow rocky soils of Valdobbiadene." He recommends contrasting its "beautiful elegance" with the classic Veneto trattoria dish *spiedo*: spit-roasted skewers of meat, poultry, potatoes, and sage.

Zanotto Rosso Col Fondo (NV; 12% ABV; $$)

Well, why not try a funky-as-heck *red col fondo*, if you can? This quirky little crown-capped number is a blend of the indigenous Italian Marzemino with Cabernet Sauvignon. It has a pungent, vinegary appeal, with notes of black pepper, green olives, and, well, veggies. Try it with Piemontese *bagna càuda*—basically, crudités, but with a garlicky sauce.

Casa Coste Piane "Frizzante . . . Naturalmente" Valdobbiadene Prosecco (NV; 11% ABV; $$)

This cloudy wine has a pastry-dough aroma and mineral palate, yes, but it's so much about pillowy texture—the bubbles are so voluminous and so perfectly suspended—that one just wants to lounge in it.

---

[14]   *In the old days, says wine expert Alan Tardi, a bottle of* col fondo *would be stored and carried upright, then decanted into a pitcher, to avoid the presence of sediment. Now that we are in the Pét-Nat era, times have changed and funk is cool.*

of these wines are often printed with a release date—typically in a 1980s bitmapped typeface, akin to old IBM computer printouts.

Then there are the smaller DOCG "Superiore" zones. Conegliano Valdobbiadene, the best-known of these, is named for the two eponymous towns, about 21 miles (34 km) from one another. The lesser-known Asolo[15] is about 15 miles (24 km) south of Valdobbiadene in the Colli Asolani, a neat row of hills with views of the Venetian Prealps.[16] Vacationers traveling from Conegliano Valdobbiadene to Asolo should leave plenty of time to visit the superbly symmetric villas and palaces designed by sixteenth-century architect Andrea Palladio.

Finally, there are the "Crus," so to speak, of Prosecco. Cartizze, just east of the town of Valdobbiadene, is a Grand Cru-ish slope, set at a precipitous angle. The Premier Cru equivalents are microzones called Rive (local dialect for "steep slopes"). If you see "Cartizze" or "Rive" on a label, you'll know you are in store for a treat. And if you want to truly geek out on Prosecco, look for the word "Millesimato," meaning "vintage," on the label. Yes, that's right: There's such a thing as vintage Prosecco, and it can gain complexity with a bit of age.

Adriano Adami "Col Credas" Rive di Farra di Soligo Valdobbiadene Prosecco Superiore (V; 11% ABV; $$)

This sublime single-vineyard Prosecco is bone-dry, with piercing acidity softened by fresh pear and lemon aromatics. Col Credas, located above the River Piave, is a term meaning "clay hill" in local dialect. Adami released the first single-vineyard Prosecco ever, in 1933.

De Faveri Brut Treviso Prosecco (NV; 11% ABV; $$)

Bright, crisp, and fresh, with ultra-fine bubbles, and a hint of sour lemon curd, this basic Prosecco is so well-made that it can sit open[17] in your fridge for three days and still be in tip-top condition. So what is the De Faveri family's secret? Well, they *are* Champagne importers as well as Prosecco producers.

---

[15] *Asolo Prosecco can be very difficult to locate in the United States, other than at Costco(!), where the devious wine masterminds have managed to bottle a $7 Asolo under the house brand, Kirkland.*

[16] *That is, baby siblings of the Alps.*

[17] *Use a Vacu Vin rubber cork or something similar.*

Nino Franco Valdobbiadene Superiore di Cartizze
(V; 11% ABV; $$-$$$)

Precious Cartizze wines can be difficult to track down in the United States, since we are so used to buying Prosecco on the cheap. You're in for a treat if you can find this peaches-and-cream delight. Also keep an eye out for "Grave di Stecca," Nino Franco's bottling from its stunning walled estate, Villa Barberini.[18]

Ruggeri "Giustino B" Valdobbiadene Prosecco Superiore (V; 11.5% ABV; $$$)

Named for winery founder Giustino Bisol, who started the operation in 1950, this is a luscious wine with a generous 16 grams per liter of sugar that's released after a few years of age.

Sommariva Conegliano Valdobbiadene Prosecco Superiore (NV; 11.5% ABV; $)

Lemongrass. Cucumber. Marshmallow root. Taro root. Parsnip. Sassafras. A wonder from winemaker Cinzia Sommariva.

Sorelle Bronca Valdobbiadene Extra Dry Prosecco Superiore (NV; 11% ABV; $$)

The Italians prefer Extra Dry[19] to Brut, so open your mind to this more generous style. This beauty from the vinetending Bronca sisters (not to be confused with the book-writing Brontë sisters) boasts aromatics of Asian pear with a hint of musk, a pillowy-soft texture, and a palate that calls to mind risotto with white pepper.

Terre de San Venanzio Fortunato Valdobbiadene Brut Prosecco Superiore
(V; 11.5% ABV; $-$$)

This delightfully floral, citrusy, weightless wine has such an outstandingly refined *perlage* that the ridiculously long name of the winery will effortlessly slide off your tongue after a few sips. (It's a reference to a local poet-bishop-saint-vinetender, 530–607 CE. RIP.)

---

[18]   *Not to be confused with the Pope's summer residence, which goes by the same name.*

[19]   *As a reminder, in sparkling-wine terms, "Extra Dry" means "actually, there's a hint of sweetness."*

Bisson Bianco Vino Frizzante (V; 11% ABV; $$)

Pierluigi Lugano is the merchant and winegrower behind the chic Ligurian Bisson label, a favorite with sommeliers. This eastern Italian side project, a partnership with his pal Eli Spagnol of Torre Zecchei in Valdobbiadene, is Prosecco as interpreted by a Northwest Coast (of Italy) winegrower: lean, salty, and dry, with mouth-puckering green tannins. Either you'll love this minimalist wine or you'll hate it . . . there's no in between.

Required Reading: The Bellini

No write-up of Prosecco is complete without a primer on the Bellini, the brunch-worthy cocktail of peach purée and Prosecco.

- Venetian Renaissance painter Giovanni Bellini (1430–1516) painted, among other things, many profiles of pale, long-nosed gentlemen, with overgrown bowl haircuts and pillbox hats.
- Sometime in the 1930s or '40s, Venetian restaurateur Giuseppe Cipriani added a purée of white peaches to Prosecco, and a drink was born. Cipriani named his beverage after the faded color of a saint's robe in a Bellini painting.
- The original home of the Bellini cocktail, Harry's Bar, is adjacent to Saint Mark's Square. Once a hangout for the rich, interesting, and famous, it is today where tourists go to drink Bellinis.
- Bottled Bellini mix *is just not the same* as fresh white peach purée.
- Those haircuts.

Friuli-Venezia Giulia

The only Italian state that borders Slovenia is mountainous and mysterious, complete with alpine lakes and the cosmopolitan coffeehouse cultural mishmash that is the city of Trieste. The perpetually stone-faced Bohemian-Austrian poet Rainer Maria Rilke composed some of his greatest work at the fourteenth-century Duino Castle, perched on a cliff overlooking the Gulf of Trieste. Sadly, even in these uplifting surroundings, Rilke was not able to smile.

Perhaps this is because the only wine at his disposal was Friulian Ribolla Gialla, aka Slovenian Rebula. Tradition here dictates that Ribolla should be crushed and macerated as though it were a red wine; the resulting "orange wine," or *ramato*, is murky, tannic, and amber-colored from spending all that time on the skins. It can be spicy, herbaceous, and confounding.

....

I Clivi "RGL" Ribolla Gialla Spumante Brut Nature
(V; 11% ABV; $$)

From the Colli Orientali ("Eastern Hills") on the border of Slovenia, the "RGL" gets its bubbles via a single fermentation, with the vat sealed partway through the process. It is bone-dry to the point where it actually tastes like a bone, but there is nothing brothy about this mineral, savory apéritif.

....

Edi Kante "Dosaggio Zero" Vino Spumante di Qualita Metodo Classico
(NV; 12.5% ABV; $$$)

When an Italian has a name like Edi Kante, you can guess he lives on the Slovenian border (in the limestone-rich Carso district, to be exact) and makes *ramato*. This is a *metodo classico* bubbly, however, made half from Chardonnay and half from the local grape Malvasia, with caramelization on the nose and some almond extract on the palate, as well as a feral, slightly smoky note.

Emilia-Romagna

Occupying the fertile southern side of the Po River, Emilia-Romagna is Italy encapsulated. It's home to all your fave automotive manufacturers (Ferrari, Lamborghini, Maserati, Ducati), opera men (Verdi, Rossini, Toscanini, Pavarotti), some poet named Dante, and the Università di Bologna, the world's oldest institution of higher learning. Museum-piece cities like Ravenna and Piacenza spawned artists like Correggio and Michelangelo, and filmmakers like Bertolucci and Fellini. And then there's the gastronomy. Towns like Reggio-Emilia, Parma, and Bologna gave us cheese, prosciutto, and, duh, bologna. And from Modena, we have Balsamic vinegar and . . . Lambrusco. Which sparkles. And goes well with bologna.

LAMBRUSCO

As is so frequently the case with wine, Lambrusco went through a period of popularity back in the 1980s when mass-produced brands left everyone with the mistaken impression that it was sweet. Then everyone stopped drinking it. Today, fizzy, fragrant, light-bodied red Lambrusco is on the rebound, as the *amabile* and *dolce* (semisweet and sweet) styles are being pushed aside in favor of *secco* (dry) wines that go with pretty much every food you can imagine.

There are ten different grapes with the word "Lambrusco"[20] in their names. The key varieties to look for are Lambrusco Salamino di Santa Croce, Lambrusco di Sorbara, and Lambrusco Grasparossa di Castelvetro. These wines tend to be *frizzante* rather than *spumante*, so although some will display an impressive head of foam, the bubbles hit the front of your tongue and then tend to dissipate. Serve Lambrusco chilled, and always bring it along on picnics.

. . . .

Antica Corte Pallavicina "Rosso Del Motto" Lambrusco (NV; 11% ABV; $)

The "ancient court" of Pallavicina is a restored castle that's now an elegant inn adjoining a farm and winery, run by celebrity chef Massimo Spigaroli and his brother

---

[20] *"Lambrusco" comes from the Latin term for wild grapes, labruscum.*

(who, incidentally, have a family connection to Giuseppe Verdi). The cellars are jam-packed with Spigaroli's famous house-cured haunches of *culatello* and wheels of fragrant cheese. This squat, jug-shaped bottle yields a pleasant red, with—dry, not sweet—notes of chocolate malt, Grand Marnier, and aloe.

Alfredo Bertolani "Delicato e Fresco" Rosé (V; 11.5% ABV; $)

This slightly cloudy, pink-raspberry-tinted beverage, made from the Lambrusco grapes Salamino and Marani, is indeed "delicate and fresh," with a subtle nose of flowers and succulents, and something savory on the palate. The Bertolanis have been Lambrusco producers in the Scandiano hills since 1925.

Cleto Chiarli e Figli "Vecchia Modena Premium" Lambrusco di Sorbara Secco (NV; 11% ABV; $$)

The Sorbara grape is considered by many to be the best of the Lambruschi, and the jewel-toned range of translucent pink-to-red colors it comes in is as uplifting as the sight of, well, sorbet. Emilia-Romagna's first commercial winery, founded in the 1860s by a Modena restaurateur, nails the genre with this watermelon-colored, wild-strawberry-scented fizz, with notes of balsamic vinegar and crumbled dry herbs on the palate.

Fattoria Moretto Lambrusco Grasparossa di Castelvetro (NV; 11% ABV; $$)

Grasparossa di Castelvetro is the smallest of the Lambrusco DOCs, occupying gently undulating hillside vineyards some 12 miles (20 km) south of Modena. Fattoria Moretto, an early adherent of organic agriculture, delivers the deep-violet color, joyful blueberry-jam aromatics, and impressive head of foam that are the classic trademarks of the Grasparossa grape. At the same time, notes of minerality and herbaceousness lift this wine to the next level.

Puianello Rosé Ancestrale Lambrusco dell'Emilia (NV; 12% ABV; $)

The blob of sediment clinging to the crown cap signals that this *"non filtrato"* bottle is an outlier, from a cantina that has been in business since 1938. The color is a cloudy pale peach, the aromatics

pull between lychee and clay, there's a snickerdoodle cookie thing happening on the palate, and the back label says "semi-dry," but the bottle I tried was dry as a bone, with a creamy froth.

purple juice smells like a Jewish deli in the best possible way (think pastrami and pickling juice), with rustic tannins and rosemary-tinged finish.

Vigneto Saetti "RossoViola" Salamino di Santa Croce Lambrusco (V; 11.5% ABV; $–$$)

Just in case the bougie black-fabric label doesn't make it clear that this wine is special, there's a small paper note tucked under the foil informing the drinker that it is natural, with no nasty preservatives. The most-planted of the Lambruscos, Salamino is thought to have earned its name from its long, cylindrical grape clusters, which form like "little salamis," and—wouldn't you know—this

Cantina della Volta Lambrusco Rosé di Modena Spumante Metodo Classico (V; 12.5% ABV; $$$)

Ah, a *metodo classico* wine from the Lambrusco di Sorbara grape. A delightful shade that's halfway between pale pink and canta-loupe, it has brioche essence on the nose, and juicy acidity, plus notes of lime, raspberry, and grapefruit pith on the palate. The only giveaway that we're in Emilia-Romagna here is a scrumptious sour black-cherry note.

Marche

with a crown cap, it's a nearly weightless Charmat-method blend of Verdicchio, Trebbiano, and Chardonnay. The nose is fresh and herbaceous, with an appealing hint of leather, making it the vinous equivalent of pilsner.

....

Alberto Quacquarini Vernaccia di Serrapetrona Vino Spumante Secco
(NV; 12.5% ABV; $$)

Like the Sunda pandolin of Borneo—aka "the artichoke of mammals"—Vernaccia di Serrapetrona is quite rare and rather quirky. There were, last I checked, a total of five wineries in the appellation, four of which were producing the utterly whimsical *spumante* version of the local red, Vernaccia. This oddity is made in the *appassimento* style, in which half the grapes are dried to make a raisin wine that is added to the original wine. Those madcap winemakers then ferment the wine yet *again* to make it bubble, then finish it *dolce* (sweet) or *secco* (dry). The aromatics and palate are straight out of ye olde Dickensian Christmas cookbook: cinnamon stick, peppermint, clove-spiced venison, and Madeira.

"Le Marche" (as the Italians call it) is sometimes translated, literally, as "The Marches." This title refers not to the month or the act of walking stiffly, knees held high, but is an archaic term for a political region, something like a county. Hilly and coastal, Marche is scenic and quiet. Likewise, the under-the-radar wine landscape is one of traditional family *cantinas*.

....

Garofoli "Guelfo Verde" Marche Frizzante (V; 11.5% ABV; $)

Like the Marche itself, this unassuming fizz—from a family winery dating back to 1871—is fresh and understated. Topped

Apulia (and Campania)

You know Campania: It's got the beautiful Amalfi Coast, eerie Pompeii and Herculaneum, delicious fresh seafood, and Elena Ferrante's riveting Neopolitan quartet of novels. But the classical Greek grape varieties are a bit more obscure, with names—like Aglianico, Falanghina, and Greco di Tufo—that could be toga-clad characters out of a play by Aeschylus or Euripides.

As for Apulia, aka Puglia, it's so far southeast that it's practically part of Greece, and indeed, in the 7th and 8th centuries BCE, there was a major Greek migration here. And while Apulia is best-known for its rich reds and hot-pink rosés, it's like Campania in that high-elevation vineyards, cooled by morning breezes off the sea, create surprisingly good condi-tions for sparkling winemaking.

Colli della Murgia "Galetto" Puglia Extra Dry Spumante Rosé (NV; 12.5% ABV; $$)

Hailing from the cave-riddled cliffside *comune* of Gravina, this *spumante* Aglianico is the color of fire-roasted-red-pepper Kool-Aid. Its sharp bubbles, savory flair, and notes of ripe strawberries, black cherries, sea salt, grapefruit pith, and bitters could cut right through a melty Apulian burrata.

SALENTO

You may know the hefty red Salice Salentino, made from the Negroamaro grape, as well as Salento's deep-purple Primitivo. But the Apulian region of Salento occupies the very sole of the heel of the Italian boot—hot and beachy year-round—so rosés and bubblies go down easy here.

Palamà "Skarabocchio" Salento Frizzante Rosato (NV; 11% ABV; $)

This juicy, raspberry-colored treat tastes of watermelon, grapefruit, sangría, and—yes!—salted french fries. The frothy *mousse* is like seafoam. The Palamà family are restaurateurs as well as winemak-ers, so I trust that their pairing suggestion for this wine— pan-roasted tuna with Apulian olive oil and tomatoes—is spot-on.

Shelley Lindgren on Why You Should Be Drinking Bubbles from Campania

Shelley Lindgren is co-owner and wine director of SPQR, A16, and A16 Rockridge, all in the Bay Area of California, and co-author of the books *A16 Food + Wine* and *SPQR: Modern Italian Food & Wine*. And she has a thing for southern Italian sparkling wine.

Contrary to what you might assume, Lindgren says, the sunny south is well-suited to bubbly production, thanks to the coastal Apennine Mountains. "In Campania, they are still vinifying the ancient grapes once grown in Pompeii—there is so much history," she adds.

De Conciliis "Selim" Spumante Brut (NV; 12% ABV; $$)

"Selim" is Miles (as in Davis) spelled backwards, and this jazzy wine from an organic farm on the stunning Campania coastline is a bubbly blend of Aglianico and Fiano, vinified in stainless steel, on the lees for softness. Lindgren describes it as "similar to Prosecco, with bracing acidity, but with generosity on the palate," with a flavor profile of tart honeycrisp apple, honeydew melon, and minerality.

Iovine "Terra del Gragnano" Penisola Sorrentina Frizzante Gragnano Rosso (V; 12.5% ABV; $)

This is a *frizzante* red in the old Neopolitan style eliciting notes of brambles, black pepper, and wet granite from the glass. Lindgren notes that Gragnano, on the cliffs on the way to Amalfi, is known for its pasta and tomatoes, so "this is the ideal wine for pizza. And it's perfect for hot-weather red-wine drinkers. You don't sip this wine, you drink it."

Ciro Picariello "Brut Contadino" Vino Spumante di Qualità (NV; 12%; $$$)

This no-*dosage metodo classico* is vinified from the ancient, high-acid Fiano grape, grown at 2,100 feet (640 m) of elevation, in the village of Summonte, dramatically situated on a lower slope of Mount Partenio. The maturation is partly in stainless steel, making for a crisp, lean wine. "There is that classic toasted brioche, but it also has notes of lemon zest, mandarin flower, green apple, and minerality," says Lindgren.

Sicily

Today's tourists, in their cargo shorts and fanny packs, can gaze up at Europe's most active volcano and see why the ancient Greeks and Romans believed that Hephaestus, aka Vulcan, must have a man-cave up there. (For, you know, all those weekend welding projects.) Because Mount Etna is rarely without its trademark ooze of red-hot lava, which makes for nice gritty volcanic soils for viticulture.

In addition to fire, Mount Etna also has ice. The peak of the mountain, at nearly 11,000 feet (3,330 m), has seen temperatures dip to 6 degrees Fahrenheit (–14.4 degrees Celsius), and the lower slopes tend to be breezy and cool, even as vacationers lounge on the Sicilian beaches below. And so it is possible to produce a wine that might erupt, volcano-like, if you shake up that bottle.

....

Murgo Metodo Classico Brut (V; 12.5% ABV; $–$$)

Italian diplomat and retired ambassador Baron Emanuele Scammacca del Murgo shook up the Etna oeno scene in the 1980s by making sparkling wines from the delightfully aromatic indigenous red grape, Nerello Mascalese. Murgo does a Brut, an Extra-Brut, and a Brut Rosé. Shelley Lindgren, who pours Murgo at her restaurants, praises this wine for its "volcanic minerality and racy acidity, with lemon verbena, honeycrisp apples, and delicate bubbles," and I couldn't say it better.

$$$

Erbaluce di Caluso
Cieck

$$$

Langhe
Vietti

$$$

Alta Langa
Ettore Germano

$$

Alta Langa
Enrico Serafino

$$$

Alta Langa
Contratto

$$

Acqui
Braida

$$$

Franciacorta
Barone Pizzini

$$$$

Franciacorta
Bellavista

$$$

Franciacorta
Berlucchi

$$$

Franciacorta
Ferghettina

$

Trentino
Pojer e Sandri

$$–$$$

Trentino
Furlani

$$

Trentodoc
Ferrari

$$

Prosecco
Zanotto

$$

Prosecco
Casa Coste Piane

$$

Prosecco
De Faveri

$$$

Prosecco
Ruggeri

$$

Prosecco
Sorelle Bronca

$$$

Friuli-Venezia Giulia
Edi Kante

$

Lambrusco
Bertolani

$

Lambrusco
Puianello

$$

Lambrusco
Vigneto Saetti

$$$

Campania
Ciro Picariello

$$

Sicily
Murgo

Iberophone Nations

Spain and Portugal share rivers and mountain ranges, climates, grape varieties, and parallel histories. And it's no accident that these two seafaring nations both mastered the art of fortified wine, which was for centuries the only *vino*, aka *vinho*, that could reliably travel overseas without spoiling.

Vinously speaking, there are still striking similarities between the two. Portugal's Vinho Verde is, if not technically sparkling, awfully fizzy, akin to Txakolí from northern Spain's Basque Country. And as we will see, the fully sparkling wines from these two regions also have a lot in common. And now for the historically awkward part.

Of all the colonized regions of the world, Central and South America have been making the European-style wines for the longest period of time. Following Juan de Grijalva's cruise ship to Cozumel in 1518, conquistadors, missionaries, and settlers wasted no time in getting viticulture going.

But at what cost? And who needs food, or an entire civilization, when there's wine? In 1542, Hérnan Cortés, governor of "New Spain," took a break from killing

RECIPE

SPARKLING SANGRÍA SPRITZ

SERVES 1

This variation on sangría represents all corners of Spain. The city of Granada in southern Spain is named after the pomegranate, which grows there, while Catalonia in the northeast is the home state of the signature sparkling wine, Cava, as well as Spanish Vermouth.

4 ounces Cava
2 ounces Spanish red Vermouth
1 thinly sliced orange wheel
1 thinly sliced lemon wheel
1 tablespoon fresh pomegranate seeds
Topo Chico sparkling mineral water, if desired

Half-fill a Mason jar or large sturdy wineglass with ice and slowly pour Cava, and then Vermouth, over the ice. Add the lemon and orange wheels to the glass, garnishing the edge of the glass with one wheel. Drop in pomegranate seeds and stir gently before serving.
Mix with mineral water, if desired, to make a lighter beverage.

off the Aztecs to command all settlers in what is now Mexico to plant not a food crop, but *vitis vinifera*. By 1532, the Portuguese were establishing grapevines in Brazil, and the year 1540 found Spanish monks making communion wines in Peru.

Today, a few hours after Spanish wine lovers sip Cava with their tapas in Barcelona, you might find their counterparts in Santiago, some 7,000 miles (11,000 km)

away, clinking glasses of bubbly vinified from the sixteenth-century Spanish Listán Prieto (aka País) grape. So, I guess, here's to the *conquistadors*, who, er, may have perpetrated terrorism, committed genocide, and obliterated the Aztec Empire, but did it with a goblet of wine in hand! *Ay caramba.*

For South and Central America map, see p. 163.

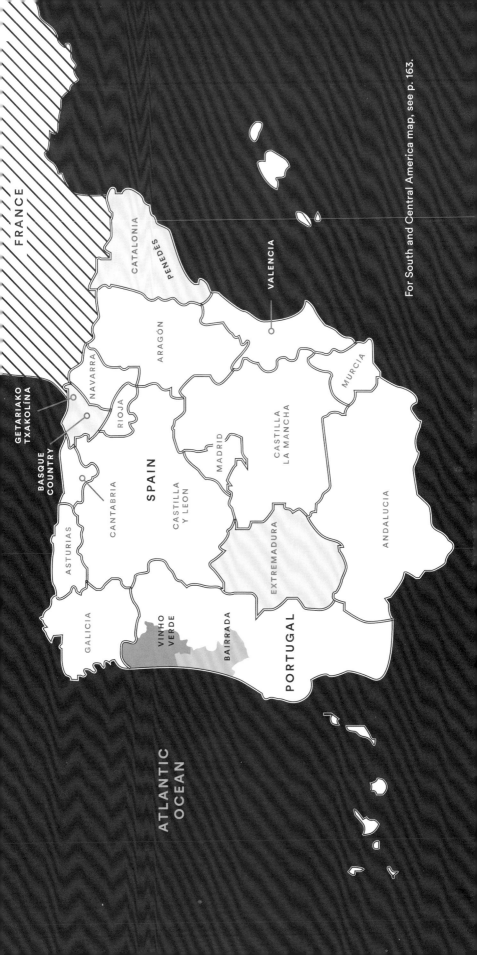

FRANCE

ATLANTIC
OCEAN

SPAIN

PORTUGAL

GALICIA

ASTURIAS

CANTABRIA

BASQUE
COUNTRY

GETARIAKO
TXAKOLÍNA

NAVARRA

RIOJA

ARAGÓN

CATALONIA

PENEDÈS

CASTILLA
Y LEON

MADRID

CASTILLA
LA MANCHA

VALENCIA

MURCIA

EXTREMADURA

ANDALUCIA

VINHO
VERDE

BAIRRADA

For South and Central America map, see p. 163.

Spain

The traditional-method *vino espumante* of Spain, Cava, is as affordable as Prosecco. But Spain is in the midst of a sparkling-wine renaissance that may result in a category better-known for quality than quantity. In addition, the natural-wine craze has settled into the Spanish sparkling scene, with some of the most exciting vintners reviving old indigenous vines and revisiting archaic winemaking techniques to capture exotic aromatics, textures, and flavors in their bottlings. All of this adds up to a feeling of excitement in the air, particularly in Catalonia, the epicenter of sparkling-wine production.

CATALONIA

You can taste Catalonian pride in the wine bars of Barcelona, where the region's bubbles are paired with tapas like *fideuà*, a paella-like plate made with short noodles rather than rice.

This pride ties into a movement to reclassify high-quality Catalonian Cava as something else. A small group of vintners has begun labeling their bubblies as "Corpinnat," for "heart of the Penedès." This unofficial designation is a guarantee of organic farming, the use of (mostly) estate-grown indigenous grape varieties, and a minimum of eighteen months[1] aging en *tirage,* as opposed to the Cava minimum of nine months.

This is because the term "Cava"[2] came into use in 1970 as a way to placate the Champenoise[3] rather than to communicate anything specific about a particular region or style. Thus, Spanish labeling laws are lax enough that "Cava" can be produced wayyyy down in Badajoz[4] so long as it's made via the traditional method and meets a bare minimum of quality standards.

So keep an eye out for Corpinnat, which is distinctly Catalonian.

---

[1]   It should be noted that there is a Reserva Cava designation for wines that have spent eighteen months en tirage, *and Gran Reserva for those that have been on the lees for a minimum of thirty months.*

[2]   It roughly translates as *"cellar."*

[3]   The rather charming term xampany, *as mentioned on page 151, continues to proliferate in the local lingo. It's pronounced* shahm-PAHN-yee, *too close to* shahm-PAHN-yuh *(that's "Champagne" in French) for comfort.*

[4]   Badajoz, *in southwestern Spain, is 608 miles (979 km) from the Catalonian center of Cava production, Sant Sadurní d'Anoia.*

Vine Wine's Coastal Finds

In Williamsburg, Brooklyn, the Vine Wine bottle shop captures the Catalonian spirit with its #vinewinesign, a sidewalk chalkboard that's regularly updated—not to advertise wine deals or special events, but to inform passersby and Instagram followers of the day's top news headlines.

In addition to sharing a sense of political engagement with her Catalonian counterparts, Vine Wine owner Talitha Whidbee is also a connoisseur of Spanish natural wines. When I asked her to recommend a couple of her fave Iberian Pét-Nats, she directed me to two intriguing pockets of coastal Catalonia.

Alta Alella/Celler de Les Aus "Bruant" Brut Nature Reserva Cava (V; 12% ABV; $$$)

Organically farmed Alta Alella inhabits the tiny coastal wine region of Alella, just north of Barcelona. Each Celler de Les Aus bottling is named after a bird species inhabiting the neighboring Serralada de Marina park; the Bruant on this label is a type of sparrow. Made with no *dosage* and no added sulfites, this wine is "everything I want in a sparkling wine," says Whidbee. "It makes me think of eating and drinking in Barcelona."

Partida Creus "GT" Penedès (V; 14.5% ABV; $$$)

In the Baix Penedès, a couple of former Italian architects revive old vineyards and resurrect obscure indigenous grape varieties. The "renegade punk-rock spirit" at Partida Creus means that "they don't have every wine every year and the names don't always stay the same, year to year," and the super-natural winemaking style calls for tasters with open minds: "Instead of looking for flaws, look for enjoyment." This red fizz is vinified from Garrut, a local clone of Monastrell,[5] and "should be drunk at 4:30 p.m., straight from your fridge," says Whidbee.

---

[5] *Known as Mourvèdre in France.*

Josep Foraster Trepat Rosat[6] Cava (NV; 11.5% ABV; $$)

The organically farmed, high-elevation Mas Foraster vineyard is in Central Catalonia's Conca de Barberà region, in the foothills of the Prades Mountains near Tarragona, noted for its collection of remarkable twelfth-century Cistercian monasteries as well as Trepat, an autochthonous (that is, indigenous, or native) red grape. Unlike in Champagne, where it's common to add still red wine to sparkling wine to make rosé, blending is not allowed for *Rosado* Cava, so all the gorgeous color you see is the result of maceration.

---

[6] *This section will include words in Catalan as well as Spanish, as it's common to switch back and forth in Catalonia.* Rosat *is the Catalan word for* rosado *(Spanish) or* rosé *(French).*

Why Catalonian Cava Is a Political Statement

Prosperous and fiercely independent, Catalonians have long demanded autonomy, griping that their tax revenue supports the rest of Spain.

During the Spanish Civil War, this attitude did not sit well with General Francisco Franco, who executed and jailed prominent Catalan community leaders. These included the successful proprietors of the sparkling-wine bodegas, whose luxury products embodied the upscale Catalonian way of life.

As was the case in Champagne during the two World Wars, the Catalonians found their way through the crisis. Women proved to be savvy entrepreneurs, running the wineries on behalf of their missing husbands and brothers. And the deep underground cellars of the winemaking town of Sant Sadurní d'Anoia provided sanctuary during air raids.[7]

Today, Catalonia's separatist streak continues to bedevil the Cava trade. With every political outburst—such as the many recent declarations of independence—the rest of Spain boycotts Catalonian products, Cava foremost among these. The only upside to this incessant domestic trade war is that foreign markets are enjoying more Penedès Cava every year.

---

[7] *Torelló Mata,* Cava, Where Are You Headed? The Legacy of Agustí Torelló Mata, *49–54.*

Penedès

Catalonia's sparkling heart and soul hugs the state's central coastline from Barcelona to Tarragona, then climbs the Garraf Mountains to high plains overlooked by the dramatic rocky cliffs of Montserrat, a range that protects the region from the cold winds of the Pyrenees.

The French varieties Pinot Noir and Chardonnay are grown in the upland, inland zones, where temperatures dip as low as they do in Champagne. But a surge of local pride has rendered native grape varieties more prominent in recent years, and for good reason, since they favor the coastal Mediterranean climate and naturally achieve high acidity in the local soils.

Foremost among these grapes is the citrusy white Xarel·lo, pronounced *chah-REH-loh*. Softer, vanilla-scented, fruity Macabeo[8] is grown in higher volumes and does best in coastal sites. Finally, Parellada favors high-elevation sites and slate soils. The last of the trio to be harvested, it's naturally acidic and makes fresh, jasmine-scented wines.

Blended, these three make such a rich base wine that the better Penedès producers use little to no *dosage*. That said, these indigenous grape varieties also impart a slight whiff of rubbery funk, a note of rusticity that can be surprisingly addictive.

....

Gramona "Celler Batlle"[9] Finca Font de Jui Brut Corpinnat
(V; 12% ABV; $$$$$)

Like a high-end Grande Marque, Gramona bottle-ages its wines under cork rather than crown cap, practices jetting to minimize sulfur additions, and maintains a solera[10] dating all the way back to 1881 to produce a fortified Xarel·lo that's used as the *dosage* for the sparkling wines. Aged *en tirage* for a minimum of 120 months, this wine is Xarel·lo and Macabeo sourced entirely from the Finca Font de Jui,[11] the family's biodynamic estate, farmed by draft horses on the outskirts of Sant Sadurní d'Anoia. This magisterial wine, produced in an eco-friendly winery, is somehow fresh on the

---

[8] *Also spelled Macabeu, and also called Viura.*

[9] *Batlle was the original family winery name. It changed to Gramona when the Batlle family married into the Gramona family.*

[10] *See page 278 for more on this term.*

[11] *This estate, named after a spring that runs through it, has been granted the status of a Paraje Calificado—Paratge Qualificat in Catalan—that is, a Cru-level lieu-dit.*

palate despite all that age, while also spicy, yeasty, creamy, and sumptuous.

Recaredo "Intens" Brut Nature Rosat Corpinnat
(V; 12% ABV; $$$)

Recaredo is devoted to long-aged, estate-grown, terroir-driven, Brut Nature bottlings. All lees aging is done under cork, and all farming is biodynamic. The house's single *lieu-dit* bottlings are well worth tasting if you can find and afford them. "Intens," a blend of Garnacha and Monastrell, gets its red-currant color from maceration, as is required for Cava and Corpinnat. Earthy and spicy, it has a roasted-tomato quality that just begs for a food pairing with the official spices of Spain, saffron and paprika.

Agustí Torelló Mata "Kripta" Gran Reserva Cava[12] Brut Nature
(V; 11.5% ABV; $$$$–$$$$$)

This old-vine *première cuvée* comes in an unusual amphora-shaped bottle, with a rounded base—said to encourage the circulation of yeast—that can't be parked anywhere but an ice bucket. The straight-outta-Aeschylus gold-accented label design is by artist Rafael Bartolozzi. The house cultivates its own *pied de cuve* yeast selections. Agustí Torelló Mata, Sant Sadurní d'Anoia's resident historian, is a staunch supporter of the traditional Cava appellation although his wines qualify as Corpinnat. The family is unusual in its commitment to Macabeo as the predominant grape in their portfolio; although more fickle in the vineyard, they find it to be more supple in the cellar. Typically available nine years past its release date, "Kripta" is still suggestive of fresh nectarine and yellow plum. The texture is silky, and a yeastiness on the palate progresses to savoriness at the finish.

---

[12] *Despite Corpinnat-eligible farming and winemaking, the Torelló family were holdouts for the Cava designation at the time of this writing.*

Lice Knowing You

When those nasty root lice, phylloxera, started gobbling up French vineyards in the 1860s, Spain stepped in and sent *vino* north to prop up the wine industry there. This being prior to the advent of refrigerated shipping containers, red Spanish table wines were fortified with brandy to stabilize them for the long train journeys. But base wines traveling all the way to Champagne from Spain had to be low in alcohol for a second bottle fermentation to be possible.

The resolution to this problem was found in Catalonia, which happened to be the major cork supplier to Champagne and was already dabbling in sparkling winemaking, anyway. It turned out that the native Xarel·lo grape possessed profound antioxidant qualities that made it a champion traveler—a fact that ancient Roman traders knew in centuries past.[13]

The connection between the two regions grew so strong that even today, you'll see signs around Barcelona for *xampanyerias* ("Champagne" bars, in Catalan) where *xampany* ("Champagne," but in fact Cava) or *xampanyet* (carbonated wine) is served.

By the time phylloxera crossed the Pyrenees, Catalonian growers acted quickly to replant[14]—but instead of the red varieties that had dominated prior to the scourge, they devoted their plantings to the three native white varieties that had proven so apt for sparkling winemaking.

Today, the people of the winemaking town of Sant Sadurní d'Anoia commemorate the role root lice have had in their culture by dressing up in gargantuan bug costumes, setting off fireworks, and drinking a ton of sparkling wine at the "Festa de la Fil·loxera" (as they spell "phylloxera" around here) every September.

---

[13] Junyent, *"Compitiendo con el Champagne."*

[14] *By this time it was known that phylloxera could be circumvented by replanting with European* vitis vinifera *vines grafted onto phylloxera-resistant native American grapevine rootstock.*

¡Raventós y Raventós y Raventós!

One of the many similarities Penedès wine country shares with Champagne is the sense that everyone is somehow related to everyone else, with the same surnames popping up everywhere. Thus, there are at least five different Cava houses with "Raventós" in their names.[15] And for all I know, there may be more . . .

But for serious aficionados, only one Raventós matters. Josep Raventós i Fatjó first made traditional-method bubbly for his family's winery, Codorníu, in 1872. His son, Manuel Raventós Domènech, was the first to blend the three indigenous grape varieties. (He also had a flair for marketing, commissioning striking modernist posters, and plotting an "accident" in which a bull cart full of Codorníu bubbly smashed into a shop window on Barcelona's famous Las Ramblas. The stunt made front-page headlines and turned Codorníu into a household name.)[16]

A few generations later, Josep Maria Raventós i Blanc[17] established the Cava denomination in 1970, then split from Codorníu and launched his own winery across the street in 1986, taking with him 220 acres (90 ha) of vineyard and farmland that had been in the family since 1497. Today the Raventós i Blanc estate is a biodynamic sanctuary, its massale-selected vines[18] plowed by draft horses. And as if to demonstrate the similarities between the Penedès and Champagne, one plot is given over to a jumble of massive chalk-white rocks riddled with marine fossils.

The Codorníu winery is currently controlled by a global asset management firm. Raventós i Blanc, by contrast, remains staunchly independent. In 2012, it was the first winery to leave the Cava appellation—ironically, the very appellation founded by Josep Raventós i Blanc—establishing its own denomination of origin, "Conca del Riu Anoia."[19]

Today, Manuel Raventós Negra[20] oversees the bodega, with his visionary son Josep ("Pepe") Raventós i Vidal running day-to-day operations and dabbling in side projects such as an elegant line of natural wines under the Can Sumoi label.

Raventós i Blanc "Manuel Raventós Negra" Conca del Riu Anoia (V; 12.5% ABV; $$$$–$$$$$)

The patriarch selects and blends his top 100 percent Xarel·lo barrels from the most exceptional vintages, then ages the bottles six years on the lees, to make this Prestige Cuvée. Creamy, salty, and luxuriant, it has intoxicating aromatics of melon and yeast.

---

[15] *Raventós i Blanc, the Raventós Codorníu corporation, Ramón Raventós, Raventós Rosell, and Solà Raventós. And for all I know, there may be more.*

[16] *Torelló Mata,* Cava, Where Are You Headed?, *39.*

[17] *In Spain, children get both parents' surnames, as in Raventós i Fatjó and Raventós i Blanc. And in the Raventós family, firstborn sons are given either the name Josep or Manuel.*

[18] *That is, selected from vineyard cuttings rather than purchased from a nursery, as is more commonly done.*

[19] *The geographic outline of this self-proclaimed appellation encompasses the Anoia River Valley, between the towns of Sant Sadurní d'Anoia and Vilafranca del Penedès, and thus could be used by other producers in the area willing to abide by the requirements, which are even stricter than those of Corpinnat.*

[20] *Yes, you read that right: Manuel Raventós Negra is the son of Josep Raventós i Blanc. Which means that Josep's mother was a "White" and Manuel's mother was a "Black."*

Codorníu "Ars Collecta" Gran Reserva Blanc de Noirs Cava (V; 11.5% ABV; $$)

Three mass-produced Catalonian Cava brands are familiar to shoppers worldwide. There is Jaume Serra's dirt-cheap Cristalino,[21] and there is Freixenet, a massive international conglomerate that is Spain's largest beverage exporter. Finally, there is Codorníu, whose solid-white-bottled, Chardonnay-based "Anna"[22] cuvée is consumed like 7-Up in Spain. But dating back to 1551, Codorníu is also the nation's oldest winery, with underground caves that drop five floors below ground and tunnel nearly 19 miles (30 km) through the earth. Its production buildings, designed by Gaudí contemporary Josep Puig i Cadafalch, have been declared a national heritage site. Today, winemaker Bruno Colomer maintains the crowd-pleasing, fruit-driven Codorníu house style while experimenting with micro-lots of more nuanced wines. This is 85 percent Pinot Noir and 7 percent Xarel·lo, with an additional 8 percent Trepat, an indigenous red grape that's used in Catalan winegrowing zones such as Conca de Barberà and Costers del Segre to make *rosado*.

Avinyó Brut Reserva Cava (NV; 11.5% ABV; $$)

Since the sixteenth century, the Esteve family has been farming Can Fontanals, an estate abutting an archaeological site where the earliest evidence of winemaking in northeastern Spain (dating back to the third century BCE) has been found. They practice organic farming, long lees aging, and on-demand disgorgement; this blend of the classic trio of grapes is satisfyingly beer-like, with barley aromatics that would pair well with stick-to-your-ribs foods.

Clos Lentiscus "N 41° 15,656 E 1° 45,086" Método Tradicional Penedès Brut Nature Rosé (V; 12% ABV; $$$)

In the shadow of the Garraf Massif range and under the watch of an ancient Pistacia lentiscus (mastic) tree, the Aviñó family[23] grows grapes biodynamically. A commitment to natural winemaking stems from a family member's stomach cancer diagnosis, and includes native yeasts, no sulfur additions, and the use of honey from the farm's own beehives to sweeten the *liqueur de tirage*. This stunning raspberry-nectarine-tinted 100 percent Samsó[24] bottling has aromatics of candied cherries and lip-smacking notes of plum and drinking vinegar that call for a match of grilled Japanese eggplant.

Llopart Método Tradicional Reserva Brut Rosé Corpinnat (V; 11.5% ABV; $$)

The Llopart (pronounced *yoh-PAHRT*)[25] family has been growing grapes since 1385 and making traditional-method bubbly since 1887. This blend of 60 percent Monastrell, 20 percent Garnatxa, and 20 percent Pinot Noir, farmed organically at elevations higher than 1,180 feet (360 m), spends eighteen months *en tirage*, showing equal parts wild strawberry and earthiness; it's wonderful with *buñuelos de bacalao* in Barcelona restaurants.

Celler La Salada "Roig Boig" Penedès Método Ancestral (V; 11% ABV; $$)

Toni Carbó, cofounder of the highly regarded Mas Candí label, farms his field-blend plantings of indigenous varieties biodynamically, following a no-till philosophy. This funky, fizzy, richly pigmented, naturally made *rosado* is a blend of the red and white varieties Sumoll, Roigenc, Mandó,

Cannonnau, Monica, Torbat, Parellada, and Xarel·lo; most of the fruit is direct-pressed, while a fraction is held back to macerate for four months.

Vinyes Singulars "Minipuça" Penedès Método Ancestral (V; 11% ABV; $$)

Cal Batlle—yes, that name sounds familiar if you've just read about Gramona (see page 149)—is a farm growing grains, fruit, olives, almonds, vegetables, and wine grapes. Vintner Ignasi Seguí sells most of the fruit from his family's historic vineyard, saving his top selections to make his own wines,

---

[21] *Just in case you pick this up at Walmart and feel like you've won the lottery, please note that Jaume Serra Cristalino is not affiliated with, sponsored by, approved by, endorsed by, or in any way connected to Louis Roederer's Cristal, which retails for upward of $250 a bottle and needs at least a decade of cellar age before serving.*

[22] *Named after Anna Codorníu, who in 1659, at the age of fourteen, married Miquel Raventós, and was the last in the family to bear the Codorníu name.*

[23] *Yes, it's a common name in the area and is spelled in different ways.*

[24] *Samsó is the Catalonian term for Carignan, or Cariñena, a grape that's prominent in Spain and has seen its reputation resurrected of late in Languedoc and Sardinia.*

[25] *At least that's how I'd pronounce it in Spanish! Catalan is outside my wheelhouse.*

which he ages in abandoned civil war–era air-raid shelters on the estate. I'm a fan of his *rosado*, called "Al Rosa, l'Amor s'Hi Posa," but this old-vine Xarel·lo is a linear, mineral delight.

Júlia Bernet "Ú" Vinyes de Muntanya Brut Nature Corpinnat (V; 12.5% ABV; $$)

Xavier Bernet farms only Xarel·lo in the western foothills of the Ordal Mountains, near the village of Subirats; he named his label after his daughter. This Brut Nature has a persistent *mousse*, clean palate, and fresh aromatics of wildflowers, hay, and pear.

German Gilabert Método Tradicional Brut Nature Reserva Cava (NV; 11.5% ABV; $)

American father-daughter importers José and Teresa Pastor curate cuvées for their Vinos de Terruños line, which focuses on native Spanish varieties. This certified-organic blend of the three classic Penedès grapes offers up aromatics of sisal, savory tarragon chicken, exotic spices, hand lotion, stones, jasmine tea, pipe tobacco, cayenne, and I could go on . . .

Totus Tuus Brut Cava (NV; 11.5% ABV; $)

Alberto Orte, the Jerez-based partner behind Olé Imports, blends this rich, smoky, viscous wine for his mother, labeling it (in Latin) "Everything for You." It is indeed a little bit of everything— Chardonnay, Macabeo, and Pinot Noir in addition to the classic trio—and it's sappy, savory, spicy, and rustic, with a hint (why not?) of coffee.

BASQUE COUNTRY

Catalonia's equal in insubordination—*down with the oppressors!*— is *País Vasco*, aka Basque Country. In both Barcelona and Bilbao, resistance flags hang from apartment windows and citizens march chanting through the streets.

I give you this bit of background to help you better understand the wine. Just as Catalonian wine labels are peppered with unfamiliar Catalan terms, the verbiage on a Basque bottle bristles with spikey *X*s and *K*s. Txakolí, the region's signature beverage, prickles too, hitting the palate like LaCroix.

It's not quite a sparkling wine, but it *does* foam when the bartenders of San Sebastián lift the bottle above eye-level as

The brilliant Basque: Cristóbal Balenciaga

they pour. Cascading from such a height, a head of froth builds. Txakolí gets its spritz from a high-tech take on the ancestral method: The juice of young, high-acid grapes is fermented in airtight steel tanks, then chilled until it's nearly freezing before bottling. The bit of fizz that's captured in the bottle is the natural last gasp of fermentation.

But it's not exactly a sparkling wine, so let's look at *vino de método tradicional* from a Txakolí producer. Don't ask me how to say that in Basque.

Getariako Txakolína

Getariako Txakolína roughly translates as "wine from the village of Getaria," a historic seaside town between San Sebastian and Bilbao boasting a charming old port and the ultramodern Cristóbal Balenciaga museum. Just as native son Balenciaga took traditional Basque forms— the nun's habit, the fisherman's slicker—and reinvented them as expertly crafted works of utter genius, Txakolí from Getaria is a totally modern wine coming from age-old autochthonous grape varieties: the pale Hondarrabi Zuri and the dark Hondarrabi Beltza. And traditional-method *sparkling* Txakolí is the vinous equivalent of Basque-born haute couture.

Ameztoi "Hijo de Rubentis" Getariako Txakolína Extra-Brut Rosé (NV; 12% ABV; $$–$$$)

Seventh-generation vintner Ignacio Ameztoi has earned fame for his Rubentis rosé Txakolí. The son (*hijo*) of Rubentis is a full-on traditional-method bottle-fermented bubbly made from the Hondarrabi Beltza grape. One can just see the windblown vineyards high in the hills above the Bay of Biscay after tasting the brine, citrus, and salsa verde notes in this rose-gold wine. Then it loosens up in the glass, revealing spices, cherries, and vanilla.

EXTREMADURA

The poorest state in Spain represents opportunity. Sure, locals still commute astride donkeys and horses, following paths carved millennia ago. But the cheap real estate and extreme weather have attracted some of Europe's largest solar and wind farms, rendering the region a leader in green energy. And the old cheap *vino de mesa* industry is being displaced by young vintners attracted by affordable vineyard land. The Ribera del Guadiana is the subzone of most viticultural interest, growing native varieties like Cayetana Blanca, Pardina, or Montúa among the fig and olive groves, with the river providing just enough natural moisture to keep vegetation alive. Cava is produced here, but given that this region's winegrowing history can be traced back to 550 BCE, let's look at an old-school vino *espumoso*.

Bodegas Cerro la Barca "Vegas Altas" Ancestral Vino de la Tierra de Extremadura (NV; 11.5% ABV; $–$$)

Since 2003, Cerro la Barca has been devoted to upping the Extremadura winemaking game, and resurrecting nearly extinct indigenous grape varieties in the Ribera del Guadiana with organic and biodynamic farming. This buttercup-colored blend of 40 percent Xarel·lo, 40 percent Macabeo, and 20 percent Cabernet Sauvignon may need a bit of initial air, but after a few minutes in the glass, it gives off aromatics of buttered noodles and river stones; the creamy palate has a maple-like sappiness to it.

Portugal

For most of us, Portuguese wines are the heady, fortified Port and Madeira; the leathery red table wines from the Douro; and the spritzy and affordable whites of Vinho Verde. Visit this ocean-front nation, however, and you'll broaden your horizons. Not only are *bacalhau* (salt cod) and *marisco* (shellfish) superb with the zesty local fizz, but in Bairrada, the top *espumante*-producing region, the classic pairing is *leitão*, or roast suckling pig. You've got to hand it to these people for trusting bubbly to stand up to a food that traditionally calls for red wine.

Alas, Portugal historically has consumed most of its own *espumante*. Today, fortified wine accounts for a quarter of Portuguese vinous exports.[26] Sparkling wine accounts for only 3 percent of table wine (that is, not fortified) exports, and most of that goes to the former Portuguese territories of Brazil, Angola, and Mozambique. But there is change in the air. After years of economic stagnation and fiscal austerity in Portugal, savvy young winemakers have moved in to take advantage of affordable land, material, and labor costs, bringing with them knowledge and a drive to innovate.

---

[26]   *According to 2015 data provided by the trade group Wines of Portugal.*

BAIRRADA

A group of Champagne enthusiasts established *espumante* as Bairrada's specialty in the late nineteenth century, when, inspired by the area's sandy, chalky soils and drizzly, mid-coastal climate, they began bottle-fermenting wines and established the Associação Vinícola da Bairrada (Bairrada Winery Association). The movement hit full speed in the 1920s, with the opening of a number of *caves*.

Even as the region has been earning buzz in the wine press lately for its monumental reds made from the native Baga grape, Bairrada continues to turn out some 65 percent of all Portuguese bubblies. Thanks in part to its convenient location between the cities of Oporto and Lisbon, most of this is consumed inside Portuguese borders.

....

Luis Pato Maria Gomes Vinho Espumante
(NV; 12.5% ABV; $$)

From a family of Bairrada vine-tenders since the eighteenth century, the eponymous Pato is a champion of indigenous varieties on *vinhas velhas*, or old ungrafted[27] vines, and single-vineyard bubblies. This summery sparkling white is made from 95 percent Maria Gomes, aka Fernão Pires—a floral, aromatic, citrusy grape—plus 5 percent Sercialinho, an extremely delicate native variety said to be extinct outside of Pato's vineyards. This wine's aromatics can vary depending on when you open it, ranging from honeydew melon-cucumber lotion to smoky and sultry.

....

Filipa Pato & William Wouters "3B" Extra Bruto Unfiltered Rosé (NV; 11.5% ABV; $–$$)

Luis Pato's daughter Filipa trained all over the world before returning home with her husband, Belgian sommelier and restaurateur William Wouters, to produce what she calls *vinhos autênticos sem maquiagem*, or "authentic wines without makeup": biodynamic practices in the vineyard and minimal intervention in the winery. There's a deft hand behind this powder-puff-pink blend of 75 percent Baga and 25 percent Bical. Its aromatics are of soft spices and *pão doce* (Portuguese sweet bread); the smooth, pleasing palate has a touch of lavender.

São João Bruto Rosé
(V; 12.5% ABV; $$)

São João is a *négociant* winery, named after the beatific patron saint of Bairrada and founded in 1920. The bubbles in this traditional-method wine are a bit clumsy and rough, the color is watermelon Jolly Rancher, and the aromatics are cotton candy. But the palate is clean, with just a touch of bell pepper and black plum, and for the price (less than $20), this is an easy-drinking blend of the high-yielding, acid-driven, purple-skinned Baga and Touriga Nacional, the low-yielding, tannic star of the Douro.

VINHO VERDE

The Minho Valley in the Atlantic Northwest of Portugal is cool, drizzly, and green. Here, adjacent to Spanish Galicia, is the Vinho Verde wine region, where the eponymous light, spritzy whites are made from grapes harvested early—or "green"—and then sold in tall, thin, green bottles.[28] These inexpensive quaffers traditionally got their light *efervescência* from an ancestral-method-type situation. These days, winemaking techniques have improved, and the injection of a bit of CO_2 achieves a similar pick-me-up effect. But Vinho Verde wines don't, strictly speaking, sparkle. So let's turn our attention back to those early accidents and talk about an ancestral-method bubbly from Vinho Verde that would kill with a plate of *bacalhau*.

Aphros "Phaunus" Pét-Nat Vinho Espumante Branco
(V; 12% ABV; $$–$$$)

Vasco Croft comes from one of the Anglo clans that established the fortified winemaking industry[29] in Portugal, and he himself has some "Phaunus" (Pan, or god of forests and wingman of Dionysus) qualities: He raises sheep, tends bee boxes, harbors endangered mountain horses called *garranos*, and makes wine in terra-cotta amphorae. His rendition of the fragrant, floral Loureiro grape makes a Pét-Nat with high-toned and bright aromatics with notes of spruce, pine, and limoncello, as well as a frothy and mouthfilling *mousse*.

---

[27] *Nearly all wine grapevines today are grafted onto American rootstock to deter the destructive root louse known as phylloxera.*

[28] *This is, it should be noted, the Vinho Verde we know best in the US, but the region produces many styles of wines, including sturdy reds.*

[29] *The Crofts founded their Port house in 1588 and sold it, in 2001, to the Fladgate Partnership.*

México

The oldest still-extant *bodega* in the Americas, Casa Madero, was founded way back in 1597, making it not much younger than Spain's Codorníu, dating back to 1551. It's located in Central México, where the potential for fine winemaking seems to be limitless. Due to its altitude, with vineyards that can reach 6,500 feet (2,000 m) and even higher, weather here can be spring-like year-round, with cool enough temperatures to achieve the acidity levels necessary to make bubbly. Cava king Freixenet runs a Central Mexican operation called Finca Sala Vivé that's a three-hour drive from México City, and visitors to México can find locally vinified fizz from smaller producers in restaurants and bars. But only Baja has managed to export its *efervescencia* north of the border.

NORTHERN BAJA

Some 80 miles (130 km) south of San Diego, and 70 miles (110 km) south of Tijuana, is the epicenter of the most exciting growing region in México, currently producing 90 percent of the nation's wine.

The epicenter of Northern Baja wine country is the Valle de Guadalupe, near Ensenada. This Eden-like setting is home to numerous boutique hotels, independent *bodegas*, and stylish restaurants turning out wine-friendly "Baja Med"—Mexican-Mediterranean—cuisine. The grape varieties here tend to be Bordeaux and Italian, and the wines tend to be meaty and red, but there are a few pockets of resistance where effervescence is achieved.

....

Bichi "Pet Mex" Tecate
México (V; 12.5% ABV; $$$)

This ancestral-method sparkler comes from the poster boys for natural winemaking in México, celebrity chef Jair Téllez, his brother, Noel, and

NORTHERN
BAJA

CENTRAL
AMERICA

MÉXICO

BRAZIL

SOUTH
AMERICA

SERRA
GAÚCHA

MENDOZA

CHILE

ARGENTINA

URUGUAY

SAN ANTONIO
VALLEY

Burgundian-turned-Chilean natural winemaker Louis-Antoine Luyt. The brothers track down heirloom plantings and bring them back to health with organic and biodynamic viticulture, then follow a natural winemaking protocol that includes stomping grapes by foot, wild-yeast fermentations, and concrete amphorae. Their winery is located at the Téllez family ranch near the border town of Tecate, but the high-elevation vineyard source for this wine is near coastal Ensenada on sandy loam soils. Dry-farmed and own-rooted,[30] it was planted more than seven decades ago to an unidentified grape variety. One US retailer describes "Pet Mex" as "pixie juice," which just about nails it.

---

[30] *That is, growing from its own roots, not grafted. See discussions of phylloxera, pages 66 and 151, for more on this.*

Our Lady and Guadalupe

Mexican wine consultant Sandra Fernández Gaytán has achieved certifications at institutions such as the Culinary Institute of America, UC Davis, the Court of Master Sommeliers, and even the Consejo Regulador of Jerez. So when she told me that there's one, and only one, Mexican sparkling wine that can stand among the best bubbles in the world, I prayed she'd tell me more . . .

Espuma de Piedra "EP + bb" Valle de Guadalupe Baja Blanc de Blancs (NV; 12.5% ABV; $$)

"Owner and enologist Hugo d'Acosta is one of the most important and influential characters in the Mexican *enológica* scene," says Fernández Gaytán. "He has rewritten the narrative." D'Acosta makes a variety of wines under multiple brands. Given his geographic reality, his grape choices for his Espuma de Piedra traditional-method wines are unusual, including Zinfandel and Barbera. The "EP + bb" Blanc de Blancs is half Chardonnay, half Sauvignon Blanc, and sits on the lees for eighteen months. "It is an elegant, dry wine with very good acidity," says Fernández Gaytán. "It's the best example of the country's traditional-method wines."

Brazil

Brazil is the fifth-largest and fifth-most-populous nation in the world, the biggest country in Latin America, and South America's third-most-prolific wine producer after Argentina and Chile. European wine-grape varieties arrived here back in 1532, on the ship of Portuguese *fidalgo*,[31] explorer, and wearer of white tights Martim Afonso de Sousa.

(Then there was that interlude when Portugal banned Brazilian viticulture in order to minimize the competition in the motherland. When the Portuguese royal family and court relocated to Rio de Janeiro between 1808 and 1821—it seemed best to stay out of Napoleon's way—wouldn't you know it, winemaking started back up again.)

After slavery—finally—was outlawed in Brazil in 1878, an influx of Italian and German immigrants got right to work planting vineyards. Today, a grape variety called Riesling Italico, or Welschriesling, brought by late-nineteenth-century Italians, continues to be one of Brazil's most-planted fine-wine grapes.

One wonders why we don't see more Brazilian wines here in the United States. The answer is multifold. First, the majority are simple supermarket *vinhos de mesa* (table wines) made from subpar grape varieties. Second, the nation's volatile economy has historically delivered more drama than its most addictive telenovelas, resulting in limited imports and exports. Since pulling out of its most recent recession in 2017, however, Brazil has been sending some interesting sparkling wines our way.

SERRA GAÚCHA

The majority of Brazil's fine wine is produced in its southernmost state of Rio Grande do Sul, on the Uruguayan border. Here, in the drizzly foothills of the "mountain cowboy" range, the Serra Gaúcha, the center of the action is the DO Vale dos Vinhedos, just west of the city of Bento Gonçalves. (If you go, be sure to stop at the Capela Nossa Senhora das Neves, constructed in 1907 during a major drought. With no water on hand to make cement, the Italian masons formed its bricks from clay, straw, and—YES!—wine.)

---

[31] *Nobleman of, in this case, royal bastard heritage.*

In 1973, the French Champagne giant Moët & Chandon opened a winery here, in the town of Garibaldi. Since then, Serra Gaúcha has been a sparkling-wine specialist, with increasing plantings of Chardonnay, Pinot Noir, and that Riesling Italico, which blends well into bubblies. In addition to traditional-method sparklers, regional wineries are experimenting with fizzy Moscato and Charmat-method Glera, à la Prosecco.

....

Salton "Intenso" Serra Gaúcha Brazil Sparkling Brut
(NV; 11.5% ABV; $$)

Antonio Domenico Salton emigrated to Brazil from Italy's Veneto in 1878 with a head full of Old World winemaking knowledge. The winery his seven sons established in 1910 is today thought to be the largest winemaking operation in the Americas, welcoming some 45 million visitors annually to its tasting room and formal gardens; the stunning mosaic over the front entrance of the massive château happens to be the world's largest solar clock. Still family-run, Salton makes a wide variety of wines, including at least twenty traditional-method bubblies, a range of Moscato-like *frisantes*, and this frothy, floral Prosecco-style *espumante*, 70 percent Chardonnay and 30 percent Riesling Italico.

Uruguay

Most of the world's winemaking regions fall between the thirtieth and fiftieth parallels—regardless of hemisphere—comfortably removed from the heat and humidity of the equator, as well as the cold temperatures and divergent daylight hours at the poles. So it follows that centrally located Uruguay should be South America's fourth-largest wine producer, even though it's the second-smallest nation on the continent.

The European influence is strong, with a fine-dining scene that's dominated by Italian, Spanish, and French cuisine due to immigrant populations from those three nations, plus you'll hear Portuguese spoken due to the influx of tourists from Brazil. Until now, Uruguay has been best-known as a producer of powerful reds made from Tannat, a brutish dark grape that hails from southwestern France and can handle the humidity, but a current movement toward cool-climate white varieties marks an opportunity for sparkling winemaking.

Canelones According to Adriana Vivián Rossi

Uruguay's most prolific wine region is a short drive north and east from the bustling capital city of Montevideo. If it sounds like it's named after a tubular Italian pasta, well, that's not too far off, because Italian names pop up frequently here. Adriana Vivián Rossi is a local who knows these names well: She's president of the Asociación Uruguaya de Sommeliers Profesionales (AUSP), as well as a partner in the artisanal brewery and wine-and-beer bar, Bestiario, in Montevideo. I asked her to tell us about a couple of her favorite Canelones sparkling wines.

Pisano "Río de los Pájaros" Reserve Tannat Brut Nature (NV; 13.5% ABV; $$)

The Pisano Arretxea brothers are Italian-Basque, which is fitting, since Basque immigrants brought the Tannat grape with them to Uruguay. They produce this traditional-method treat in very small volumes and call it Black Beauty among themselves. "It's deep-purple in color, with a subtle light-purple foam on the top of the glass," Rossi notes. "I'm pretty sure that it is the only Tannat sparkling wine in the world." Given its classic Tannat aromatics of "violets, blackberries, and blackcurrant, with hints of licorice," Rossi suggests matching it with oven-roasted sweetbreads.

Pizzorno Uruguay Reserva Brut Nature (NV; 13.5% ABV; $$)

Like Salton in Brazil, Pizzorno winery was established by Italian immigrants in 1910. Twelve grape varieties grow in the family vineyards, but this "soft and elegant" Brut Nature is the classic Chardonnay–Pinot Noir combination. "It has twenty-four months of aging on the lees, which gives it unctuosity and roundness," observes Rossi, who admires this wine's "charm and brightness."

Argentina

God bless those Christian missionaries. Not only did they plant wine grapes in 1556, but, taking measure of the high-and-dry terrain, they diverted glacial runoff into irrigation trenches, ensuring that their vines didn't dry up. In short, the brothers had their priorities in order.

Roving French wine consultant Michel Aimé Pouget arrived in the mid-nineteenth century, established an agronomy school, and started pushing French grape varieties, particularly Malbec, which is now Argentina's national grape. A few decades later, a wave of European immigrants arrived, having fled the phylloxera epidemic back home. Their brains full of Old World viticultural knowledge, they hit the ground running, and thanked the heavens every day that said ground was sandy and thus inhospitable to those nasty little root lice.

Today, Argentineans have a particular thing for fizzy drinks. They mix Fernet Branca liqueur with Coca-Cola and serve wine from soda siphons, carbonated on the spot, over ice. Thus, the Moët & Chandon and Mumm Champagne houses both maintain busy outposts here. Open a bottle alongside a platter of doughy empanadas and you've got a party.

MENDOZA

Argentina's best-known wine region hugs the eastern slopes of the Andes, near the Chilean border. Due to a perfect storm of European investment and ideal

Post-Nazi Intrigue in Argentina

In the 1950s, Baron Bertrand de Ladoucette, owner of an eponymous winery in the Loire Valley, and his wife Élisabeth de Vogüé moved part-time to Argentina to invest in ranch land, partly out of fear of a possible postwar Soviet invasion of France.[32]

One thing led to another, and soon Élisabeth's uncle, Count Robert-Jean de Vogüé—director of Moët & Chandon—was spending his vacation time sniffing around Argentina looking to plant sparkling-wine grapes.

De Vogüé had even more reason to want to diversify his assets in far-flung Argentina. A leader of the Resistance, he had been arrested and imprisoned by the Gestapo during the war.[33] So in 1959, de Vogüé convinced Ladoucette to head up a new winery far from the turmoil of postwar Europe: Chandon Argentina.

Unbeknownst to both men—but known to us now—Nazi war criminals like Adolf Eichmann had also secretly fled to Argentina after the war, not so much to protect assets as to, oh, maybe escape prosecution by the United Nations War Crimes Commission. Fascism-friendly Juan Perón left the door wide open, and Argentina's sizable German immigrant population provided plenty of camouflage.

One wonders if the opponents ever crossed paths in the Pampas, or if Eichmann ever tipped back a glass of Chandon Argentina to celebrate his temporary escape[34] from the authorities.

---

[32] Mount, The Vineyard at the End of the World: Maverick Winemakers and the Rebirth of Malbec, 243.

[33] Illson, "Count de Vogüé Dies."

[34] He was captured in 1960.

Andrés Rosberg on Argentina's Next Big Things

Andrés Rosberg cofounded the Argentine Association of Sommeliers, and, through 2020, serves as president of the Association de la Sommellerie Internationale, among many other honorifics. He's also managing director of the Los Arbolitos Vineyard Trust, a 1,000-acre (405 ha) *finca* (vineyard estate) in Mendoza. He tells me there are tons of boutique bubblies we should try the next time we visit Argentina; here are a few we might be able to find in the US. "Most of Argentina's larger producers also run respectable sparkling wine [in addition to still wine] programs," Rosberg says.

Bodega Cruzat Método Tradicional Vallé de Uco Mendoza Extra-Brut (NV; 12.5% ABV; $$)

Argentinean bubbly master Pedro Rosell, who learned his craft in Champagne, is "crafting some cracking sparkling wines," Rosberg says. The fruit for this blend of 75 percent Pinot Noir and 25 percent Chardonnay is grown at 4,590 feet (1,400 m) of elevation.

Zuccardi "Cuvée Especial" Mendoza Blanc de Blancs (V; 12.5% ABV; $$–$$$)

"This brilliant cuvée, Zuccardi's top sparkling, is made with 100 percent Chardonnay grapes from Tupungato in the Uco Valley, and aged for a minimum of four years on its lees before it is released," says Rosberg. "It combines amazing complexity with vibrant tension and verticality."

Luigi Bosca "Bohème" Mendoza Brut Nature (NV; 12.3% ABV; $$–$$$)

According to Rosberg, Bodega Luigi Bosca's Las Compuertas vineyard is "the highest in the area, planted almost one hundred years ago." He describes this wine as one of "great complexity and balance," unusual in its inclusion of Pinot Meunier along with Pinot Noir and Chardonnay in the *cépage* (blend of grape varieties).

climatic conditions, the western-most and highest-elevation Uco Valley subzone is turning into a powerhouse for sparkling wines made from early-harvested Pinot Noir and Chardonnay. (Mendozans aren't afraid to make moody Malbec into a bubbly, either.)

There's so much sunlight at these high elevations that the alcohol levels are higher than what we're used to. The flavors, however, are still in balance, thanks to the sharp acidity that comes with the sort of ice-cold nighttime temperatures that can be achieved only in the mountains. These wines are so simultaneously rich and invigorating that a person might feel as strong and swift as the Argentine "Atomic Flea" *futbolista*, Lionel Messi, after downing a glass.

Alma Negra Mendoza Argentina Brut Nature
(NV; 13% ABV; $$)

Fourth-generation winegrower Ernesto Catena—scion of the Mondavis of Argentina—is the mastermind behind Alma Negra ("black soul"), which is devoted entirely to "black" grape varieties.[35] This traditional-method blend of Malbec and Pinot Noir spends just eight months on the lees and is barely tinged pink with color. The aromatics are subtle and yeasty, with a surprising pineapple note.

Reginato Mendoza Argentina Rosé of Malbec
(NV; 13.5% ABV; $$)

This easy, pale-salmon-colored, Charmat-method bubbly has a touch of powdered sugar on the nose, but that's soon pushed aside by the true underlying nature of Malbec: fierce, earthy, even a touch animal. It works, and could easily stand up next to a *churrasco* platter.

Domaine Bousquet Mendoza Argentina Brut Rosé
(NV; 12% ABV; $)

The Pinot Noir (75 percent) and Chardonnay (25 percent) that went into this Charmat-method fizz were farmed organically at 4,000 feet (1,200 m), and there's nothing not to like about its white peach, strawberry, and citrus notes. There's a touch of residual sugar, but hey—this was all of $11 last time I checked.

---

[35] *"Black" wine grapes make red wines, as in Pinot Noir or Grenache Noir.*

Chile

Cape Horn, the toenail of the *en pointe* ballerina's foot that is Chile, is just about as far south as an average person can go on this planet, nearly as close to Antarctica as San Francisco is to San Diego.

While Argentina warms up all morning on the sunrise side of the Andes, Chile shivers in the mountains' shadow. While Argentina gets the South Atlantic winds off Africa, Chile gets the Southern Ocean winds off . . . well, there's really nothing there until you hit New Zealand.

All of which is to say that Chile is chilly. As in icebergs. But, as with Argentina, the high-elevation winegrowing regions of this nation are also noted for their clear skies and intense mountain sunlight.

SAN ANTONIO VALLEY

One of Chile's newer wine regions is fast becoming known for Chardonnay, Pinot Noir, and Sauvignon Blanc, thanks to the influence of the refreshing Humboldt Current trade winds. Add to that a remarkable diurnal shift—a wide divergence between daytime and nighttime temperatures—and you've got wines that could be a magical realist creation of Isabel Allende. How can a wine with such searing acidity, fresh tropical-fruit flavors, and light weight on the palate pack full-strength alcohol?

....

Apaltagua "Costero" Extra-Brut San Antonio Valley Chile Sparkling Wine
(NV; 13% ABV; $$)

The Chardonnay and Sauvignon Blanc in this affordable traditional-method bubbly were sourced from the Coastal Mountains. Pale-gold in color, its aromatics are like "a really fun bar," as my assistant, Zoe, put it. Notes of jalapeño, papaya, coconut, and banana all speak to the sunny side of Sauvignon Blanc. Take note that this winery also produces an interesting sparkling pomegranate wine.

Amanda Barnes Feels Chile

The founder and editor of the online *South America Wine Guide*, British-born Amanda Barnes is based in Mendoza, Argentina, and writes for numerous international wine publications.

"Sparkling wine is seeing a real boom in Chile over the last decade," Barnes tells me. "Chile has so many climates and conditions that are ideal for making good quality bubbly at an affordable price point that it has become a staple in every bar and restaurant across the country." Here are some of her picks.

....

Bodegas RE "Re Noir: Nature Virgen" Método Tradicional Casablanca Blanc de Noirs (V; 12.5% ABV; $$$)

Winemaker Pablo Morandé, who has been making "rich, classic bubblies" at his primary Viña Morandé winery for decades, is behind this experimental partnership with his winemaker son Pablo Jr. Barnes describes the "bone-dry," unfiltered "Re Noir" as "thrilling." The first fermentation is spontaneous, in large wooden casks, making for a "creamy, perfumed, and complex" wine.

....

Viña Aquitania "Sol de Sol" Malleco Valley Traiguén Brut Nature (V; 12% ABV; $$$)

Globe-trotting celebrity winemaker Bruno Prats launched this fab partnership with friends from Bollinger Champagne and Château Margaux in Bordeaux. As one does. "Viña Aquitania was one of the first to plant so far south, in Malleco," says Barnes. More than two years on lees "leave a lingering complexity underpinned by taut acidity," alongside "flinty," "citrus, apple, and brioche" notes.

....

Azur Método Tradicional Valle de Limarí Brut (V; 12% ABV; $$$)

"This traditional-method sparkling wine is a special side project from Emiliana (the world's largest organic winery) and shows just how far sparkling-wine production in Chile has come," observes Barnes, adding that the coastal climate and limestone-rich soils of Limarí favor Chardonnay and Pinot Noir. This wine spends three years *sur lie*, and is "floral and bready on the nose with a delightfully delicate finish and fine bubbles."

$$$

Alella

Alta Alella

$$$

Penedès

Partida Creus

$$

Catalonia

Josep Foraster

$$$$$

Corpinnat

Gramona

$$$

Corpinnat

Recaredo

$$$$–$$$$$

Penedès

Agustí Torelló Mata

$$$$–$$$$$

Conca del Riu Anoia

Raventós

$$

Penedès

Codorníu

$$

Penedès

Avinyó

$$

Penedès

Llopart

$$

Penedès

Celler La Salada

$$

Penedès

Vinyes Singulars

$$

Corpinnat

Júlia Bernet

$

Penedès

Totus Tuus

$$

Bairrada

Luis Pato

$$

Bairrada

São João

$$

Valle de Guadalupe

Espuma de Piedra

$$

Canelones

Pisano

$$

Mendoza

Bodega Cruzat

$$

Mendoza

Alma Negra

$$

San Antonio Valley

Apaltagua

$$$

Casablanca

Bodegas RE

$$$

Malleco Valley

Viña Aquitania

$$$

Valle de Limarí

Azur

Central
AND
Eastern
Europe
AND THE
Middle
East

If you looked at this chapter heading with a raised eyebrow, you are in for a big surprise. The world's third-highest-volume sparkling-wine producer, after Italy and France, is none other than Germany. Yes, that's right. (Germany is also the world's third-most-prolific Pinot Noir producer, which fits nicely with this picture.) The fourth-biggest bubbles factory is Spain, and then the fifth is another shocker: Russia.

RECIPE

COLD DUCK PUNCH (KALTE ENTE)[1]

SERVES 8–10

Clemens Wenzeslaus of Saxony invented this beverage when he mixed together various wines with lemon balm. He called it a Kalte Ende—perhaps envisioning it as a "cold end" to a hot summer day—but at some point he was misheard and the punch became the much more delightful Kalte Ente, or "Cold Duck."

1 750-ml bottle
  sparkling mineral
  water
1 750-ml bottle dry
  Riesling
1 750-ml bottle
  Sekt
3 lemons
Simple syrup or
  citrus soda,
  optional
Ice
Lemon balm, or
  mint, for garnish

Combine all liquid ingredients in a giant pitcher or punch bowl. Slice the lemons thinly and add to the mix. If desired, refrigerate the punch for a few hours to allow the lemons to macerate. (If you'd prefer it sweeter, you can add simple syrup or citrus soda, like 7-Up, to taste.) Add ice to your punch bowl and garnish with sprigs of lemon balm or mint when ready to serve.

---

[1]   *In the late 1930s, Detroit's Pontchartrain Wine Cellars produced a premixed and bottled red Cold Duck that was quite popular. Today, a gawd-awful company called André California Champagne makes a Cold Duck (also red) that I am sure graces many a gas-station shelf. Do not, under any circumstances, drink this.*

"But," you are protesting, "I can't remember the last time I saw a German sparkling wine, I didn't even know that Russian fizz existed, and why should I read about bubbles from Croatia or Israel unless I'm going there on vacation?"

Why? Because this chapter is bubbling over with wine regions that have bounced back from periods of conflict, closed markets, and economic uncertainty. And they're ready to export wines to your doorstep.

Setting aside the far eastern parts of this chapter for the moment (we'll get to Greece and beyond beginning on pages 206 and 207, where you'll find another map), Germany, Russia, and Austria were hit hard in World Wars I and II. The aftereffects of these conflicts plunged Central Europe into a vinous downward spiral.

Noble winemaking traditions were lost—or at least set aside—in favor of Eastern Bloc–style industrial production. And while West Germany and Austria remained democratic, Teutonic wines fought an uphill battle for acceptance in foreign markets in decades past due to the reputations of saccharine German white blends, an Austrian antifreeze scandal—don't ask—and a tradition of classifying wines in a way that confused consumers.

Russia's wine industry has remained insular, but the breakup of the former Yugoslavia following the Balkan wars of the 1990s led to an oenological renaissance. It turns out that the Hapsburg Empire was once a bastion of fine winemaking, its villages ranked for their vineyard quality long before Bordeaux was ever classified. And, wouldn't you know it? Central European nations, just like the rest of Europe, boast centuries-old plots that were tended by diligent monks throughout the Middle Ages. If not for all those wars, Slovenia might be considered the equal of France or Italy today.

A new generation of Balkan winemakers are reviving those vineyards of yesteryear just as a new generation of vintners in Germany and Austria are doubling down on quality and exporting more bottles overseas. All of which means that Central Europe may soon be giving Champagne a run for its money.

Let's Talk About Sekt, Baby

Both the Germans and the Austrians refer to sparkling wine as Sekt, inviting all sorts of Sekt-ual play regarding well, you know, the *joy* of Sekt. For example, when I feel like talking to a Sekt machine, I say to my wine fridge, "I want your Sekt, you Sekt-y thing!" And my wine fridge says, "I want to Sekt you up!" And then I self-administer some Sekt-ual healing.

Why are you looking at me like that?

Germany

So you know now that Germany is the fourth-biggest sparkling-wine producer. Turns out it's *also* the fourth-thirstiest importer of Champagne in the world. All that adds up to a nation that drinks a LOT of bubbles—in fact, Germans consume the most per capita of any nation on the planet. According to the trade organization Wines of Germany, Germans consumed 3.7 liters per capita of sparkling wine in 2016—that's about twenty-five glasses for every woman, man, and child. *Wait, what? Since when did children drink sparkling wine?*

Anyway, the German government is well aware of this fact: A special sparkling-wine tax, called the *sektsteuer*, which has been in effect since 1902, adds more than a euro to the price of every bottle, and no one seems to complain about it. Not even the kids.

Now for a language lesson: *Schaumwein* is a generic term for sparkling wine, although the term "Sekt" is used more often. The volume-oriented houses, called *Sektkellereien*, tend to make tank-fermented wines, the German analogs of Prosecco. There's also a simple *frizzante* style of Sekt, called *Secco*, with only 1 to 2.5 bars of atmospheric pressure. This is not hit with the *sektsteuer* tax and tends to be quite inexpensive. In Austria, it goes by the name *Perlwein*, a term that crops up in Germany, as well.

Winzersekt is produced by a winegrower from estate fruit, and it must be a *klassischen*

How Shakespeare Named Sekt

Nearly two centuries ago, "Berlin was a hot spot for actors, artists, fashion people, and so on," says Romana Echensperger, MW. "There was always a vivid cultural scene, and everyone was drinking sparkling wine." One of those people was then-famous Shakespearean actor Ludwig Devrient, who, channeling Falstaff, demanded that his waiter, "Give me a cup of sack, rogue!" In Shakespeare's time, "sack" was Sherry, but the waiter knew his customer's predilections and brought sparkling wine. According to Echensperger, "sack" became "Sekt" at that moment, and the rest was history.

Flaschengärung, or a product of classic bottle fermentation. (I promise you will care more about these terms once you have read about the Austrian producer Malat, on page 196.) Producers of these *méthode traditionnelle* Sekts tend to be members of the VdP (Verband deutscher Prädikatsweingüter), a self-regulating association of approximately two hundred of Germany's top producers. Since 2017, the VdP has dictated and monitored various quality categories for bottle-fermented Sekt.

These include *Gutssekt* (from an estate's vineyard holdings within a single region) and *Ortssekt* (from a winery's best vineyards within a single village), which must remain on the lees for at least fifteen months, and the single-vineyard *Erste Lage* and *Grosse Lage* Sekts. Finally, there's vintage-dated Sekt, which must come from hand-harvested, estate fruit and spend a minimum of three years in the bottle before disgorgement.

And there you have Teutonic wine in a nutshell: Impossibly inscrutable.

Teutonic wine in a nutshell is also: Riesling. Germany's top grape is considered (by the Germans, at least) to be the noblest variety of *vitis vinifera* in its clarity, transparency, and ability to transmit *terroir*. Some German wineries proudly proclaim on their websites that they are "100 percent Riesling." Unfortunately, any further discussion of the supposed "purity" of the white Riesling grape comes off sounding just plain wrong, so I will leave it there. Just know that, while some German Sekts are Champagne-style blends of Chardonnay and Pinot Noir, you will find that high-acid Riesling rules in Germany.

MOSEL

The Mosel River—along with its tributaries, the Saar and the Ruwer—carves out Germany's most celebrated wine region, noted for its cold-but-sunny climate and steep, steep, *steep* slate slopes that cause harvest workers to swear like sailors every autumn. Majestic and graceful, it stretches from the city of Koblens, where the Mosel meets the Rhine, to the France-Luxembourg border.

The Romans got the German wine industry kicking here, at the city of Trier, where there are still impressive ruins. The eighteenth-century Archbishop Clemens Wenzeslaus of Saxony sent it into high gear during his stint in Trier by commanding that the noble grape, Riesling, be

planted in place of less-impressive varieties.

By the time the Romantic painter J. M. W. Turner showed up, in the nineteenth century, the Mosel was a romantic, Riesling-soaked place indeed. It still is . . . especially if you've got a glass of Sekt in hand.

....

Dr.[2] Loosen Brut Rosé Sekt
(V; 12.5%; $$$)

Ernst Loosen has his hand in many labels and is known well in the US for his inexpensive "Dr. L" ($) spar-kling Riesling. But Loosen has a particular soft spot for Pinot Noir, and he puts it to excellent use in this rosé. It has a golden apricot color, a wonderfully interactive *mousse*, and smoky stone-fruit flavors that get earthy and hempy as it sits in the glass. This Sekt has

staying power, thanks to five years on the fine lees and hand-riddling and disgorgement.

....

Maximin Grünhaus Brut Sekt
(V; 12% ABV; $$$)

This estate, near the juncture of the Ruwer and Mosel rivers, has been used for wine production since 966; the property has been in the current family's hands since 1882. This is a rich and satisfying

---

[2] *Brief aside: Many vineyards and wineries have "Dr." in their titles. According to Ernst Loosen—whose family has been running his winery for more than two centuries—this is because the Germans place a high value on education, and a PhD, or doctorate, is a mark of prestige. And you will notice that the two experts I quote in this chapter are MWs, or Masters of Wine—basically the doctorate of the wine world. These Germans are studious volk.*

Romana Echensperger, MW, on Sekt Every Sunday

"My granny had eight sisters," recalls Romana Echensperger when I ask her why so much Sekt is drunk in Germany. "They always met on Sundays for coffee and cake (loads of buttercream cake—you can't imagine!). However, you can't drink coffee for more than two hours. So, the logical drink after coffee was always Sekt."

In her past life—perhaps due to the priorities instilled by her granny—Echensperger was a sommelier at highly regarded restaurants in Germany and Spain. Today, she is a Master of Wine, working as a consultant, educator, and journalist in Germany and internationally. I asked Echensperger to share a couple of her fave Sekts with us so that we might drink a toast to her granny.

Schloss Vaux "Cuvée Vaux" Sekt (V; 12% ABV; $–$$)

Though their titles may only be ceremonial these days, a German count and a German prince oversee sparkling winemaking operations at the striking brick Schloss Vaux palace in Eltville. (If you're wondering why "Vaux" sounds French, the vineyards used to be in Alsace . . . Those wars again.) Echensperger describes Vaux's most basic cuvée as "the German darling," equally beloved by wine aficionados as it is by casual weekend imbibers. "It's not too dry, with a very creamy froth," she says of this *méthode traditionnelle* blend of Weissburgunder (Pinot Blanc), Spätburgunder (Pinot Noir), and Riesling, sourced from Rheinhessen and Pfalz.

Raumland "Cuvée Marie-Louise" Rheinhessen Brut Blanc de Noirs (V; 12% ABV; $$)

Echensperger describes Volker Raumland as "the German Yoda for sparkling wine" due to his vast knowledge and diligent study of the subtleties of bubbly production: "A lot of premium producers bring their base wines to Raumland and Volker makes their sparkling wines for them." The Blanc de Noirs is sourced from Raumland's estate-grown, organically farmed Pinot Noir.

It's Time to Get Sekt-Positive

Before World War I, Germany was renowned as a producer of fine sparkling wines, perhaps even on par with Champagne (see Chapter 2, page 54, for more on this). "What a flourishing, enterprising business this once was," remarks Master of Wine Anne Krebiehl when I ask her what happened to Sekt. "Two world wars completely flattened it. What came out of the ashes was an industrial manufacturing approach to winemaking."

As Krebiehl sees it, the annihilation of the Jewish merchant class obliterated the market for quality, bottle-fermented Sekt, while the postwar German emphasis on process and industrial engineering paved the way for Charmat-method wines to be produced in large quantities. "During my childhood," she recalls, "'Sekt' was kind of a dirty word."

Even today, "Sekt" continues to have negative connotations: "In 2017, Germans consumed 400 million bottles of sparkling wine. Of that, they produced 368.8 million bottles themselves. The vast majority of that is plonk," Krebiehl admits. "In Germany, certain drug stores have a license to sell alcohol. You can buy the cheapest sparkling plonk at these places for less than 5 euros. That is, Sekt made from wine sourced from throughout Europe, that was made sparkling and sweet in Germany."

"You find a lot in German literature about Sekt," adds Romana Echensperger, MW. "When people couldn't afford Champagne, they were drinking Sekt. Thomas Mann wrote a book called *Confessions of Felix Krull, Confidence Man* . . . He describes the father of this character as the owner of a Sekt house and makes a joke out of it."

People. It's time to explode these old stereotypes. Try some of the wines recommended by Krebiehl and Echensperger in this chapter. Let's bring Sekt-y back.

méthode traditionnelle, with fragrances of honeycomb, apple and orange blossom, brioche, and a hint of Riesling-appropriate petrol. The *dosage* is composed of the winery's own Auslese (off-dry) Riesling.

Reichsgraf von Kesselstatt "Majorat" Brut Riesling
(V; 13% ABV; $$)

Even if you didn't know this was one of the Mosel's OG wineries, you'd still identify this cuvée from vineyards along the Mosel, Saar, and Ruwer as a super-OG wine with the first sniff. It's unabashedly butter yellow, with the gasoline aromatics of legit German Riesling. The von Kesselstatts were court sommeliers, vineyard managers, and/or cellar masters for the Prince-Bishopric of Trier beginning in 1362 and own some of the most storied vineyards in Germany, so it's no surprise that this wine reeks of history.

Hild Mosel Elbling Sekt
(NV; 12.5% ABV; $$)

We're in the Upper Mosel now, which is confusing because it's to the south of the Lower Mosel (but it's higher in elevation, so there you go). Here near the Luxembourg border, the key grape variety isn't Riesling. Instead, the limestone soils favor the obscure, ancient, low-sugar, high-acid Elbling, which makes an ideal candidate for sparkling wine, and in fact was the preeminent Sekt grape in the nineteenth century. Light, fun, frothy, and peachy, with some floral and honeydew melon notes, this little number is reminiscent of Prosecco. Who said German wine had to be all *sturm und drang*?

RHEINGAU

As befits its name, the Rheingau wine region follows the northern banks of the river Rhine, from

---

Sure, I'll Take a *Schorle*!

There is a strong German tradition of drinking effervescent wine that dates back to the eighteenth century; it's just not the tradition you might be imagining. A *Schorle* is a bubbly summer beverage made by mixing wine (or juice, if you are underage) with sparkling water.

the jazzy town of Bacharach to Hochheim am Main, where the river meets its tributary, the Main. And while Riesling, again, holds court, the red Spätburgunder (aka Pinot Noir) accounts for more than 12 percent of plantings. Speaking of court, Queen Victoria was a fan of Rheingau wines, particularly from the aforementioned Hochheim, which explains why the Brits traditionally referred to German wines as "Hock."

The Rheingau is also renowned as the home of the oenological program at Geisenheim University and the Grape Breeding Institute, where some of your favorite grapes (let's hear it for Müller Thurgau!) were born and bred. Fitness freaks should take note that the area around the scenic city of Wiesbaden is chock full of hiking-and-tippling opportunities: Witness the Rheingau Riesling Trail, the Wine Experience Trail, and the Wiesbaden Wine and Nature Trail. Why drink and drive when you can drink and walk?

....

Leitz "Eins Zwei Zero" Sparkling Riesling (NV; 0% ABV; $$)

Surprise! OK, if you're an oeno geek, this alcohol-free bubbly does *not* taste like a fine fermented Riesling, even though it's from a highly respected producer. But for those off-the-wagon types looking to celebrate, it beats sparkling cider by a longshot. It's dry, frothy, and mouthfilling, with notes of apricot, spearmint, jasmine tea, figs, and—here's the part where it rings untrue—powdered lemonade. No matter. Your pregnant friends will thank you for this truly adult beverage.

....

Robert Weil Rheingau Riesling Brut (V; 12.5% ABV; $$$)

Robert Weil acquired his first vineyards in 1867 when he saw the Franco-Prussian War coming and got his hide out of Paris. His estate focuses entirely on Riesling, and this bubbly is all business. Dry, smoky, and weighty, with notes of apple skin and yellow fruit, it's a ponderous example of *klassischen Flaschengärung*, aka classic bottle fermentation. I find it to be *weltschmerzy*,[3] but my wine-trade friends assure me that this is the German equivalent of Champagne.

---

[3] *World-weary.*

Anne Krebiehl, MW, on Proper Riesling Sekt

German-born, London-based Master of Wine Anne Krebiehl is infectiously enthusiastic about the state of Sekt, seeing great hope in the Riesling grape. Here are some of Krebiehl's favorite Sekts right now.

Von Buhl Pfalz Riesling Brut Sekt (V; 12.5% ABV; $$$)

Von Buhl was all the rage in the nineteenth century, toasted at the opening ceremonies for the Suez Canal. The brand has recently been revived with Mathieu Kauffmann, former *chef de cave* of Champagne Bollinger, as managing director and winemaker. "Mathieu was born in Alsace, with Riesling running through his veins," notes Krebiehl, adding that the wines "manage to unite masterful creaminess and a dreamlike texture of very, very fine *mousse* with exquisite purity of varietal fruit."

Solter Rheingau Brut Riesling Sekt (NV; 12% ABV; $$$)

This all-female-run *sekthaus* produces bubblies for other wineries as well as its own, from a historic house where lullaby composer Johannes Brahms[4] used to spend his summers. Krebiehl particularly admires Solter's long-aged, single-vineyard Riesling Sekts, which get their *dosage* from sweet Riesling, making for intense petrol aromatics. And you can't go wrong with their basic *méthode traditionnelle* Brut.

Barth Rheingau Brut Riesling (NV; 12% ABV; $$$)

"Winemaker Mark Dunn loves the expression of his Sekt so much that often he uses no *dosage* at all. I admire him for that," says Krebiehl, adding that Dunn was also instrumental in creating the new VdP Sekt statutes, along with Mathieu Kauffmann of Reichsrat von Buhl. "I am looking forward to tasting whatever is slumbering in his cellar right now."

---

[4]   *There's a musical theme here, because Von Buhl bubbly (above) was a favorite of wedding-theme composer Felix Mendelssohn.*

NAHE

Nahe, pronounced *nah-uh*, means "near." It's a 33.5-mile (54 km) long valley on a diagonal axis that follows the line of the Nahe River. So what is it near? It lies between the villages of Bingen, on the River Rhine, and Meisenheim. And the bad, bad town of Bad Kreuznach marks its center.

This valley rocks. That is, it's marked by many rocky outcroppings, it once harbored a thriving gemstone-mining industry, and multiple soil types crop up in individual vineyards. If the following two Sekts are any measure of the place, Nahe may also be my new favorite undiscovered sparkling-wine region.

Kruger-Rumpf Germany Brut Rosé (NV; 12% ABV; $$$)

The house style at Kruger-Rumpf, which dates back to 1708, emphasizes minerality and precision. This Sekt has that, but it also has fresh-off-the-cane raspberry aromatics to die for. I am told that this wine is available only in limited amounts in the US. This is my appeal to bring in more, because it makes me happy.

Schlossgut Diel "Goldloch" Brut Nature Riesling Sekt (V; 13% ABV; $$$$)

Miners never did find gold at Goldloch vineyard—a site so steep that one false step could send one tumbling down to the road below—but it has been a fine investment for Schlossgut Diel. This winery is housed in a castle dating back to the 1200s that sits on a ridge overlooking the storybook-scenic Trollbach Valley, which is where trolls go to relax. This wine is left on the lees in the bottle for a whopping sixty months after extended lees aging in locally sourced barrels, and gets no *dosage*, so expect apple-peachy notes of Riesling, counterbalanced by dry minerality and a creamy texture.

Stuart Pigott Is All for Exports

London-born Riesling evangelist Stuart Pigott is based in Germany, where he is wine columnist for the newspaper *Frankfurter Allgemeine Zeitung* and also contributing editor for JamesSuckling.com. He is also the author of *The Best White Wine on Earth: The Riesling Story*.

"These are just three examples," Pigott responded when I asked him to share his three favorite German bubblies with us. "I could give many more, but, many of them don't make it to the US." Let's hope that this state of affairs changes soon.

Van Volxem "1900" Saar Brut Riesling (V; 11–12% ABV; $$)

In the third century Van Volxem was a villa and vineyard on a slatey site. Today, a spanking-new cellar is outfitted with oak casks hewn from estate forests. Pigott describes this bubbly as inspired by the winemaking style of 1900 vintners: "seductive," with "textural richness" and "notes of candied and dried fruit . . . It can easily compete with vintage Champagnes from good producers."

Peter Lauer "Réserve Nature" Saar Crémant (V; 11.5% ABV; $$$)

"When Florian Lauer took over the family's wine estate a little more than a decade ago, he found there was a considerable stock of sparkling wines still on the lees. Rather than just drink it himself, every now and again he releases a seriously mature vintage," explains Pigott. As I wrote this, wines as old as thirty-six years were available for purchase. "Yes, the 1984 vintage is currently available, although in small quantities," confirms Pigott. "This has gigantic lees autolysis character balancing the characteristic steely acidity of the Saar."

Shelter Winery Baden Brut (V; 12% ABV; $$$)

Pigott is a bullish about this label, named for the winery's original cellar, a grass-covered abandoned bunker at a former Canadian army base. This "powerful" old-vine sparkling wine, according to Piggott, "has more than enough freshness to carry the fullish body and generous berry aromas."

PFALZ

It's not the fault of Pfalz that it's so prolific and maybe doesn't always turn out top-notch wines. It's just fertile as all get-out here, and the vines sometimes overproduce. This region hugs the slopes that follow the path of the Rhine River from Mannheim to the border with Alsace, France, and the Vosges Mountains. Pundits point out that the Pfalz is more the soulmate of Alsace than any other German region, turning out Rieslings that tend to be dry and powerful rather than fruity and delicate.

....

Dr. Deinhard "Deidesheim" Pfalz Extra-Brut Riesling
(NV; 12.5% ABV; $$)

The Von Winning winery was founded in 1849 by the die-hard Dr. Deinhard and flourished under his winning son-in-law, Leopold von Winning. Today, the "Dr. Deinhard"–labeled wines are vinified in stainless steel for thirst-quenching zippiness, while the wines labeled Von Winning are very traditionally barrel-fermented and aged. The Von Winning take on Sekt offers delicate notes of orange blossom, lime peel, and peach; the Dr. Deinhard has a bracing, fierce acidity and floral aromatics, with notes of pineapple, white pepper, and apricot.

....

Theo Minges Pfalz Brut Riesling (V; 12.5% ABV; $$)

The Minges family has been at this for six generations, and their Old Worldy sparkling wine is bottled-aged on the lees for three and a half years, making for fine bubbles and complex aromatics. That's long enough, too, to impart robust and distinctive dry Riesling characteristics, like petrol on the nose and sour lemon on the palate.

Austria

The Germans claim that Riesling is the purest, noblest grape variety. And, funnily enough, the Austrians claim the same thing about Grüner Veltliner. That said, Austrians aren't Grüner purists. They tend to experiment a bit more, since their climate and geography are able to support a wide array of grape varieties. So within the realm of

Austrian sparkling wines, you'll tend to find the old standards Pinot Noir and Chard, as well as fruity Riesling *and* grassy Grüner.

While Austria is nowhere near Germany in its volume of bubbly production, Austrian producers have done a smashing job of getting their fizz into overseas markets. In part, that's because they were ahead of their neighbors in putting the word "fine" in front of their sparkling wines. Although the members-only VdP[5] may be making the loudest declarations about sparkling-wine quality in Germany, *all* wine labeled as Austrian Sekt is by definition a *Qualitätsschaumwein* as of 2017, which means that it has met certain basic standards. And there's an Austrian version of grower Champagne, called *Hauersekt*, which is a wine made on-site by the vinetender.

A term to look for on Austrian Sekt labels is g.U., which stands for *geschützte Ursprungsbezeichnung*, which I hope to never have to spell again, and don't ask me why the "U" is capitalized while the "g" is not. It translates as "protected designation of origin," and means a wine is from *somewhere* rather than everywhere. There are three tiers of somewhere: *Klassik* wines are sourced from vineyards in one state and have aged at least nine months on the lees; *Reserve* Sekts are sourced from one state and are made according to quality methods, i.e., hand-harvested and bottle-fermented, with a minimum of eighteen months on the lees; and *Grosse Reserves* are from a single village and must sit on the lees for at least thirty months. Got all that? Good.

....

Dürnberg[6] "Erdenlied" Österreich Sparkling Rosé
(NV; 12% ABV; $)

Österreich is the general "Austria" designation; because this wine doesn't appear to be sourced from any specific subzone, it's a terrific price. It's vinified from the Austrian-born-and-bred grape Zweigelt, which is a cross of two other reds you may have never heard of, St. Laurent and Blaufränkisch. This pink beauty is dry and herbaceous, with notes of dried lavender and candied rose petal, lemongrass, white pepper, and nutmeg.

---

[5] *See page 181, if you must, for a reminder of what VdP is.*

[6] *Note: This wine is bottled specifically for Astor Wines & Spirits in New York, but can be purchased online through Astor.*

WIEN (VIENNA)

Before we get to Austria's big wine regions, let's take a quick peek at the tiniest one. Believe it or not, the urban metropolis of Vienna boasts as many vineyards as there are mimes in Paris, pretzel stands in New York City, double-decker buses in London, and dim sum joints in Hong Kong.[7] Thus, the city is its own self-contained appellation, surrounded by—but not technically part of—Niederösterreich, which you'll read about on the next page.

In the city, the thing to do is to go to a *heurigen*—a tavern that gets its name from "this year's wine"—and guzzle *Wiener Gemischter Satz*, a Viennese field blend of traditional white varieties, all thrown together in a fermentation tank to make a zippy, refreshing beverage. For fine sparkling wine, you're better off going to a *vinotheque*, which is a bottle shop-cum-wine bar, and sadly not related to a *discotheque*, although one can always hope that "Funky Town" will make an appearance on the playlist.

Before you go, it might be worth noting that the German word *wein* translates as "wine." The city of Vienna, in German, is spelled *Wien*. And just to confuse matters, *weinen* means "to cry." Please, don't cry! Visit Vienna, take a boat ride down the Danube, and laugh about how delicious the sparkling wines around these parts are.

---

[7]   *This is a rough estimation.*

NIEDERÖSTERREICH

The northeastern chunk of Austria, hugged up against the Czech Republic and Slovakia, is the nation's biggest and best-known fine-wine production area. Its name translates as "Lower Austria," because it's downriver from its western neighbor "Upper Austria" (Oberösterreich), which should seem obvious, but isn't until you look it up.

Within its borders lie the highly regarded winegrowing subappellations of Kamptal, Kremstal, and Wachau, and at its center is the perfectly round bubble that is the separate Wien region—that is, the city of Vienna, encircled by its elegant ring-shaped boulevard,

Sekt in the City at Schlumberger

For Austrians and Germans, the name "Schlumberger" means bubbles.[8] Stuttgart native Robert Alwin Schlumberger served as *chef de cave* and production manager at Champagne maison Ruinart before introducing Austria's first sparkling wine in the 1840s. Within a couple of decades, the royals of the Austrian Empire, as well as England and the Kingdom of Hungary, were sipping Schlumberger's "Sparkling Vöslauer." The urban Schlumberger cellars are three centuries old and were modernized by nineteenth-century architect Carl Ritter von Ghega, the mastermind behind the Semmering railway (see Steiermark, on page 198), so schedule a visit the next time you're in Vienna.

Schlumberger Burgenland Méthode Traditionnelle Brut Rosé (V; 11.5% ABV; $$–$$$)

Although the winery is in the big city, the vineyards are located in Burgenland, the wine region directly south of Niederösterreich. This fruity blend of Pinot Noir and St. Laurent (a native Austrian red grape that's related to Pinot Noir) does not pretend to be complex, but it's pleasantly fruity, with ripe nectarine notes, and would be a refreshing quaffer if one were, let's say, waltzing to Strauss.

[8] *Note: There is a different wine producer by the same name, in Alsace, France.*

the *Ringstraße*. You can use the city as your base from which to explore Niederösterreich, as most wineries make an easy day trip.

Kamptal

About an hour's drive northwest of Vienna, the Kamptal is bisected by the Kamp River. And, yes, in case you are wondering, there is good camping in the Kamptal. A scenic, if somewhat creepy, spot for your tent is adjacent to the Dobra Castle ruins in Pölla, on the pristine Dobra Reservoir . . . the ideal setting for a murder mystery.

If you're seeking more sophisticated digs, check out the Loisium Wine & Spa Resort, designed by famed American architect Steven Holl and featuring a future-forward wine museum, all over a creepy-cool labyrinth of wine cellars dating back nine centuries.

....

Loimer Niederösterreich Reserve Brut Rosé
(NV; 12% ABV; $$$)

Loimer is the producer behind the popular "Lois" Grüner Veltliner, which graces many a wine list in the US. The Zweigelt and Pinot Noir in this bottle (rounded out with a touch of Chardonnay) were biodynamically grown. The wine

sees ten months of barrel aging, followed by a year in the bottle, for a minimalist style: Dry and mineral, with a snap-pea freshness, and a note of dried rose petals, which must be the Zweigelt talking.

....

Jurtschitsch Österreich Méthode Traditionnelle Brut Rosé (NV; 12% ABV; $$–$$$)

Stefanie Hasselbach—whose family owns the renowned Gunderloch estate in Germany's Rheinhessen—and Alwin Jurtschitsch are quite the Teutonic winemaking power couple. They have converted the Jurtschitsch vineyards to organic agriculture and practice natural winemaking, but there's nothing hippie-ish about this cotton-candy-pink delight, bottle-aged for thirty months, with smoky, slatey, sultry, and creamy lemon curd notes and a powerful *perlage* that fades gently at the finish. The Jurtschitsch family has been running its eponymous winery since 1868, although its origins go back at least three hundred years earlier. But don't listen to me, listen to wine importer and expert Terry Theise, whose eloquent recommendations grace the following page.

Terry Theise on Killer Kamptal

Back when most other American wine importers were focused on old standards like Chianti and Bordeaux, Terry Theise was enlightening us on the beauty of German Riesling, the nuance of Austrian Grüner Veltliner, and the joys of grower Champagne in his compellingly written wine catalogs. Theise is also the author of two wine memoirs, *Reading Between the Wines* and *What Makes a Wine Worth Drinking*. In short, I had to quote him in this chapter. So I asked him about the Kamptal.

"The Kamptal is noteworthy for its concentration of outstanding producers in a small area, in and around the town of Langenlois. This tends to spur 'competition' if you're the hard-nosed type, and 'achievement' if you're a little more idealistic," says Theise. "Where sparkling wine is concerned, most of the Kamptal's top growers are as serious about their Sekt as they are about all their wines."

Although the following two labels are not printed with the Kamptal geographical designation, the wineries and vineyards are located there.

Bründlmayer Niederösterreich Brut Sekt (NV; 11.5% ABV; $$$)

"First among equals, perhaps, is Bründlmayer, who was also the first in Austria to take Sekt seriously," says Theise. While there are other, pricier sparkling wines in the Bründlmayer lineup, Theise describes this blend of Pinot Gris, Blanc, and Noir, with Chardonnay and Grüner Veltliner for good measure, as "the most suave of the range, with the salty-sweet-umami savor of a perfect piece of Parmigiano Reggiano." It spends its first year in Austrian oak barrels, then eighteen months in the bottle on the lees prior to *remuage*.

Schloss Gobelsburg Niederösterreich g.U. Extra-Brut (V; 12% ABV; $$$$$)

A $99 Austrian Sekt? Yep. According to Theise, this beauty "spends around ten years *en tirage*, and if you have a streak of mischief in your nature you'll have wicked fun bamboozling your wine friends if they taste this blind. For it is every bit as searching, intricate, and refined as Champagne but tastes nothing like it." Just a couple of miles from Bründlmayer, Schloss Gobelsburg is a former Cistercian monastic estate dating back to 1171. The grape blend (aka *cépage*) is Pinot Noir, Riesling, and Grüner Veltliner, and it works.

Steininger "Young" Austria Sparkling Rosé

(NV; 12.5% ABV; $–$$)

Sometimes, the least-expensive and least-serious wine in a lineup is the one that captures my heart. Unlike its peers—the other Steininger sparkling wines come in wide-bottomed, weighty green bottles, and their flavors strike me as similarly clunky—the "Young" is presented in a clear bottle, with no foil and a devil-may-care label design. It's mostly Zweigelt, with 20 percent Pinot Noir and 20 percent Cabernet Sauvignon, and has a Prosecco-ish winsome character, with nectarine and cantaloupe notes on the nose and palate. The release date is noted on the label, just in case you wish to verify its youth.

Kremstal

Flanked by its besties, the equally admired Kamptal and Wachau, Kremstal is sitting pretty on its reputation for producing elegant Grüner Veltliners and Rieslings. It follows the northwest-southeast line of the Krems River and is bisected by the Danube. The heart of the zone centers around the colorful town of Krems, renowned for its wine since the Middle Ages and also the world HQ of *Marillenschnaps* (a type of apricot brandy).

A wine region that doesn't take itself too seriously has its priorities in order, so bravo for the culturally minded people of Krems: Despite all the great medieval architecture and world-class vineyards here, the don't-miss destination in Krems is the Karikaturmuseum, devoted to cartoons and satirical art. As for the sparkling wine, if there's one name to know, it's Malat.

Malat Niederösterreich Brut Reserve (V; 12.5% ABV; $$$$)

When Gerald Malat, whose family's winegrowing tradition goes back to 1722, produced the first Austrian estate-bottled Brut Sekt in the 1970s, the powerful Austrian *négociants* tried to stop him, and he had to fight a legal battle against The Man that went all the way to the Supreme Court of Justice, where he finally prevailed. Thanks to Gerald, Austria now has *Winzersekt*, or estate-grown, traditional-method Sekt. Gerald's son Michael bottle-ferments his bone-dry sparkling wines with no *dosage*, but there is a key-lime-and-marzipan softness around this wine's edges. And don't miss the delicate pink

Blauburgunder (aka Pinot Noir) rosé, which also sits on the lees for at least three years.[9]

Wachau

As if we needed to read about yet *another* verdant river valley. But while the Kamptal is on the Kamp River, and Kremstal stretches north from the Danube to follow the line of the Krems River, Wachau follows the big blue: the wide, slow Danube, between the towns of Melk and Krems. Cool breezes from the northwest are in a constant state of smackdown here against warm ones from the Pannonian Plain to the east. The conflict is like the famous 1837 piano duel between Viennese concert-circuit regulars Franz Liszt and Sigismond Thalberg— imagine an epic rap battle, but

---

[9] *Bonus: Malat also has a chic contemporary boutique hotel, surrounded by vines, offering views of the historic Göttweig Abbey.*

with pianos. What comes out of all that tension? Wine that's as dramatic as Liszt's "Dante Symphony": high on acid and punchy with ripe-fruit flavor.

At any rate, this section of valley is so scenic and historically significant that the whole dang thing is a UNESCO World Heritage site. Winemaking can be traced back to Roman times, but the region really kicked into high gear in the Middle Ages, when the Benedictine monks dialed down on viticulture. Among the monasteries, castles, and ruins are terraced vineyards, cut into the steep riverbank slopes, which emanate an almost holy quality, and *heurigen* (wine gardens) packed with happy oeno enthusiasts.

....

Nikolaihof Wachau Riesling Sekt (V; 12% ABV; $$$)

This estate traces its history back nearly two thousand—yes, that's right—years. The current owners (as of 1894), the Saahs family, have been practicing biodynamics in the vineyard and cellar since 1971, and their wines are so pure and downright seraphic that one can see—or, taste?—why they produce a biodynamic skincare line as well. This sparkling Riesling does not disappoint. It holds its own against Champagne while being its own uniquely Austrian, uniquely Riesling thing. Note: The standard bottling is an Extra-Brut; there is also a Brut Nature.

▬▬▬▬▬▬▬▬▬▬▬▬▬▬▬

STEIERMARK

OK, so Steiermark is the German way of saying "Styria," but when you get down to Slovenia (page 202), you'll see why it's best to go with the German here. Austrian Styria is divided into three wine-growing zones: southern Styria, western Styria, and Vulkanland, which is not only where Dr. Spock goes to drink sparkling wine, but also translates to "volcano land." German can be SO much fun!

Austro-Styrian highlights, according to UNESCO, are the scenic and historic Semmering railway,[10] which tiptoes between and through heartbreakingly scenic mountains at nearly 3,000 feet (900 m) of elevation, from Gloggnitz to Mürzzuschlag. And the city of Graz—rhymes with "hots," as in, "I have the hots for Graz"—where you can tour the Eggenberg Palace, which was designed following a mathematical model to represent the cosmos.

---

[10]   *Designed by nineteenth-century architect Carl Ritter von Ghega, also mentioned on page 193.*

Weststeiermark

Western Styria is notable for its allegiance to an unusual grape, the native Blauer Wildbacher, which makes the regional specialty, a rosé called Schilcher. Previously thought to be too acidic to make anything other than simple pink wines, the variety is currently in a period of rediscovery as growers up their viticultural games.

Langmann Vulgo Lex Schilcher Frizzante (NV; 11.5% ABV; $$)

Here's your chance to taste a Schilcher, and it's fizzy as an added bonus. I'm not going to pretend this Charmat-method wine is anything more than a frivolity, cantaloupe-colored and fluffy in its consistency, with peach and nectarine aromatics, a bit of minerality, and that's all, folks. But who can turn away a wine label with some good old Latin on it? And the Langmann family has been at this wine thing since 1746, so they know from Blauer Wildbacher.

Hungary

Alas, Hungary is struggling. As an importer acquaintance put it to me, "After you leave Budapest, it gets really rural, really fast. There may or may not be electricity. And Hungary is a dark political place right now." Indeed, as I was penning this very classic of wine literature, prominent newspapers had just been shut down and the ruling regime's modus operandi was being described as "soft fascism."

In cosmopolitan Budapest, Hungarian wines rule the *extremely* patriotic restaurant lists, the sole exception being Champagne. (Which fits right in with the fascism thing. See: *weinführer*, Chapter 1, page 53.) Today's Hungarian vintners are working to displace this interloper, however, with sparkling wines of their own.

These are most exciting—in my opinion—when made from the indigenous grapes of the region, such as the native Carpathian variety Hársleveulű.

This land-bound nation is better known for its world-renowned sweet wine, Tokaji Aszú, which was praised by monarchs and famous writers as far back as the sixteenth century for its outstanding quality and complexity. Also: the old-style red blend known as "Bull's Blood." Hungary is also famous for its fine oak barrels, which are said to add spice, weight, and texture to wines. At any rate, if it's OK with His Eminence, the Prime Minister Viktor Orbán, I'll get back to the bubblies.

SOMLÓ

Some 30 miles (48 km) from the popular vacation destination of Lake Balaton in western Hungary, the Somló (pronounced *SHOME-loh*) winegrowing zone is Hungary's smallest but fiercest: It's a former volcano, with vineyards hugging its steep sides, and the ruins of a castle on top. The wines from these vineyards were thought to have curative properties in centuries past. This area has a history of producing sparkling wine, but don't get too excited: Back in the days of Communism, Somló churned out buckets of cheap, sweet bubbly. Over the past three decades or so, however, vintners have been reviving this historic winegrowing region's reputation, which last peaked in the eighteenth century, when aristocratic vinetenders poured Somló wines for royalty.

Kreinbacher "Classic" Somló Méthode Traditionnelle Brut
(NV; 12% ABV; $$$)

József Kreinbacher, an importer of high-end Burgundy and Champagne into Hungary, wisely brought in the cellar master of Champagne Paul Bara, Christian Forget, to oversee winemaking at his namesake *maison*. The mod property boasts a boutique hotel and chic contemporary bistro. (Apparently, Somló gets electricity.) This blend of 85 percent Furmint with 15 percent Chardonnay is bright yellow, with a smoky nose and a creamy texture that honor the intrinsic richness of the Furmint. The complex palate ranges from plum skin to kiwi to sour lemon to white pepper.

TOKAJ

Hungary's best-known wine region occupies a slice of the far northeast, spilling over into Slovakia. Its claim to fame is a precious wine squeezed from—yes— rotten raisins, thanks to a rainy early autumn that is almost invariably followed by dry sunshine, creating the ideal conditions for a beneficial fruit fungus called *Botrytis cinerea*. The resulting sweet, nectar-like wine, called Tokaji Aszú, was once so highly prized that Tokaj's vineyards were the first in the world to be judged and classified for their quality. In recent years, however, enterprising winemakers have begun to explore the dry side of Tokaj's white grapes, picking them before they dry up and grow mold, and vinifying light, lively white wines, and even bubblies.

Kikelet Tokaji Pezsgo
(V; 12% ABV; $$$$)

French winemaker Stéphanie Berecz grew up in the Loire Valley and learned her craft in Bordeaux before moving to Tokaj to make wine and marry a hunky Hungarian. She sticks to classic practices like whole-cluster pressing and native yeast fermentations. This barrel-ferment-based *pezsgo*—which simply means "sparkling wine"—will taste peculiar to Western palate. The Hársleveulű grapes give it a highlighter-yellow color and aromatics of pine sap, honey, roasted parsnips, and pineapple. Add mouth-puckering acidity and smoky notes, and you've got something truly out of the ordinary.

Slovenia

Most Americans can only conjure up two words about Slovenia: Melania Trump. Western Europeans might think of another two words: ski holiday. The booming wine industry, happily, is chipping away at our narrow-mindedness. For oeno geeks, Slovenia is a nation with a long and noble history and an iconoclastic present, where some of the most interesting *terroir*, techniques, and grape varieties make distinctive wines. The following bottlings are about as far removed from Melania Trump on a ski holiday as one can imagine: Earthy, funky, and primal, they're more like Janis Joplin at Woodstock. At any rate, Slovenia is a quiet and picturesque nation with untold promise in viticulture.

PRIMORSKA

Slovenia can be broken into three major wine regions—the three Ps—each with its own subzones. (Each of these regions has a name that ends with the *-ska* suffix, unless the *-je* suffix is used. This is just to confuse you. So Primorska and Primorje are the same thing. And sometimes Primorska is spelled "Primorski." And now, back to our regular programming.)

Primorska is the area best-known by Westerners because it is the most Western, in its way. It borders Italy, boasts a humming economy, and produces the most wine. And it's well-situated for viticulture, being both mountainous and Mediterranean. Although it's also referred to in English as the Slovene Littoral,[11] more than half of Primorska does *not* literally hug the coast of the Gulf of Trieste. Most of it is buffered from the bay by approximately 3 miles (5 km) of Italy, and the beautiful Austro-Hungarian-Slovene-but-technically-Italian city of Trieste.

Kras

Not to be kras—I mean crass—but methinks Italy got the better deal. The world's first binational wine region is called Carso in Italia, where it hugs the balmy Mediterranean coastline. Its Slovenian counterpart, Kras (also called Karst), by contrast, occupies a high plateau—former oak forest, rendered barren centuries ago by Venetian ship builders. The central attraction? Tourists go to Kras to look at sinkholes and explore caves. And no, these are not Champenoise caves.

These are drippy, deep, dark karst[12] caves.

Kras (pronounced *krowsh*, actually) also has a less-than-forgiving climate going for it. Summers are hot, winters are chilly, and there's a nasty cold wind called the *bora*, or *burja*, that is so strong that it literally blew away the paltry precious soil in the region until farmers and vine-tenders got smart and built stone walls. What little iron-rich *terra rossa* (red soil) there is, punctuated by outcroppings of white limestone, is excellent for growing grapes such as the regional red specialty, Teran, which is known elsewhere as Refošk or Refosco. Snap some up if you see it, since most Slovenian wine is white.

. . . .

Štoka Kras Teran Penece
(V; 12.4% ABV; $–$$)

How better to taste Teran than in the form of a *penece* (that's Slovenian for Pét-Nat), from a Slovenian winery dating back to 1839? This is deep-purple in color, with old Bordelaise aromatics—menthol, eucalyptus, leather, black pepper, apothecarian herbs and spices—and, OK, maybe just a hint of cheese. (Štoka fertilizes solely with cow manure, and, hey, I guess it shows.) The winery also makes a smoky, pleasantly

sour, herbaceous *penece* from the region's signature white grape, Vitovska; it's accented by notes of white pear granita and banana.

_____

Slovenian Istria

Vacationers might know Istria better as a Croatian coastal paradise, but thanks to those dang wars and the resulting border delineations, the northern chunk of the Istrian Peninsula is not Croatian but *Slovenska Istra*, as the Slovenes say. The "Slovene Riviera" is also a paradise, where bright-green vineyards spill into the blue sea. The Romans called this region *terra magica* for good reason.

. . . .

Rodica "Bela" Istra Brut Sparkling Malvazija
(V; 12.5% ABV; $$)

At this organic family winery in the village of Truške, just south of the sea and on the north side of the fire-breathing Dragonja River Valley, the house specialty is the white grape Malvazija, aka Malvasia. The spontaneously fermented base wine is mellowed

_____

[11] *The term "littoral" refers to land that hugs a shoreline.*

[12] *This is the geological term for these types of caves.*

over five months in low-key acacia barrels. No disgorgement makes for a murky appearance to go along with the cider vinegar-tobacco-pineapple juice aromatics. But even if you aren't a fan of funk, you might enjoy the gently frothy palate, with its notes of creamy mango lassi and quince paste.

PODRAVSKA

Posavska and Podravska sound like they should be fairytale twins, but they are in fact those other two Slovenian wine regions. Posavska, to the southeast, borders Croatia. Podravska,[14] in the northeast, adjoins Croatia, Hungary, and Austria, and is of most interest to us since sparkling wine is a specialty there. Also, nearly all the wine of Podravska is white. And wait, there's more: In the beautiful city of Maribor, you can visit The World's Oldest Grapevine, as per the Guinness Book of World Records. It has its own museum and its own anthem and it is more than 450 years old making it a positively posh progenitor.

Slovenian Styria

We all learned in high school history class that the assassinations of Austro-Hungarian Archduke Franz Ferdinand and his wife, Sophie, Duchess of Hohenberg, started World War I. A visit to Styria will stir up textbook memories, because there are, these days, two Styrias where there once was one Austro-Hungarian Styria. Austria got Upper and Central Styria, while Slovenian Styria (*Slovenska Štajerska*) is Lower Styria. And now you know why I went with the German on page 198.

. . . .

Kobal Štajerska Extra-Brut Yellow Muscat (V; 12.5% ABV; $$)

In Italy, Moscato Giallo is often made into a dessert wine. In Slovenia, it makes flavorful dry wines redolent of rich tropical fruit. Bone-dry but aromatic with muskmelon notes, this bubbly version is sourced from the steep, verdant, cool, and sun-soaked Haloze Hills. Insider tip: The adorably squat-bottled half-size version of this wine is too charming to pass up.

---

[14]   *Note: While the English term for this geographical region is Drava Valley, wine enthusiasts know it by its Slovenian name.*

Croatia

Everyone's new favorite vacation destination boasts a long stretch of coastline, just across the Adriatic from six different Italian states; multiple ferries run between the two nations. Breathtakingly beautiful Croatia boasts an astonishing number of islands—more than twelve hundred—that continue to grow in number as a couple of busy tectonic plates continue to rub up against one another.

As with so many central European nations, Croatia has a long tradition of winemaking, but the craft stagnated under Communist rule. By the end of the Croatian War of Independence in 1995, the nation was in tatters, its shell-shocked population recovering from trauma. But today, much has been rebuilt, and a new generation of winemakers are resurrecting their old family vineyards and revisiting the grape varieties and

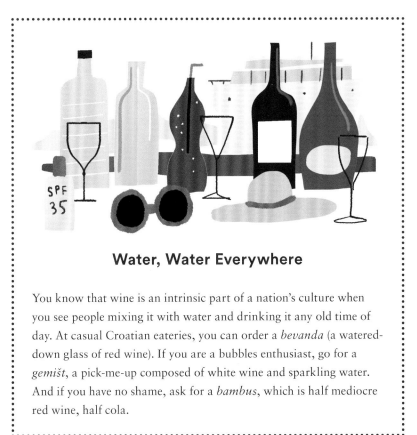

Water, Water Everywhere

You know that wine is an intrinsic part of a nation's culture when you see people mixing it with water and drinking it any old time of day. At casual Croatian eateries, you can order a *bevanda* (a watered-down glass of red wine). If you are a bubbles enthusiast, go for a *gemišt*, a pick-me-up composed of white wine and sparkling water. And if you have no shame, ask for a *bambus*, which is half mediocre red wine, half cola.

classic winemaking techniques their great-grandparents knew so well. And now, let us just lift a glass of Croatian bubbly.

· ·

Bibich Croatia Méthode Traditionnelle Brut Rosé
(NV; 12.3% ABV; $$)

The label is printed with a national appellation, but the winery, dating back to 1906, is located in Dalmatia, in the hills above the town of Skradin, overlooking the Krka River and the national park by the same name. The crumbly limestone here barely qualifies as soil, but it's ideal for growing the indigenous red grape Plavina, a variety with qualities of acidity and freshness that make it well-suited to sparkling winemaking. This bubbly's translucent peachy hue is a delight to behold; the elegant *mousse* starts out prickly and builds into a plush foam on the palate. Unusual strawberry yogurt-like aromatics confirm the fact that this is a grape you've never tasted before but want to try again.

Greece

A leisurely ferry ride across the Adriatic from Brindisi, Italy, Greece is one of the OG nations of wine production, with an oenological history that dates back to at least 4500 BCE, if not well before. As we learned in Chapter 2 (page 35), there's some evidence to suggest that the ancient Greeks knew how to stop a fermentation and capture natural effervescence in wine.

And yet, Anglophone oenophiles don't know a whole lot about Greek wines, mostly because exports didn't really begin in earnest until about a decade ago. Economic factors played a role, sure, but the language barrier also presents a problem. As with the Republic of Georgia and Israel, Greece has its own distinct alphabet, making translations on wine labels doubly cumbersome. I mean, το αφρώδες κρασί είναι το καλύτερο, right?

Translators have been hard at work churning out Greek wine labels using the Latin alphabet so that we may learn about the fascinating indigenous grapes of Greece that make such flavorful, food-friendly wines. Alas, spellings vary: The Amyntaio region, referenced below, is also

REPUBLIC OF GEORGIA

IRAQ

SYRIA

TURKEY

ISRAEL

GALILEE

MEDITERRANEAN SEA

BULGARIA

NAOUSSA

AMYNTAIO

GREECE

SANTORINI

IONNINA

It's All Greek to Tara Q. Thomas

Tara Q. Thomas is an author, the executive editor of *Wine & Spirits* magazine, and wine columnist for the magazine *Culture: The Word on Cheese.* She's also an expert on the wines of Greece and travels there frequently.

Tourists, according to Thomas, can often be seen guzzling cheap fizz from Compagnia Agricola Industriale Rodi (CAIR), a commercial winery on the island of Rhodes that has been churning out bubbly for decades. And for good reason: "In general, sparkling wine fits really well with Greek cuisine—there are so many salty flavors and fried foods," she says. "They make fritters out of everything—fish, leeks, any vegetable you can think of, actually. And there's fresh seafood everywhere you go. It tends to be prepared very straight-up, with olive oil and lemon."

But more and more high-end producers are getting in on the game, according to Thomas, and these wineries are worth watching. In addition, new sparkling-wine bars are popping up in Athens. "I even tasted a sparkling retsina last year," she reports, referring to the famous white wine that's flavored with pine pitch. "Which, for the record, was delicious."

I asked Thomas to tell us about some of the most exciting native-grape sparkling wines from Greece that she's drinking right now. Here are a few of her faves.

Kir-Yianni Amyntaio "Akakies" Naoussa Sparkling Wine (NV; 12% ABV; $$)

First, some disambiguation: Western Macedonia is a state in northern Greece, not to be confused with North Macedonia, which is its own nation, just north of Western Macedonia. Also: There is a scenic tourist town called Naoussa on the sunny southern isle of Paros, but the wine town of Naoussa (also spelled Naousa) is in Western Macedonia. And all of these place names are spelled about twelve different ways. At any rate, Western Macedonia "looks very much like Piedmont: It's very green, moist, and foggy," says Thomas. And it's here, near Naoussa, that Amyntaio/Amyndeon, Greece's sole rosé-only appellation of origin, is located. Double points go to "Akakies" for being both bright pink *and* bubbly. Thomas describes this sim-

ple pleasure as "silly" and "fun." It's vinified from a grape called Xinomavro, meaning "sour black." It's "a name that came from the grape's really high acidity in this region—which makes it great for sparkling wine," points out Thomas.

Karanika Amyntaio Extra Cuvée de Réserve Brut Nature (V; 12.5% ABV; $$$)

This is a more serious, zero-*dosage*, traditional-method bubbly, also made from the Xinomavro grape, and also from the Amyntaio region. A Dutch couple obsessed with Champagne farms their grapes biodynamically in the high-elevation environs of Amyntaio to produce what Thomas declares to be "sophisticated" and "possibly the best sparkling wine in the country." This bone-dry brut is earthy and clean, with forest-floor notes, says Thomas, that take on a "truffly characteristic" with age.

Santo Wines Santorini Méthode Traditionnelle Brut (NV; 11.6% ABV; $$–$$$)

"When I think of Santorini, I think of these little tomato fritters called *domatokeftedes*," says Thomas. "Santorini is famous for its tomatoes and has a tomato-paste industry. These sweet, delicious, fried fritters are heaven with sparkling wine." Especially if that wine is made from the naturally high-acid Assyrtiko grape. Santo is the island's co-op, a fifty-year-old union of twelve hundred small grape growers who provide fruit to one centralized winery, and operate a chic gourmet store-cum-tasting room overlooking the sea.

spelled Amintaio, Amyndaio, and Amyndeon, just to confuse us.

At any rate, in the coolest parts of Greek wine country, some of these native grapes develop such brisk acidity that they are perfectly suited for the sort of sparkling wine one should sip whilst, say, viewing one of the *Mamma Mia!* films or contemplating at the azure waters off Corfu.

....

Domaine Glinavos "Paleokerisio" Ioannina Traditional Semi-Sparkling Orange Wine (V; 10.5% ABV; $)

Paleokerisio translates roughly as "traditional wine," and it's made in the style of an old-country village draught, then packaged in an old-fashioned squat brown 500-ml bottle. A couple of weeks of maceration on the skins renders the juice of the indigenous white grape, Debina, gold. Add to that a whisper of the red grape Vlahiko,

and this fizzy, semisweet beverage gets its distinct orange color. And—holy nose!—the aromatics are all apple cider and licorice, the palate nougaty, figgy, and clovey without being cloying.

Serve this quirky delight with baklava or shortbread, and only to those who have a sense of humor. The fruit comes from the hilly district of Zitsa, which, as Tara Q. Thomas pointed out to me, is Greece's chilliest appellation, as well as the oldest devoted to sparkling wine.

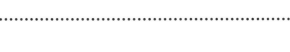

A Few Words in Support of World Trade

I'd like to take a few lines here to shout out to Romania, Bulgaria, Turkey, and Lebanon. These nations have burgeoning sparkling-wine scenes worth celebrating, but I conferred with a couple of top sommeliers from these parts of the planet and was informed that the brands worth covering are not yet exported to the US.

Republic of Georgia

All the way across the Black Sea from Central Europe is the nation boasting the earliest archaeological evidence of winemaking, dating back some eight thousand years. Georgia's botanical scholars have fastidiously catalogued this country's thousands of unique native grape varieties, and its committed vintners have kept alive archaic winemaking methods, to the delight of the many curious sommeliers and students of wine who make the pilgrimage to Georgia every year.

UNESCO has declared the old-school Georgian winemaking technique to be a treasure of cultural heritage, and it actually is a very sensible way to vinify, so why change? The trick is to bury dinosaur-size amphorae, called *kvevri*,[13] underground, where the temperature and humidity levels are ideal, dump all the grapes in there to percolate, then seal things up for a few months. The finished wines are weird and wonderful, which is why all the avant-garde wine bars have a Georgian bottle on their lists these days. Which also explains why we can get a few Georgian *bubblies* way over here . . . importers and buyers have Georgia on their minds.

Bagrationi 1882 "Georgian Royal Tradition" Georgia Brut Sparkling Wine (NV; 12% ABV; $)

The Bagrationis were the royal rulers of Georgia from 780 all the way up to the nineteenth century. Beginning in 1882, Prince Ivane Bagrationi-Mukhraneli, an Imperial Russian general, devoted his retirement to turning some of his vast landholdings into vineyards and recruiting French oenological experts to make a Champagne-like beverage—just as a little Georgian boy named Joseph Stalin was developing his lifelong dislike of princes. Today, Bagrationi's wines are ubiquitous at celebrations throughout the Caucasus. The lineup includes traditional-method bubbles as well as this Charmat brut. The white native grapes Tsitska, Chinebuli (also called Chinuri), and Mtsvane throw off strong scents of lilies and apple blossom. The palate is surprisingly dry and Rhône-like (think Viognier), and the bubbles are less than impressive . . . still, this is an inexpensive taste of history.

---

[13] *Also spelled* qvevri.

Lapati "Kidev Erti" Georgia Chinuri (V; 10% ABV; $$$)

A couple of guys from France were so obsessed with natural winemaking that they moved to Georgia make this pert pick-me-up in their all-*kvevri* winery, where they crush the grapes with their bare feet. If you haven't drunk the natural-wine Kool-Aid, skip this disjointed Pét-Nat. If you have, delight in its bare-bones, deconstructed, maybe-it's-still-fermenting style. The native Chinuri grape gives up some distinct vanilla wafer notes on the nose and chamomile on the palate. Recork it and stick in your fridge for a day or two, then come back to it to discover its mellow, sake-like qualities.

Israel

And now for the Holy Land. There is, of course, a long history of winemaking in the nation of Israel, wine being a common theme uniting both the Old and New Testaments. But Israelis don't see sparkling wine as a symbol of celebration the way Westerners do. On Rosh Hashanah Eve—Jewish New Year's Eve—culinary magazines suggest cider and mead as appropriate beverages for the occasion.

As for Western New Year's Eve, it's called "Sylvester" here—a nickname for Saint Sylvester's Day—apparently because central and eastern Europe go by this nomenclature, and the Israeli population is heavy with expats from that part of the world. Problem is, Pope Sylvester was a serious anti-Semite. So why break out the sparkling wine?

This may in part explain the false start in traditional-method Israeli winemaking in the 1960s and '70s that eventually—forgive the pun—fizzled out. But today, bubbly is back on the scene. There's a newish wine bar in Tel Aviv called Brut—a sign that there's a healthy thirst for good bubbly in the land where water was, so they say, once turned to wine.

GALILEE

Israel's subtropical climate might give a sparkling-wine connoisseur pause. Where in this hot, arid nation could temperatures possibly dip low enough to capture the

fresh acidity necessary to make a lively bubbly wine? Why, north of the Sea of Galilee. Here, in the mountainous Golan Heights, it snows in the winter, and vineyards are planted at elevations as high as 4,000 feet (1,200 m). The vines are lovingly tended by *moshavim* and *kibbutzim* (cooperative farms).

....

Yarden Galilee Blanc de Blancs (V; 12% ABV; $$$)

This sparkling Chardonnay comes from the Golan Heights Winery, one of Israel's finest, with vineyard plantings dating back to 1978. Yarden is one of six distinct labels from this producer; its chief winemaker worked a stint at Jacquesson in Champagne, where he learned a thing or two. This wine doesn't have the biscuity notes one might expect from a traditional-method wine, bottle-aged on the lees for *seven years*, but it's quite pleasant and refreshing—the perfect thing to sip at an al fresco eatery by the beach in Tel Aviv or Haifa.

$$$

Mosel

Dr. Loosen

$$$

Mosel

Maximin Grünhaus

$$

Mosel

Reichsgraf von Kesselstatt

$$

Rheingau

Leitz

$$$

Rheingau

Robert Weil

$$$

Pfalz

Von Buhl

$$$

Rheingau

Solter

$$$

Rheingau

Barth

$$$

Nahe

Kruger-Rumpf

$$$$

Nahe

Schlossgut Diel

$$

Pfalz

Dr. Deinhard

$$

Pfalz

Theo Minges

$$
Saar
Van Volxem

$$$
Saar
Peter Lauer

$$–$$$
Burgenland
Schlumberger

$$$
Kamptal
Loimer

$$–$$$
Kamptal
Jurtschitsch

$$$
Kamptal
Bründlmayer

$$$$$
Kamptal
Schloss Gobelsburg

$–$$
Kamptal
Steininger

$$$$
Kremstal
Malat

$$
Amyntaio
Kir-Yianni

$$$
Amyntaio
Karanika

$$–$$$
Santorini
Santo

USA

Spanish Franciscan monks established vineyards in what is today New Mexico back in 1629. They found their way to current-day California in 1769. But American winegrowing went through fits and starts as European settlers struggled to identify which vine varieties would take well here. When we finally hit our stride, we were sidetracked by two World Wars and utterly ruined by Prohibition, which shut down the alcoholic beverage industry between 1920 and 1933 and led growers to abandon their vines.

Thus, only over the past five or six decades has there been a truly functional oenological and viticultural practice in the United States. And so today, while there are wineries in all fifty states in the Union, *sparkling* winemakers are surprisingly sparse.

Given the relatively young average age of the American winery, our industry hasn't been around long enough to establish much of a tradition of putting bottles away for years on end. In addition, the majority of American winery owners didn't inherit estates that were in the family for decades or centuries, a common theme you may have noticed in previous chapters. If you're paying

RECIPE SWEET STARS & STRIPES

SERVES 1

Because, let's face it: Americans talk dry, but they drink sweet. And the combination of sugar and cucumber is inexplicably refreshing on a hot summer day such as July 4. Recipe courtesy of Domaine Chandon, Napa Valley, USA.

2 to 3 ultra-thin
  cucumber slices
Ice cubes
4 ounces demi-sec
  (semisweet) spar-
  kling wine

Place cucumber slices over the ice cubes in a wineglass or short rocks glass. Pour in the sparkling wine and serve.

---

a hefty mortgage or monthly rent, it doesn't make sense to just sit on fragile inventory—bottles *sur lattes* that can't be disturbed—for years on end before selling it.

Oh, and there's the fact that US consumers know their Champers: We are Champagne's number-one export market by value. Which means we not only drink a lot of it, but we also know the good stuff. We will see right through those high-end American wineries charging Champagne prices for their as-yet-unproven *méthode traditionnelle* wines.

Meanwhile, starry-eyed young winemakers—who can barely afford to rent out a fraction of a shared winery space—have figured out how to circumvent the aforementioned obstacles. Pét-Nats can be made from less-desirable young vines that may not be able to reach full ripeness. They don't have to sit around in the bottle for years before sale. And they can be priced within reach for the next generation of oenophiles.

Finally, there's the just-carbonate-it route, which—after all my talk about how sophisticated our palates are—resonates in the land of Coke and Pepsi. Because someone's gotta pay the bills.

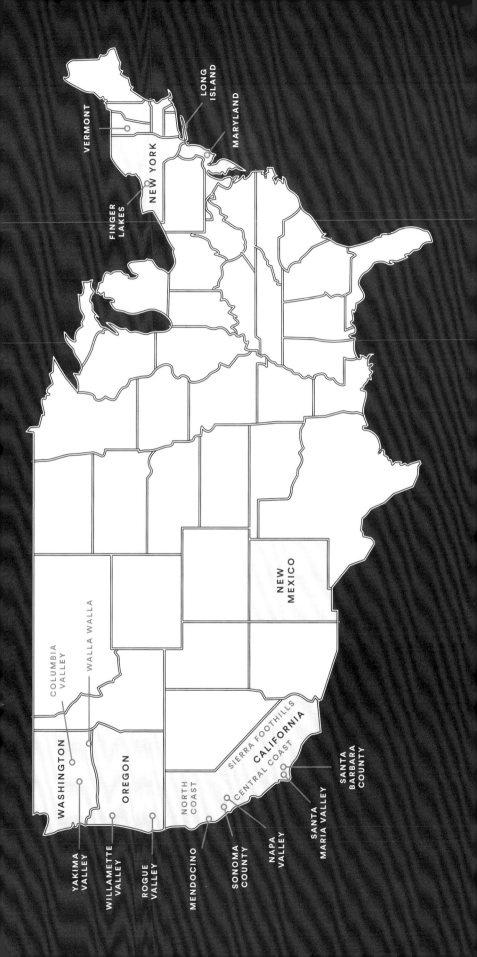

VERMONT

LONG ISLAND

MARYLAND

NEW YORK

FINGER LAKES

NEW MEXICO

COLUMBIA VALLEY

WALLA WALLA

SIERRA FOOTHILLS

CALIFORNIA

CENTRAL COAST

WASHINGTON

OREGON

NORTH COAST

SANTA BARBARA COUNTY

YAKIMA VALLEY

WILLAMETTE VALLEY

ROGUE VALLEY

MENDOCINO

SONOMA COUNTY

NAPA VALLEY

SANTA MARIA VALLEY

Effervescence in the Executive Branch

While President Thomas Jefferson was giving lip service to the idea of ending slavery, he was also amassing a fabulous Champagne collection and trying to grow his own *vitis vinifera*, at Monticello. (The aforementioned slaves were, of course, the ones doing all the heavy lifting.)

Alas, Jefferson's vines succumbed to rot and pests. Virginia's hot, humid summers don't make for ideal grape-growing conditions, let alone sparkling wine–growing conditions. But a couple of Champenoise vintners today run a boutique sparkling winery, Thibaut-Janisson, in Charlottesville. Their micro-lots of Chardonnay-based wines are impossible to find outside the DMV (that's DC-Maryland-Virginia, for all you Beltway outsiders) zone, but receive glowing reviews.

Oh, and there's another Virginia winery that bottles bubbles: the former Kluge Estate, now the Trump Winery, which churns out effervescent wines ($34 to $80/bottle) from fruit grown in the Monticello American Viticultural Area (AVA). So, Thomas Jefferson, an American president is finally bottling Virginia bubbly. Are you happy now?

California

As we learned in Chapter 2, Californians have been trying to make sparkling wine since the 1840s. But all the fun ended when Congress enacted Prohibition. The American wine industry came skittering to a stop, and the knowledge and tools necessary for bottle-fermented sparkling wine were lost.

Fizz returned to California in a big way when Moët & Chandon launched Chandon California in 1973. Seeing an opportunity, other Champenoise Grandes Marques *maisons* moved into the Napa Valley and found success, both with tourism and with supermarket-shelf sales.

Alas, the increasingly sultry Bordelaise climate in Napa isn't well-suited to Champenoise wine-growing and methods, making for increasingly early pick dates. As one independent producer confided to me, "We have too much sun. Accordingly, producers here have combated this issue by being handed apples and making lemonade."

Today, a new generation of winemakers are applying deductive reasoning to the situation, finding stashes of undervalued old vines and treating the fruit as it wants to be treated. In response, the French-held houses will no doubt be upping their games over the next decade, as they have in Champagne, where the growers have pushed a region-wide agenda of greater transparency and authenticity.

NAPA VALLEY

Champagne is not an easy place to visit if you don't have a working knowledge of French. The Napa Valley, on the other hand, is a terrific place to vacation, particularly during the off-season when the traffic is manageable. So here's your trade-off: The sparkling wines you will taste in the Napa Valley just won't be as good as those you might taste in Champagne. But if you're looking to go on a luxe tour de bubbles, the hospitality teams of the Napa Valley are ready and waiting for you, no matter what style of sparkling you desire.[1]

The wineries are aware that California's best-known wine region is better-suited to growing Cabernet Sauvignon than Pinot Noir and Chardonnay, so in many of the sumptuous tasting rooms

you'll visit, you'll be told that the grapes maybe aren't grown right here. Maybe they're grown somewhere else, somewhere cooler. That's a good thing—embrace it.

That said, the Carneros subzone, which straddles the south ends of both Napa Valley and Sonoma County, enjoys a cooler climate thanks to the chilly winds and fogs that blow through here off San Pablo Bay, and produces some luscious bubblies.

Frank Family Vineyards Carneros Napa Valley Blanc de Blancs (V; 12% ABV; $$$$)

The stone Frank Family winery was built in 1884; an early owner of the estate was the legendary Lillie "Firebelle" Hitchcock Coit, philanthropist, supporter of firefighters, and cross-dressing gambler. The incomparable Ms. Coit surely would have loved this brash, broad-shouldered bubbly made from Carneros Chardonnay. Current owners Rich and Leslie Frank are a past president of Walt Disney Studios and a former Emmy Award–winning broadcast journalist.

[1] *A shout-out here to Hagafen, on the Silverado Trail, which offers a kosher sparkling wine ($$$).*

Domaine Carneros by Taittinger "Le Rêve" Carneros Blanc de Blancs

(V; 12% ABV; $$$$$)

California's architectural copy of Taittinger's Louis Quinze–era Château de la Marquetterie[2] features a grand entrance, formal gardens, and marble floors that make a person hanker, strangely, for a fur coat and bonbons. Leesy and luscious, "Le Rêve" is the American counterpart to Taittinger's Prestige Cuvée, "Comtes de Champagne," made entirely from estate fruit.

Mumm Napa "DVX" Napa Valley Méthode Traditionnelle

(V; 12.5% ABV; $$$$$)

G. H. Mumm is the third-best-selling Champagne in the world and the top-selling Champagne in France, and its California outpost turns out half a million cases of wine per year, in the form of an absurd number of cuvées (I counted forty when I visited). The 120 base wines are sourced from 45 farmers, mostly located in Carneros. The best of the best goes into the DVX Rosé—named after founding winemaker Guy Devaux—which offers bold aromatics and flavors of cherry and raspberry that are balanced by focused minerality. It gets a rather decadent *dosage* of 11-plus grams per liter of sugar and spends a full forty-three months *en tirage*.

Onward Wines Suisun Valley Pétillant Naturel Malvasia Bianca (V; 12.4% ABV; $$)

Frank Family Vineyards (see page 221) alum Faith Armstrong Foster now vinifies unusual grapes using timeworn techniques for her Onward and Farmstrong labels. Her bubbly selection includes everything from a red Pét-Nat of Carignane to a Charmat-method Malvasia sold in cans.[3] This Malvasia is sourced from the Suisun Valley, a small southern appendage of the Napa Valley[4] that's cradled between the Twin Sisters and Vaca Mountains. Somehow simultaneously irreverent and polished, it has notes of mango, peach purée, black licorice, nectarine pit, and pink peppercorns that linger on the long finish.

---

[2] *The château is not a winemaking facility. Taittinger's impressive* crayères *and cellar are in Reims and well worth a visit, even if you get stuck doing the French-language tour.*

[3] *Note: I maintain my stance on sparkling wines in cans.*

[4] *It is a separate appellation, however.*

The Real Deal

If you only have time to visit one Napa Valley sparkling winery, book a tour at Schramsberg, where the more than two miles of caves make for a *très Champenoise* experience. In 1862, German immigrants Jacob and Annie Schram purchased this 200-acre (81-ha) Diamond Mountain property and began digging deep cellars and planting vineyards. When husband and wife Jack and Jamie Davies purchased the estate in 1965, it was ready for a sparkling-wine-fueled turn-around. By 1972, President Richard Nixon was toasting Chinese premier Zhou Enlai with Schramsberg.

Esther Mobley, the *San Francisco Chronicle* critic who is quoted on the following pages, is a fan of the "gorgeous, rich, textured" Schramsberg Reserve, a long-*tirage*, mostly Pinot Noir bottling that becomes available a decade after its vintage date. At $120 a bottle at the time of this writing, it's a bit steep, as is the J. Schram line of bubblies ($120 to $185), presented in squat Ruinart-style bottles. Made from the cream of the crop of base wines, these are wonder-fully nutty, with the autolytic notes of a long rest *sur lie*, and have an avid following among collectors.

Schramsberg North Coast Méthode Champenoise Brut Blanc de Blancs (V; 12.4% ABV; $$$)

In the manner of a Grande Marque, Schramsberg sources the Char-donnay for this cuvée from 120 different vineyard blocks spread throughout Napa, Sonoma, Mendocino, and Marin Counties. The three hundred base wines made annually go in various directions depending on the nature of the fruit: some in tank, some in barrel, some finishing malolactic, some prevented from going through it. The end result is balance: No acid additions are needed, there is vibrant intensity to the pineapple fruit notes, and winemakerly skill has rendered the texture whipped-cream silky.

Esther Mobley on (Obscure but) Consummate California

If there's a new California winemaker to watch, or a classic label to reconsider, Esther Mobley has it covered. The way the influential wine critic for the *San Francisco Chronicle* sees it, "a movement like grower Champagne" is happening in California right now. "It's exciting to see these winemakers coming out who are really forging their own paths," she says. At the same time, "they are inspired by the countercultural movement that has been happening in Champagne over the past decade or two."

I asked Mobley to share some of the most compelling grower-style California with us.

Ultramarine Charles Heintz Vineyard Sonoma Coast Blanc de Blancs (V; 12% ABV; $$$$$)

Michael Cruse (see also page 240) studied a vintage Champagne-making manual from 1860 to teach himself how to vinify traditional-method bubbly by hand; his Ultramarine bubblies sell out every year within a couple of hours. "He is working with a really renowned site for Chardonnay on the Sonoma Coast, the Charles Heintz Vineyard," Mobley notes. She describes Cruse's winemaking style as "more oxidative," making for "open-knit honeyed, nutty" aromatics and flavors, with lemon curd, brioche, and briny notes.

Château Beaux Hauts "En Tirage" Extra-Brut Recently Disgorged Carneros Blanc de Blancs (V; 12.5% ABV; $$$)

"Beaux Hauts" may mean "beautiful peaks," but it sounds like "bozo," which gives one a sense of the winking good humor that permeates this project. The only problem is, you may not be able to find this wine, made in the early 1990s, disgorged in—yes!—2011, and then more or less forgotten. But Mobley has a hunch that enough Californians have fallen so hard for this "really interesting, and delicious, super-long-*tirage* wine," that the vintner will be back with more. "The wines only existed for this fleeting moment out in the world. Once I figured out what was up with them, they were gone—they were extraordinary," Mobley says wistfully.

Caraccioli Santa Lucia Highlands Brut Rosé (V; 12% ABV; $$$–$$$$)

Longtime Roederer Estate winemaker Michel Salgues produces single-vineyard, single-vintage, traditional-method fizz in Monterey County on the Central Coast, "trying to transmit that sunny, ripe, beautiful vibe into his sparkling wines," says Mobley. The Brut Rosé, which is about 60 percent Pinot Noir and 40 percent Chardonnay, is made from partially barrel-fermented base wine. "It's really fleshy and beautiful, and has a lot of that cherry earthiness that is characteristic of Pinot Noir."

Under the Wire Bedrock Vineyard Sonoma Valley Sparkling Zinfandel (V; 12.5% ABV; $$$$)

"Sparkling Zinfandel sounds like it will be sweet, weird, or lowbrow," says Mobley. But this rosé is "gorgeous," with its brambly fruit aromatics. Under the Wire is a side label from Morgan Twain-Peterson and Chris Cottrell of Bedrock Wine Co. that is devoted entirely to traditional-method sparkling wines; this pink Zin is sourced from Bedrock's century-plus-year-old estate vines. "To me, this is the perfect example of expressing that grower Champagne idea of terroir, vintage, and vineyard through a quintessential California grape variety," says Mobley.

SONOMA COUNTY

Next to inland Napa, with its posh tasting rooms and restaurants and luxe resorts, coastal Sonoma's vibe is more Western-casual: ocean vistas, dirt roads, native decorative grasses, cowboy hats, fresh local produce.

And with its maritime breezes and morning fogs, Sonoma fans say it's the better location for growing Pinot Noir and Chardonnay. Within the Sonoma County viticultural area, the prime subappellations for sparkling wine are the very coolest Sonoma Coast and Russian River Valley, due to their proximity to the Pacific Ocean, as well as their respective subzones, Fort Ross-Seaview and Green Valley.

True Sonoma Style

You know you're in Sonoma when you belly up to the outdoor bar at Iron Horse, made of tree-trunk planks set on wine barrels. Who needs walls when the beauty of Sonoma's Green Valley is all around you?

The cooling Pacific Ocean is just 13 miles (21 km) away, and the Goldridge sandy loam soil here is particularly well-suited to Pinot Noir and Chardonnay. Each of twenty-eight blocks of vines is farmed and vinified separately, and the winery releases twelve different sparkling cuvées annually, with a variety of *dosage* levels and late disgorgements, depending on the vintage.

Over the years, the brand has been served at White House and State Department dinners as a symbol of western American hospitality. Longtime philanthropists and activists, the proprietors, the Sterling family, also release special bottlings to support favorite causes.

Iron Horse Green Valley of Russian River Valley Sonoma County "Classic" Brut (V; 13.5% ABV; $$$)

With a restrained *dosage*, the "Classic" expresses the robust savory flavor of Sonoma Pinot Noir and Chardonnay. Oak-barrel fermentation and lees stirring bring creaminess and toasty notes to this, yes, classic California wine.

SEPPI California Brut
(V; 12% ABV; $$$)

Kelsey Phelps recently launched this label focused entirely on sparkling wine, entitling it after her childhood nickname for her grandfather, Napa Valley icon Joseph "Giuseppi" Phelps. With longtime Schramsberg vintner Keith Hock making the wines from mostly Sonoma-sourced fruit, SEPPI shows great promise.

MENDOCINO COUNTY

Between the Mendocino National Forest and the Pacific coastline, there's a long stretch of epic tranquility. Vineyards hug the slopes of steep foothills and cliffs tower over the ocean while redwoods reach for the sky. The bucolic beauty is over-the-top, with winding roads, blooming gardens, bounteous farmers markets, peace-loving hippies, and plenteous pot farms at every turn. (As a staunch wine drinker, I can do without the marijuana, myself, but hey . . . you do you.)

Pack a puffy jacket if you plan to visit, because even if it's warm during the day, this wine region cools off dramatically at night, by as much as 40 to 50 degrees Fahrenheit (22 to 28 degrees Celsius). This wide diurnal shift is the secret to the zingy acidity in the wines, and it makes Mendocino an ideal place for—you guessed it—bubbly production. The Anderson Valley subzone is a particular hot spot for cold sparkling wine, following the path of the Navarro River through the towns of Navarro, Philo, and Boonville, and the growers take pride in their eco-friendly organic and biodynamic practices.

Scharffenberger "Brut Excellence" Mendocino Méthode Traditionnelle
(NV; 12% ABV; $$)

For $20 a bottle, it's hard to do better than Scharffenberger's simple, lively brut, with its notes of almond and white pepper on the palate. The blend is 60 percent Pinot Noir, 40 percent Chardonnay and spends two years *en tirage*. John Scharffenberger founded the winery in 1981, then moved onto making chocolates under the Scharffen Berger brand. Today it is owned by Maisons Marques & Domaines, the American sales and marketing arm for Louis Roederer. Roederer Estate (see following page) is its luxury bubbly brand, while this crisp sipper is priced for daily indulging.

Roederer Estate "L'Ermitage" Anderson Valley Brut

(V; 12% ABV; $$$–$$$$)

Now that I've mentioned the Roederer-led takeover at Scharffenberger, let's drive 4.5 miles (7 km) north and visit Roederer Estate. The vertically planked, worn-wood barn, its interior sturdy with timber beams, is about as far from a Champenoise château as one can get and inviting in its own charming Californian way. "L'Ermitage," which is just about half Pinot Noir and half Chardonnay, is released approximately seven years after the vintage date, making for a pinpoint fine *perlage*. The palate is decadent, evoking golden raisins and banana cream pie.

CENTRAL COAST

The landscape of the Central Coast of California is so raw and sweeping that one expects a mythical beast to come loping down a hillside at any moment. Maritime winds roll in and over these wide, undulating hills— dotted with California sagebrush, accented by manzanita, and punctuated by the occasional lone oak tree—keeping vines cool and dry and encouraging grape skins to grow thick, making for brooding, profound wines.

But that's a gross generalization, because the area is so dang huge. Reaching from Santa Barbara in the south all the way to Silicon Valley in the north, it's a vast expanse of drop-dead gorgeous coastline between Los Angeles and San Francisco. So let's take a closer look at a few distinct pockets of this epic place.

Santa Barbara County

Where other parts of the Central Coast may do better with Rhône grape varieties like Syrah or Grenache, the area to the northwest of the charming seaside town of Santa Barbara generally favors Pinot Noir and Chardonnay (although the diversity of microclimates is such that it's possible to grow just about anything here, just as it's possible to spot anything from a great white shark to its one predator, the orca, off the Channel Islands just offshore).

The southern border of the region is the Santa Ynez mountain range, which rises right out of the coastline, running west to east. The San Rafael Mountains define the northern line, creating a half-opened fan shape, and the Sierra Madre Mountains run behind them, making a valley-shaped fold

in the fan, with the Santa Maria River and Sisquoc River forming another deep fold. These depressions grab morning fogs and channel winds off the Pacific Ocean every afternoon.

Within the greater wine region are the subappellations Santa Maria Valley and Santa Ynez Valley, and within the latter are the further subzones Sta. Rita Hills, Ballard Canyon, and Happy Canyon.

could be the love child of the Douro and the Jura? Combe is a partnership between wunderkind sommelier-turned-itinerant vintner Rajat Parr, and Peter Stolpman, second-generation winegrower at Stolpman Vineyards, where irrigation is not necessary thanks to clay topsoil that captures morning dew. Yeasty and bone-dry, with notes of beeswax and coconut, this is a conversation starter.

....

Combe Stolpman Vineyards Ballard Canyon "Pét-Nat" Trousseau (V; 11.5% ABV; $$$)

The Trousseau grape is known as Bastardo in Portugal's Douro Valley, but in the Jura, in mountainous eastern France, it's used to make *crémant* (sparkling wine) and pale, cloudy reds that are like delicate versions of Pinot Noir. What better place to grow it than Ballard Canyon, which

J. Brix "Cobolorum" Kick on Ranch Santa Barbara County Riesling Pétillant Naturel (V; 11.2% ABV; $$)

"Cobolorum" is apparently Latin for "naughty goblin," and this wine apparently had a reputation for exploding in previous vintages. No matter—these days, this cloudy, funky, treat has plenty of fans thanks to a glowing endorsement from the *New York Times*.

Oregon

This author may be a bit biased, given that she lives in Portland, but there is no denying that Oregon is a raging hotbed of food and beverage culture. And the level of craftsmanship across the liquid spectrum—from kombucha to coffee beans to IPAs to gin—is unparalleled.

Due to a unique combination of factors—one being that Peter Liem[5] opened a groundbreaking grower Champagne bar here with a couple of pals before anyone was using the term "grower Champagne"[6]—the relatively modest city of Portland has a bottomless thirst for top-shelf bubbly, fed by an ecosystem of local importers who built relationships with the Champenoise decades ago and purveyors who are more interested in geeking out with their clients than making a fast buck.

And then there's the locally produced wine. Over the past decade, investors have been pouring in from France, California, and elsewhere, drawn by the moderate maritime-influenced climate and diversity of soil types, as well as an artisanal culture that promotes quality over quantity. It may be expensive to grow grapes here, but Oregon wines command one of the highest average-per-bottle prices of any vinous region in the world. And consumers are willing to pay our prices, with $75 being the new normal for a bottle of high-end Pinot Noir or Chardonnay.

Oregon sparkling-wine sales are going strong, too; they grew by more than 50 percent in 2018.[7] Unfortunately, there's a tendency among overenthusiastic Oregon vintners to charge Champagne prices for some *méthode traditionnelle* bottlings that don't taste quite ready for prime time. I suspect consumers won't be so willing to pay top dollar for subpar sparkling wine over time, and this very new problem should self-correct. Perhaps more members of the establishment should take a cue from the millennials and dabble in simple, affordable Pét-Nat?

---

[5] *Author of the oft-mentioned (in this book) tome* Champagne: The Essential Guide to the Wines, Producers, and Terroirs of the Iconic Region.

[6] *Cole, "Why Portland Is America's Champagne Capital,"* SevenFifty Daily.

[7] *According to Nielsen data provided by the Oregon Wine Board.*

Jordan Michelman on the New Oregon Cool

Jordan Michelman is the cofounder of *Sprudge*, the über-hip international online coffee journal, and the author of the book *The New Rules of Coffee*. But *Sprudge* has a buzzy natural wine section, proving that I'm not the only person who consumes aromatic caffeine and aromatic alcohol on a daily basis. Sometimes together.

When I asked Michelman to bring me up to date on the avant-garde edges of winemaking, he zeroed in on some really out-there Oregon Pét-Nats. Because, as he puts it, "the kids like them."

Division Winemaking Co. "Gamine" Mae's Vineyard Applegate Valley Pétillant Grenache Rosé (V; 11.3% ABV; $$)

Michelman is "blown away" by this buttercup-colored (no, not pink) Pét-Nat, from Portland urban winemaking doyenne Kate Norris. "It's Southern Oregon Grenache, made into this beautiful, finely pointed, delicate sparkling wine." I'd also like to butt in and put in a good word for Division's "Crémant de Portland" ($$$), an uplifting, golden, fizzy Chenin Blanc.

Johan Vineyards Willamette Valley Pétillant Naturel Pinot Noir (V; 13% ABV; $$)

Johan is noted for biodynamically growing curious varieties such as Blaufränkisch and Grüner Veltliner in addition to the requisite Pinot Noir and Gris. While the winery produces a traditional-method bubbly and an ancestral-method Melon de Bourgogne, this Pét-Nat is cloudy, funky, and front-porch refreshing. "One glass will nuke your expectations for Oregon Pinot Noir," enthuses Michelman.

Art + Science "Symbiosis" (V; 11% ABV; $$)

Longtime Johan Vineyards winemaker Dan Rinke has reduced his role to vineyard manager so that he can focus his attentions on the burgeoning "natural cider scene fused and overlapping with the winemaking scene," as Michelman explains it. "Symbiosis" is a cofermentation of half Johan Willamette Valley biodynamic Grüner Veltliner, half foraged apples. "Nothing else tastes quite like it. It wakes up your tastebuds," says Michelman.

WILLAMETTE VALLEY

Oregon's Coast Range acts like cheesecloth, absorbing some of the rain and fog blowing in off the Pacific before it passes through and cools the Willamette Valley. Thus, while Seattle feels like it's misty, cold, and damp all the time, Portland only feels misty, cold, and damp most of the time. Which makes a big difference if you're trying to grow grapes . . . or stay sane.[8]

Given the Burgundian climate and favorable soils here, it follows that the Willamette Valley's calling card is Pinot Noir. Its most exciting variety is Chardonnay. Oh, and Pinot Meunier? The Valley grows that, too. This all adds up to a region that will soon emerge as an American epicenter for sparkling winemaking. Days are still young, but the raw materials are all in place, and the will and the knowhow are there. As we went to press, a new South African–funded sparkling venture was launching, with rumors of yet more outside investment in bubbles on the horizon. Watch this space.

Soter Mineral Springs Yamhill-Carlton Brut Rosé
(V; 12.8% ABV; $$$$)

Napa Valley superstar winemaker Tony Soter makes wine on the breathtaking 245-acre (99-ha) Mineral Springs Ranch, an oak woodland and biodynamic paradise replete with fruit and vegetable gardens, an orchard, hen houses, and a goat pasture. Gulp down the leesy, refined, honeysuckle-scented Blanc de Blancs if you catch sight of a bottle. The classic rosé, from a barrel-fermented base wine, spends four years *en tirage* and gets very little *dosage*. It grows silky with cellar age, the fresh notes of wild strawberry giving way to minerality and sweet-sour citrus notes.

R. Stuart & Co. "Rosé d'Or" Oregon[9] Sparkling Wine
(NV; 13.5% ABV; $$$)

When Rob Stuart was seventeen, he tasted a 1961 Bollinger that changed his life. In pursuit of a rich, oxidized "Bollinger or Krug" style, Stuart has maintained a solera[10] since 1999. He barrel-ferments and maximizes lees contact in the barrel stages for maximum creaminess. The color of this 70 percent Pinot Noir and 30 percent Chardonnay blend is more of a rose-gold than pink, very much in keeping with its name; the aromatics are rich, with a touch of sherry. On the palate there are layers and layers of savory appeal, with notes of mango and fermented tea.

....

Corollary Momtazi Vineyard Willamette Valley Carbonic Rosé (V; 11.7% ABV; $$$$)

Along with Lytle-Barnett (see page 271 for more on this), Corollary is an exciting new star in the Oregon sparkling scene. This rich, spicy, red-tinted wine is the product of a technique, called carbonic maceration, that extracts color and pure fruit flavor from whole clusters of Biodynamic Pinot Noir grapes.

....

Elk Cove Vineyards "La Bohème" Yamhill-Carlton Brut Rosé (V; 12% ABV; $$$$)

The Campbell family's favorite opera is *La Bohème*, so when they found a farm originally homesteaded by pioneers named Bohème, they knew they could make great wine from it in the rustic Willamette Valley subappellation of Yamhill-Carlton. The deep watermelon color of this wine comes from a special dedicated "color ferment" developed by winemaker Adam Campbell; and in place of a sugar solution, Campbell uses the winery's "Ultima" dessert wine as a *dosage*. This rosé's raspberry, cranberry,

pomegranate, and earth notes would please any Pinot Noir lover.

....

Argyle Artisan Series Knudsen Vineyard "Julia Lee's Block" Oregon Blanc de Blancs (V; 12.5% ABV; $$$)

Oregon's original sparkling wine-grower, cofounded in 1987 by Rollin Soles, is known nationwide for its workmanlike basic brut ($$–$$$). All wines are vintage-dated, and the house keeps a library of bottles under *tirage* dating back to the beginning. The house style is rich, rustic, and all-American. Knudsen Vineyard's "Julia Lee's Block" (in the Dundee Hills) is believed to be the first 100 percent Dijon-clone block[11] of

----

[8] *The author of this book grew up in Seattle.*

[9] *While I was researching this book, many Willamette Valley sparkling-wine producers were labeling their wines with the overall "Oregon" appellation even if they qualified for the Willamette Valley appellation, or even a subappellation. This may change.*

[10] *See page 278 for more on this term.*

[11] *"Dijon clones" are cultivars of Chardonnay sourced from Burgundy rather than California. It is thought that these vine cuttings do better in cooler climates like Oregon's. That said, some growers prefer to work with California "heritage clones." A "block" is a parcel of vines that makes up a distinct section of a vineyard.*

Chardonnay vines, dating back to 1990. This alluring wine has plenty of acidity, and aromatics of lemon curd and a garden in springtime.

....

Gran Moraine Yamhill-Carlton Oregon Brut Rosé
(NV; 12.5% ABV; $$$)

Jackson Family Wines[12] has built itself into a luxury winemaking conglomerate in recent years under the savvy leadership of Barbara Banke, widow of company founder Jess Stonestreet Jackson. Banke's portfolio of investments in Oregon's Willamette Valley exhibit an appreciation for elegance, as evidenced by this spot-on charmer clad in golden-tinged pink, which caresses the palate with delicate raspberry and strawberry notes.

....

RMS "Rollin Michael Soles" Willamette Valley Brut
(V; 12.5% ABV; $$$$)

When mustachioed Texan Rollin Soles left Argyle winery (below), his rabid fans followed him, demanding more sparkling wines, which he releases in small quantities under the RMS label. This 70 percent Pinot Noir, 30 percent Chardonnay brut spends thirty months *en tirage* and the style is creamy and refined, with restrained floral notes. The *dosage*, at 8 grams per liter, might be a bit generous, but my only complaint about this wine is that there's not more of it to go around.

COLUMBIA GORGE

The Columbia Gorge is—sorry about this—drop-dead gorgeous. The big, bad Columbia River delineates the border between Washington and Oregon, and maritime winds from the Pacific howl down a deep trench dug out by biblical-scale floods eons ago, making this stretch a haven for windsurfers and kiteboarders. On the hillsides above the water, abandoned apple and pear orchards are quickly being converted to vineyards as word of this region's untapped potential spreads among oenophiles.

The more arid inner stretches of the Gorge share similarities, weather-wise, with the Rhône or parts of Italy, while the windblown western end can feel an awful lot like Savoie or the Jura: Vineyards tend to hug the foothills of Mount Hood, which attracts skiers year-round to its gleaming-white glacier. The locals who aren't already on the river or the slopes are ready to hike, fish, or mountain bike with a moment's notice.

Analemma Atavus Vineyard Blanc de Noirs (V; 12.5% ABV; $$$$)

Analemma is a noted biodynamic producer in the Gorge, and the fifty-year-old Atavus Vineyard is organically farmed under the watch of the peaks of Mounts Hood and Adams. Aged *sur lie* in the bottle for more than three years, this wine is part apple orchard in springtime, part artisan bakery. It's starting to develop a cultish following, so grab it if you can find it. Or, better yet, plan a trip to the Gorge to visit the winery, and don't forget to bring all of your outdoorsy gear.

ROGUE VALLEY

The Rogue River watershed follows the path of the namesake river from Crater Lake, the nation's deepest, to the Pacific Ocean, twisting and winding its way rogueishly through mountains, forest, and even lava tubes, attracting hikers, kayakers, fly-fishers, and white-water rafters. The climate is dry and warm in spring, summer, and fall, and buried under snow in the winter. And while the most promising grapes here seem to be the Rhône-ish Syrah, Grenache, and Viognier, higher elevations, with their promise of supporting cooler-climate varieties, have yet to be explored.

Maison Jussiaume Rogue Valley Blanc de Blancs (NV; 12.5% ABV; $$$$)

Jean-Michel Jussiaume's day job is winemaker at Del Rio Vineyards[13] in the Rogue Valley; his side gig makes use of the seas of Chardonnay grown in that sunny spot, enjoying plentiful water from the Rogue River. Due to these favorable conditions, Jussiaume can farm a higher crop load (more fruit per vine), as is done in Champagne. Thus his Chardonnay leans more toward acidity than fruit and phenolics; this Blanc de Blancs is pale, lean, and lemony, with aromatics of fresh herbs and ruby-red grapefruit on the palate. Just as one would expect from the winemaker's acid-hound upbringing in Muscadet (see page 103 for more on this region), Jussiaume's wine begs for a plate of fresh oysters.

---

[12] *The family-held company behind the ubiquitous American Kendall-Jackson Chardonnay, as well as many other brands.*

[13] *Jussiaume previously made sparkling wine at Dr. Konstantin Frank in New York's Finger Lakes (see page 242).*

Hello, New Mexico?

Of all the places for a Champenoise family to emigrate to, one would not imagine it would be New Mexico. High-altitude, bone-dry, and cracked into cliff faces, rock towers, and mountain ranges, with a tan topography that looks like a crinkled walnut, this is the scene of Wile E. Coyote's eternal pursuit of the Road Runner.

Nonetheless, in 1984, a few members of the Gruet family—owners of a French nightclub as well as the Champagne house Gruet et Fils— found themselves camping out and planting vines in the Wild West, attracted here by the chilly nighttime temperatures, dry air, and well-draining, calcium-rich sandy soils. Today, Gruet is a household name in the US. The Gruets bottle year-round, producing some 275,000 cases of wine annually under a few different brands, including Sauvage and "Madame Liberté."

It still isn't easy for this immigrant family to farm in New Mexico; irrigation water is extremely limited in this arid region, forcing the Gruets to source grapes from other states. But a recent partnership with the Santa Ana Pueblo tribe has resulted in a new vineyard (with full First Nations water rights) called Tamaya, after the tribe's traditional, pre-Hispanic name. It's hard to conceive of a more all-American vinetending project.

Gruet "Gilbert Grand Reserve" Méthode Champenoise Brut (V; 12% ABV; $$$)

Since I'm willing to bet you've tasted Gruet's basic brut, why not try the Grand Reserve, which ferments slowly in oak barrels, ages *en tirage* for approximately three years, and is complex and rich enough to go head-to-head with other American bubblies at twice the price? With its elegant touch of blood orange on the palate, this wine makes a compelling case for New Mexico viticulture.

Washington

Just as the people of Washington range from crew rowers to rodeo bull riders, this state's wine regions are as diverse as those of an entire European nation, forming a giant horseshoe that hems in both sides of the Cascade Mountains and touches the borders of both Oregon and British Columbia.

The eastern fork of the horseshoe, hugging the foothills of the Cascades, feels a bit like Germany, what with all the Riesling vines and lederhosen (google "Leavenworth" and you'll

see what I'm talking about). On the Idaho side of this prong, it's more like Bordeaux or the Rhône as it passes through the evocatively named Channeled Scablands—desert-like grassland that was carved into canyons and coulees (long channels) by the aforementioned apocalyptic floods—en route to Canada.

The western side of the U shape traces the fragmented lines formed by the Puget Sound and its many inlets. Here, in the chilly, damp rainshadow, the grape varieties tend to have long, Teutonic names—Siegerrebe, Müller-Thurgau—but Pinot Noir is up-and-coming on the horizon, and given how positively British the weather is (see United Kingdom, page 253, to learn why British weather is a good thing), the islands off Seattle may be prime sparkling-wine country within a few decades.

COLUMBIA VALLEY

The southern trough of the aforementioned horseshoe follows the path of the Columbia River Gorge, where the fast-flowing, Pacific-bound water, lined on either side by cliffs, regulates temperatures and acts as a wind tunnel that keeps grapes cool and dry. As the line of the river runs east, the climate changes from maritime to continental, allowing for a stunning variety of grape varieties to grow.

It's pretty much Alsace, Burgundy, Piedmont, Puglia, and about twelve other European regions combined, except that there are only three languages spoken: farmer's English, farmer's Spanish, and the laid-back lingua franca of the international windsurfing-kiteboarding-snowboarding contingent that dwells here. Duuuuuuuuude.

The views are epic, and so are the proportions. Coyote Canyon's vineyard, mentioned at right, covers 1,125 acres (455 ha)—a number that would cause jaws to drop in Champagne, where the average vineyard size is 5 acres (2 ha). This is winemaking on a truly Western scale.

....

Domaine Ste. Michelle Méthode Champenoise Columbia Valley Brut Rosé (NV; 11.5% ABV; $)

Despite being owned by Altria[14] and churning out millions of cases annually, Ste. Michelle Wine Estates makes some quite lovely wines under an array of labels.

This brut rosé is bottle-fermented, and made mostly from Pinot Noir, with a bit of Pinot Meunier. A pleasant quaffer, it's gently floral, peachy, and creamy—and sells for less than $15. SMWE imports the world's third-most-popular Champagne brand, Nicolas Feuillatte, into the United States, so perhaps there has been an exchange of ideas.

....

Coyote Canyon Winery "El Chispear" Méthode Champenoise Horse Heaven Hills Albariño (V; 12% ABV; $$)

In Prosser, a sleepy town with a Wild West feel that's built around a bend in the Yakima River, Coyote Canyon planted the first Albariño in Washington State, along with many other French, Italian, and Spanish varieties. Known for making a refreshing white wine in northwestern Spain and Portugal, Albariño expresses itself a bit more richly in this traditional-method wine, with notes of almond, caramel, hay, and Meyer lemon. Horse Heaven Hills is a grassy subappellation of the Columbia Valley that overlooks the Columbia River.

---

[14] *Yes, that's right, the former Philip Morris.*

New York

The Empire State's sparkling winemaking history is long, if not entirely glorious. In 1860, the Pleasant Valley Wine Company launched in New York's northern Finger Lakes region with the sole purpose of making sparkling wine.[15] And Brotherhood Winery (founded in 1839 and still extant) began producing fizz in the early 1900s.

Ever since, the Finger Lakes, east of Niagara Falls, has been acknowledged to be a promising place for traditional-method production, its cool climate favoring Riesling, Cabernet Franc, and the fine art of secondary fermentation in bottle. Then there is Long Island, where the city goes to party, and winemakers are working with what they've got to make some brilliant bubblies.

Unsurprisingly, New York City is the nation's thirstiest sparkling-wine market. Alas, New York's strength is also its Achilles' heel. The consumer base in the big city has money to burn, and some prolific wineries in New York State are churning out overpriced, over-packaged fizz that's more fun to look at than taste. To find the best, look not for the vinous equivalent of a Hamptons gala, but for those bottles that, like the milieu at Grey Gardens, are outré, original, and speak of another time.

FINGER LAKES

Being born with a supernumerary digit is said to be good luck. Thus, the Finger Lakes, which number eleven, must be worth celebrating with a sparkling toast. From above, these long, narrow, deep lakes look like they're ready to grab a wineglass. From ground level, they're surrounded by scenic waterfalls and happy hikers.

It gets really, really, really cold in upstate New York in the winter, but similar to the Mosel or Rhine, these eleven bodies of water regulate temperatures on the hillsides above them. On top of that, nearby Lake Ontario and Lake Erie are so big, they have an almost oceanic effect on the whole western side of the state, which includes the cities of Rochester, Buffalo, Syracuse, and Ithaca. The result is a cool, breezy environment that's optimal for growing the high-acid minerally grapes that are best for sparkling winemaking.

---

[15] *The company still makes its "Great Western American Champagne" (try it if you dare).*

Pét-Nat Par-Tay with Marissa A. Ross

Here at sparkling-wine-guzzling central HQ, we are big fans of humorist, social media darling, and *Bon Appétit* magazine wine editor Marissa A. Ross, who blogs at *Wine. All the Time.* and has written a book by the same name. In addition, she's the cohost of the entertainingly discursive wine podcast *Natural Disasters.*

We asked Ross to fill us in on which funky American single-ferment *Pétillant Naturel* wines she's drinking right now.

Cruse Wine Co. Deming Vineyard Napa Valley Pétillant Naturel Valdiguié (V; 9.5% ABV; $$$)

Once known as "Napa Gamay," Valdiguié indeed has some similarities with Gamay, the Beaujolais grape: It retains excellent acidity levels, and makes fresh, quaffable styles of wine that taste delicious chilled (even the reds). Over the past few years, a new guard of California winemakers has been rediscovering old Valdiguié vines. Michael Cruse (whose other label, Ultramarine, is recommended on page 224) is at the forefront of this revival movement; his vineyard source for this Pét-Nat is approximately sixty-five years old. "It's juicy and bursting with blackberry, hibiscus, and twangy acidity, and has a *mousse* that could easily be confused for that of Champagne," Ross says about this wine.

ZAFA/Counterspell "Jungle Fever" Ellison Estate Vineyard Vermont Sparkling Wine (V; 11.5% ABV; $$$)

Krista Scruggs's innovative and electrifying wines and cider-wine coferments using foraged apples (more on this new trend in the Oregon section, page 230) have made her the It Girl of American natural winemaking. She's "an absolute game-changer," according to Ross. On Grand Isle, an island in Lake Champlain in upstate Vermont, Scruggs biodynamically grows American hybrid grape varieties; "Jungle Fever" is vinified from one called La Crescent. Ross says of this bottling, "It will hit you like a lightning bolt and fill you with warm tropical vibes of salty pineapple."

Chëpìka Pét-Nat "Catawba" Finger Lakes (V; 9.5% ABV; $$$)

Finger Lakes winemaker Nathan Kendall has teamed up with Master Sommelier extraordinaire Pascaline Lepeltier to vinify—most years[16]—Pét-Nats from the native New York grape varieties Catawba and Delaware. "Chëpìka" is the word for "roots" in Lenape, the language spoken by the local Delaware tribe. Their early-harvested, half-fermented winemaking approach squelches the "foxy"[17] tendencies of the grapes that so flummoxed the early sparkling winemakers of Ohio and New York. This bottling, says Ross, "showcases the potential of the Finger Lakes, tasting like biting into the freshest Granny Smith apple with an Italian lemon-zest core that races down your palate like an acidic zip-line."

---

[16] *Note that due to the natural approach, the wines aren't the same every year; the 2018 vintage was vinified as a dark still rosé, not a bubbly, due to the warm, wet conditions during the growing season.*

[17] *See Chapter 2, page 49, for more on Catawba's "foxiness."*

Dr. Konstantin Frank "Célèbre" Méthode Champenoise Riesling (NV; 12% ABV; $$)

Ukrainian immigrant Dr. Konstantin Frank arrived in the United States fluent in nine languages, English not being one of them, but nevertheless secured a position as a professor at Cornell University's upstate Geneva Agricultural Experiment Station. In 1962, he established his groundbreaking vineyard, planting dozens of varieties of European *vitis vinifera* in a region that was thought capable of growing only native American and hybrid grapes. At the winery's old stone château dating back to 1886, the lineup of impressive traditional-method sparkling wines includes Célèbre, which balances ripe fruit notes with plenty of acid. The yeast expresses itself with the aromatics of buttered noodles, while the palate is bright with lively notes of pear and lemon.

Ravines Méthode Classique Finger Lakes Sparkling Brut (V; 12.5% ABV; $$$)

Morten Hallgren grew up at his family's winery in Provence, worked at the renowned Bordeaux estate, Château Cos d'Estournel, after oenology school, and eventually ended up as winemaker at Dr. Konstantin Frank. Hallgren's own sparkling style is classic traditional-method. His Pinot Noir and Chardonnay bottle-age *en tirage* for a full seventy-two months, making for a fine *mousse* and deliciously doughy notes.

Hermann J. Wiemer Vineyard Finger Lakes Blanc de Noir[18] (V; 12% ABV; $$$)

Immigrants: They get the job done! The eponymous vintner Wiemer (now retired) came to the US from Germany, where his family had been making wine in the Mosel for three centuries. Thus, when he planted his classic vineyard on Seneca Lake back in 1976, the focus was on Riesling. Today, Wiemer's former apprentice Fred Merwarth runs the winery along with his business partner, Swedish agronomist Oskar Bynke. Their Pinot Noir–based Blanc de Noir is deft, with bright, appley notes, spending forty-one months *sur lie* to achieve its sophisticated texture.

---

[18] *This winery goes with the singular "Noir" rather than the more commonly used plural, "Noirs." See footnote, page 275, for more on this.*

LONG ISLAND

It's hard to believe that a two-hour drive from Brooklyn, and just minutes from Southampton, there is bucolic countryside dotted with sheep, with rolling lavender fields, cheerful pumpkin patches, and vineyards. A remarkable number of vineyards, in fact.

While the sweltering humidity of summertime can be challenging, and most experts agree that

Long Island has more in common, weather-wise, with Bordeaux than Champagne, the well-draining sandy soils and sea breezes that grace the far-eastern forks of Long Island make it possible to squeak sparkling wine out of this soil.

And given the rich-and-famous composition of the vacationers who hang out in these parts, there's major demand for local wineries to produce party juice, aka rosé and bubbly. In fact, there's a winery called Sparkling Pointe, in Southold, that produces nothing *but* bubbles (and one brandy). The wine prices are a bit steep here, but then, so is the cost of real estate. But who's paying attention when everyone is wearing $500 flip-flops and a $1,000 sarong?

Paumanok North Fork of Long Island Blanc de Blancs (V; 12% ABV; $$$)

Just about a mile from Flanders Bay, and the adjacent Great Peconic Bay, this 127-acre (51-ha) estate manages to support Merlot and Cabernet Sauvignon as well as highly rated Chenin Blanc and Sauvignon Blanc. The Massoud family's serious traditional-method sparkling Chardonnay spends more than three years

bottle-aging on the lees and is made in a crisp, citrusy, linear (submarine, as I like to say) style.

Channing Daughters Sylvanus Vineyard Long Island Pétillant Naturel Tocai Friulano (V; 10% ABV; $$)

Walter Channing had the remarkable foresight to purchase 28 acres (11 ha) of land in Bridgehampton and plant it with more than two dozen experimental grapes as early as 1982. Today, the divergent array of offerings at Channing Daughters includes quirky varieties, like Dornfelder and Blaufränkisch, and ten Pét-Nats. Of these, the Tocai Friulano is most readily available. It's made from the northeastern Italian grape Friulano,[19] which has thin skins and thus must be harvested early in a humid environment to avoid rot, making it a good candidate for bubbly in southern New York State. It's vinified to dryness and hits the palate like bottled seafoam.

---

[19] *Formerly called Tocai Friulano. The name was shortened because Hungary's signature grape, Tokaji, is pronounced the same way. Friulano is grown in Friuli, so the name fits.*

Hawaii

All fifty states produce wine, and that includes the tropical paradise of Hawaii. But while—yes—there's plenty of pineapple wine, there's fine *vitis vinifera* bubbly, as well. As we know from *Moana*, Hawaii was formed by volcanic eruptions, with five volcanoes currently active and spewing lava at this time. Mauna Kea, on the Big Island, rises 13,803 feet (4,207 m) above the ocean and welcomes skiers and snowboarders on its slopes. Thus, Hawaii *does* get cold enough to produce a very nice sparkling wine. Which is fully drinkable on your hotel-room porch after a long day at the beach.

MauiWine "Lokelani - Rose Ranch" Hawaii Sparkling Wine (NV; 12.5% ABV; $$$)

A Napa Valley winemaker helped establish the 23-acre (9-ha) vineyard here, on a ranch once frequented by Hawaiian royals, at 1,800 feet (550 m) of elevation. Tasting this traditional-method blend of Pinot Noir and Chardonnay, you'd never guess it came from a tropical climate. It sits *en tirage* for twenty to twenty-four months prior to disgorgement; a splash of Grenache provides the pink color.

A Master Curator on Maryland, Vermont, and More

The hottest category in hipster winemaking today is *méthode ancestrale*. Young sommeliers say these fizzy, crown-capped bottles are easy sells to millennial and Gen Z audiences who want character, affordability, and quirkiness from their wine experiences. Like their customers, Pét-Nat winemakers tend to be young and open to experimentation, so this is an area where an expert's recommendation can make a big difference.

Matthew Plympton's Oakland, California–based business, called Revel Wine, curates some of the most interesting and unusual winemakers in the United States. Plympton sells wines to retailers and restaurateurs in California and is a tastemaker among industry insiders, so I asked him which Pét-Nat producers he's got his eye on.

La Garagista "Ci Confonde" Vermont Pétillant Naturel Rosé (V; 12% ABV; $$$)

"Vermonter Deirdre Heekin is breaking the stereotypes of what many thought was possible with American hybrids. This lovely wine made from Frontenac Gris is all about rose hips and evocative of its alpine locale. Walking with Deirdre through her vineyards is like being on a botany class field trip," Plympton says. Frontenac is a hybrid grape variety that was cross-bred to survive very cold winters; the "Gris" version has amber-to-lavender skins.[20]

Broc Cellars Mendocino Pétillant Valdiguié (V; 11% ABV; $$$)

"There is just something about Valdiguié in its pink form. As a rosé, it screams watermelon Jolly Rancher and this *pétillant* is no exception," says Plympton. "Winemaker Chris Brockway is thought by many to only be making wines for the 'cool kids,' but this is a perfect example of Chris's ability to make a clean, ethereal wine that is all about a picnic in the park or a day at the beach."

Scar of the Sea Méthode Ancestrale Paso Robles San Juan South Vineyard Chardonnay (V; 10.5% ABV; $$)

"Scar of the Sea is making really lovely, transparent versions of Chardonnay that showcase what the grape variety is capable of from a few different locales on California's Central Coast," Plympton notes. The winery typically releases three different Pét-Nat bottlings annually. Insider tip: "Keep an eye out for the tiny production non-vintage 'Solera',[21]" Plympton advises.

Fausse Piste "Fish Sauce" Eola-Amity Hills Méthode Ancestrale (V; 12% ABV; $$)

"When chef-turned-winemaker Jesse Skiles said he wanted to make a sparkling wine from Muscat Blanc à Petits Grains, I was on board 100 percent," says Plympton. "The fruit for this crisp, airy sparkler comes from the Eola-Amity Hills of the Willamette Valley (an area known much more for Pinot Noir than anything else). It's really versatile at the table and a nice foil for cuisine with a bit of salt and heat."

Old Westminster "Field Blend" Pétillant Naturel Maryland Piquette (V; 7% ABV; $$)

In centuries past, peasants who couldn't afford wine drank *piquette*, a beverage made by adding water to just-pressed grape pomace (skins, seeds, and pulp) and refermenting this soup via *méthode ancestrale*. This example is a juicy semi-sparkling blend of red grapes that's best enjoyed chilled, with picnic foods. While not exactly a "field blend"[22] in the traditional European sense of the term, the *cépage* is an indiscriminate mix of Cabernet Franc, Syrah, and Chambourcin, a French-American hybrid that's responsible for this wine's bright acidity and electric color. According to Plympton, the folks behind Old Westminster, the Baker family of Maryland, "are inspiring countless numbers of producers on the East Coast (and in the US) to think differently."

---

[20] As mentioned in the footnote on page 105, the term "Gris" refers to in-between-colored grapes that are in the pink-to-lavender "gray" zone, as opposed to blue- or purple-skinned grapes, which are called Noir, or "black." When the skins soak in the juice, the result is a rosé wine.

[21] See page 278 for more on this term.

[22] Historically, grape varieties were all planted together, interspersed, rather than separated into blocks by variety. This was, in part, an insurance policy for ripeness and vine health in times when less was known about viticulture.

$$$$

Napa Valley
Frank Family Vineyards

$$

Napa Valley
Domaine Carneros

$$

Napa Valley
Mumm Napa

$$

Suisun Valley (Napa Valley)
Onward Wines

$$$

North Coast, CA
Schramsberg

$$$-$$$$

Santa Lucia Highlands
Caraccioli

$$$

Russian River Valley
Iron Horse

$$

Mendocino
Scharffen-berger

$$$-$$$$

Anderson Valley
Roederer Estate

$$$

Santa Barbara County
Combe

$$

Applegate Valley
Division Wine-making Co.

$$

Willamette Valley
Johan Vineyards

USA

$$$$
Yamhill-Carlton
Soter

$$$
Willamette Valley
R. Stuart & Co.

$$
Yamhill-Carlton
Gran Moraine

$$$
Willamette Valley
Elk Cove

$$$
Willamette Valley
RMS

$$$
Willamette Valley
Argyle

$$$
New Mexico
Gruet

$
Columbia Valley
Domaine Ste.
Michelle

$$$
Napa Valley
Cruse

$$
Finger Lakes
Dr. Konstantin
Frank

$$$
Finger Lakes
Hermann
J. Wiemer
Vineyard

$$$
Hawaii
MauiWine

More Anglophone Nations

Ah, colonialism. It introduced cricket to India and rugby to New Zealand. It also brought slavery, racism, outright theft, famine, brutality, taxation without representation, the loss of cultural identities, stagnant economic growth, and—oh yes—the English language to the far corners of the earth. Nearly four million Bengalis may have died of hunger in 1943 while the Brits were eating Indian bread,[1] but, hey, the ones who survived learned English!

RECIPE

FRENCH 75

SERVES 1

During the First World War, at the famous Harry's New York Bar in Paris, legendary Scottish mixologist Harry MacElhone invented a hard-hitting cocktail that married London-style gin with French Champagne. He named it after the French 75, the world's first quick-firing field artillery piece. Developed by the French army, this weapon was also used by British and American forces in World Wars I and II.

1 ounce gin
2 dashes simple syrup
½ ounce fresh lemon juice
2 ounces sparkling wine, plus more for topping off
Lemon twist, to garnish

Combine the gin, simple syrup, lemon juice, and sparkling wine in a cocktail shaker filled with ice. Shake vigorously and strain into a chilled flute. Top off with more sparkling wine and garnish with lemon twist.

And so, the United Kingdom, Canada, New Zealand, Australia, and South Africa[2] share a lingua franca as well as a taste for French Champagne. These disparate nations also share vinous similarities. All are enjoying a moment right now as exciting new frontiers for winemaking, especially when it comes to bubbly. And yet, at the same time, all of these nations boast surprisingly long winemaking histories.

For example: Although it's quite possible that Roman interlopers got the ball rolling a few centuries previously, the monk-historian known by the quill handle of the Venerable Bede was the first person to sit down and write about vinification in Britain, back in 731 CE.[3]

---

[1] *Ferriter,* Irish Times.

[2] *Of the countless languages spoken in South Africa, English, not Afrikaans, is the most widely used. The Brits controlled the Cape of Good Hope for much of the nineteenth century.*

[3] *According to the website jancisrobinson .com.*

OKANAGAN
VALLEY

CANADA

UNITED STATES

NIAGARA
PENINSULA

PRINCE
EDWARD
COUNTY

ATLANTIC
OCEAN

NOVA SCOTIA

IRELAND

WALES

CORNWALL

UNITED
KINGDOM

SUSSEX

And around about 1000 CE, Icelandic Norseman Leif Eiríksson landed on the east coast of Canada and dubbed the continent "Vinland." Because "Finland" was already taken. Scholars believe that this "vin" refers to *currant* wine—not grape wine—which Leif et al. sipped out of unicorn horns whilst feasting on rendered whale blubber, roasted puffin, fermented shark, and smoked sheep's heads. (I am only kidding about one of these things.)

South Africa's Constantia winery is still going strong today, having been established in 1685. Grapevines were planted in Sydney in 1788, and by 1836, British soldiers were drinking New Zealand wine.

But while they do have long histories with vine growing, these nations don't have entrenched bubbly traditions. That's changing right now, though. There are beautiful traditional-method cuvées coming out of New Zealand, Tasmania (Australia), South Africa, and Canada, all with their own burgeoning movements of winemakers who are redefining sparkling-wine style to fit their own growing conditions.

And England, of all places, looks like it may someday be the equal of Champagne. Blimey! And Bob's your uncle!

United Kingdom

Of all the nations in the world, the UK is the most single-mindedly sparkling-wine obsessed. It was, as I was typing this, second after the United States in total Champagne imports, despite having one-fifth of the population.[4] And the Brits—traditionally staunch supporters of the Grandes Marques—are beginning to discover the growers.

More interesting than what *les Britanniques* are importing is what they're exporting. Because nearly 70 percent of the Isles' fast-growing domestic wine trade[5] is *méthode traditionnelle* fizz. The chilly UK has the right climate for it. In fact, it's almost *too* cold: "Sometimes the acidity can be quite off-putting in English wines, causing winemakers to add too much *dosage*," confides sommelier

---

[4] *Although, as its economy was also teetering on the brink of total Brexit-caused collapse, that may have changed by the time this book is published.*

[5] *Sales of British wines grew by a hearty 31 percent between 2015 and 2017, according to the website WineGB.*

Sandia Chang, of London's Bubbledogs, whom we'll meet on page 257. But soon enough, climate change will make jolly old England feel more like balmy new California, so everyone is getting into the fizz biz. Even the royal family! (Their sparkling wine label is called Windsor Great Park.)

The Champenoise have duly noted the situation, and slid into Britain's DMs, so to speak, by purchasing and planting vineyards. Champagne Pommery has pounced, *of course*, because everyone knows that the Brits are called "Pommies" in Australia, New Zealand, and South Africa. And Taittinger has a buzzy project called Domaine Evremond. It's for everyone. Everyone who can afford Taittinger.

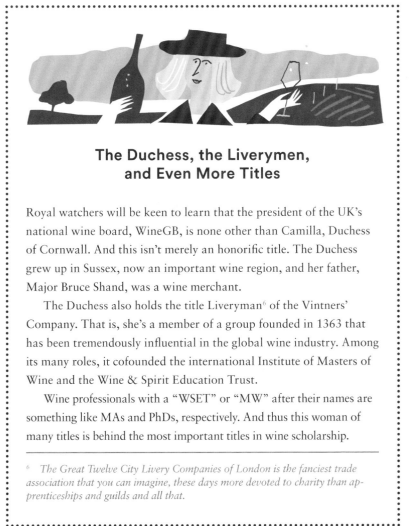

The Duchess, the Liverymen, and Even More Titles

Royal watchers will be keen to learn that the president of the UK's national wine board, WineGB, is none other than Camilla, Duchess of Cornwall. And this isn't merely an honorific title. The Duchess grew up in Sussex, now an important wine region, and her father, Major Bruce Shand, was a wine merchant.

The Duchess also holds the title Liveryman[6] of the Vintners' Company. That is, she's a member of a group founded in 1363 that has been tremendously influential in the global wine industry. Among its many roles, it cofounded the international Institute of Masters of Wine and the Wine & Spirit Education Trust.

Wine professionals with a "WSET" or "MW" after their names are something like MAs and PhDs, respectively. And thus this woman of many titles is behind the most important titles in wine scholarship.

---

[6] *The Great Twelve City Livery Companies of London is the fanciest trade association that you can imagine, these days more devoted to charity than apprenticeships and guilds and all that.*

SOUTHEAST ENGLAND

As fans of Jimmy Cliff and William Shakespeare know, the cliffs of Dover are a gleaming white indication that there is chalk, chalk, everywhere in Southeast England. And you know what that means, because you've read the Champagne chapter (pages 58–81).

While Southeast England isn't an official wine appellation—yet—it encompasses the four hot spots for bubbly production: the counties of Hampshire, Kent, Surrey, and Sussex. Collectively, their picturesque vineyards are all an easy enough driving distance[7] from London to make for a nice weekend wine-country getaway, complete with a scenic hike along those breathtaking white cliffs.

Proximity to a world banking capital is good news for the British wine industry, as it guarantees a moneyed consumer base. But investment in Southeast England wineries is happening so rapidly these days that one worries that some character might be lost along the way.[8]

Sussex

What's the best wine region in Britain? At this point, it's anyone's guess. But Sussex is the most prominent, being first in line for its own appellation designation, and being the home of the nation's sole higher institution (Plumpton College) offering viticulture and winemaking courses. It's also where most of the newish South Downs National Park is located. And it's got those chalky soils, replete with yet more white cliffs.

....

Nyetimber "1086" England Brut (V; 12% ABV; $$$$$)

As long as London maintains a healthy population of posh bankers, supermodels, film stars, blue bloods, and Russian oligarchs, Nyetimber's $200 (£150) bottling—released only in exceptional vintages—is a safe bet. Winemaker Cherie Spriggs was the first female and the first non-Champenois to win the Sparkling Winemaker of the Year title in the International Wine Challenge Awards. This storied estate on the eastern edge of the aforementioned national park

---

[7]   *Most "cellar doors," or tasting rooms, are less than ninety minutes from London by car; the drive to Dover is less than two hours.*

[8]   *One bubbly producer, for example, is now churning out gin, vodka, brandy, beer, and cider in addition to sparkling wine. I lost interest when I saw that its website has a section entitled "Corporate."*

was catalogued in the Domesday Book,[9] published in 1086, hence the proprietary name for this brut. Six years of bottle age, plus two additional years after disgorgement, lend it sleek finesse.

Ridgeview "Cavendish" England Brut (NV; 12% ABV; $$$)

Unlike many competitors, who bottle still Pinot Noir and Chardonnay, the Roberts family focuses entirely on sparkling wine. For a while there, team Roberts was gunning for all British sparkling wine to be called Merret, after the scientist Christopher Merret (see page 42), who documented sparkling winemaking techniques back in 1662. But the idea of a British "Champagne"/ "Prosecco"/"Cava"/"Sekt" equivalent has lost momentum, despite the support of the Duchess of Cornwall. At any rate, this bottle delivers an opulent experience for a basic brut, with caramel, alder smoke, and biscuits on the nose and a strawberry-pear tart-like palate with a finish of anise.

Wiston Estate South Downs Brut (NV; 12% ABV; $$$)

The chalky slopes of South Downs build finesse into this blend of the three classic sparkling-wine grapes. Wiston Estate has been the Goring family farm since 1743, and I'd call this elegant wine a deal at approximately $30.

CORNWALL

The tip of Southwestern England extends like a finger, pointing west at the Isles of Scilly, and, much farther out, the Azores, in what appears to be British upper-crusty accusation. This rugged peninsula was the setting for *The Pirates of Penzance*. Which is actually the name of a town. The highest point in Cornwall is called Brown Willy, and Cornwall is also home to the UK's most southerly point, called the Lizard. Who comes up with these names? Gilbert and Sullivan?

For those who aren't into musical theater tourism and don't want to climb Brown Willy, there are lots of other attractions, including a massive glass-domed tropical rainforest called the Eden Project,

[9] *The book's name is the archaic spelling of "doomsday." Why? Because eleventh-century readers were so shocked by the length and thoroughness of this exhaustive handwritten catalog of every place in England that they compared it to the Book of Life in the biblical Last Judgment. Clearly, these people had not experienced the Internet.*

Bubbledogs Doyenne Dishes on Top Brit Fizz

American-born sommelier Sandia Chang has proffered bottles at some of the world's finest restaurants, from Noma in Copenhagen to Per Se in New York. Today, she lives in London, where she and her husband run the intimate fine-dining spot Kitchen Table and a jaunty wine bar called Bubbledogs. The concept at Bubbledogs is simple, and brilliant: gourmet hot dogs and grower Champagne. Oh, and tater tots. What more is needed in life?

Although Bubbledogs was envisioned as a portal for boutique Champagne producers, Chang does typically include a British bubbly or two on her list. "The level of quality is amazing right now," she tells me. "The winemakers here go off and train in Champagne and come back with expertise."

Here are two of Chang's favorite English sparkling wines. I'll also include her Welsh wine pick a little later in this chapter.

Gusbourne Traditional Method England Reserve Brut (V; 12% ABV; $$$)

Chang describes this easy-drinking blend of the classic Champenoise trio of grapes as a true reflection of the chalky *terroir* of the Kent region. It's "delicate" and "really well balanced," thanks in part to a minimum of three years bottle-aging on the lees. The original de Goosebourne (as they spelled it back then) estate dates back to 1410, and the family's heraldic crest had three geese on it, which explains the charming goose on the neck of the bottle.

Hambledon Vineyard "Première Cuvée" English Sparkling Wine (NV; 12%; $$$)

Advised by friends at the Champagne house Pol Roger, Major General Sir Guy Salisbury-Jones planted England's oldest still-working vineyard all the way back in 1952. The village of Hambledon is also in the history books because it was the birthplace of cricket—hence the winery's double-bat-and-wicket logo. Due to its relatively balmy southerly location in Hampshire, "the wines tend to be a little bit more fruit-forward and rounder in style," notes Chang. "The Première Cuvée is bottle-aged for four years and has a vintagey, rich, warm, velvety texture, with notes of toffee and hazelnut."

and the ridiculously picturesque seaside town of St. Ives. And wineries, as well. Given that the region enjoys drying winds off the Atlantic and the sunniest weather in Great Britain, it's surprising that there aren't more. Someone should talk to the Duchess of Cornwall about this.

....

Camel Valley Cornwall Pinot Noir Brut Rosé
(V; 12.5% ABV; $$$)

The Lindo family's hillside estate, overlooking the Camel River, was the first British winery to earn a coveted Royal Warrant, and the first to receive a Protected Designation of Origin (PDO) from the European Union. That PDO went to Camel Valley's Darnibole Vineyard, a spot uniquely suited to the Bacchus grape.[10] This rustic *saignée*-style rosé radiates pure glee with its fragrant notes of red berries.

WALES[11]

While nearly 90 percent of Welsh land area is used for agriculture, seemingly better suited to roving herds of sheep and dairy cattle than grape cultivation. That's why, when London sommelier Sandia Chang first tasted the Ancre Hill

Estates Blanc de Blancs (below), she admits, "It was so good—I was in shock that it was from Wales!"

But the tiny Welsh wine industry is growing, offering a change of pace for British consumers, since the soils tend toward clay and loam rather than chalk, making for different aromatics and flavors. "With its hills and mountains, Wales has the altitude and slopes for vineyards," Chang enthuses. "The Welsh have so much potential going for them."

....

Ancre Hill Estates Wales Blanc de Blancs (V; 12% ABV; $$$)

This Chardonnay Blanc de Blancs from an under-the-radar family winery is "just like Champagne," gushes Chang. "It is so well-balanced. It has the minerality, and the acidity is so well-integrated." Visitors can order a platter of Welsh cheeses and while away an afternoon at the charming stone farmhouse tasting room on this biodynamic farm.

---

[10] A cross between Sylvaner, Riesling, and Müller-Thurgau, Bacchus thrives in the UK, and plantings are on the increase.

[11] Wales, like Scotland, is a semi-independent nation-state, while Sussex and Cornwall are counties. They are given equal weight in this chapter since there are so few wineries in Wales at this time.

Canada

Like the Abominable Snowman, the Great White Bubbly of the North is out there . . . But we can't see it.

Our northerly neighbor represents only 0.3 percent of total worldwide wine production, and bubbly accounts for less than 4 percent of that minuscule output. In addition, Canada's protectionist laws have traditionally favored a semi-closed market, so most of the rare, delicate fizz that's up there is hoarded for internal consumption.

Canada's calling card is ice wine, an ambrosial nectar made from grapes that have naturally frozen to be rock-solid marbles at harvest. Because it's so unusual, ice wine is the beverage that other nations want to import. And anyway, the Chinese buy more than three times the amount of Canadian wine than we Americans do. So even though we are the world's number-two importer of Canadian wine, that's not saying much.

Thus, it might seem like an exercise in futility to even write up Canadian wines that we may not be able to find in American stores. But enough of us pop across the border to ski at Whistler Blackcomb, hike at Banff or Lake Louise, or take in the culture in Toronto or Montreal that this is a worthwhile list to have on hand.

And keep in mind that Vancouver, British Columbia, is at about 49.3 degrees latitude. As is Reims, France. As climate change heats up our planet, look for the big Champagne houses to open outposts in the maple-leaf nation.

The Sparkling Winos Make Bubbly More Fun for Everyone

We all complain about social media, but then there are those moments when a glimpse of a photo brings us pure joy and we remember what's wonderful about it. And on that note, allow me to introduce you to the Sparkling Winos. They are Jeff Graham and Mike Matyjewicz, wine writers, media personalities, and "experts on all things effervescent," as they like to say.

Stop what you are doing right now and google these guys. Check out their blog at sparklingwinos.com and their Instagram feed. They are, I'm fairly certain, the happiest, most photogenic sparkling-wine connoisseurs—and cutest couple—in the world. So when it came time to work on the Canada section of this book, I knew exactly whom to hit up for informative, upbeat recommendations.

Benjamin Bridge Méthode Classique Nova Scotia Reserve Brut (V; 11% ABV; $$$$)

The sea-breezy peninsula of Nova Scotia, on Canada's east coast near the state of Maine, is ideal for bubbly production. "The cool climate and the vineyard's *terroir* bear a striking resemblance to the Champagne region of France," the Sparkling Winos tell me (they speak as one). Made from organically grown estate fruit, Benjamin Bridge wines have a "distinctive saline quality" that makes them ideal matches for the local seafood. The Brut Reserve "spent five years on its lees, so it's rich and complex, but the acidity is still absolutely electric."

Blue Mountain Vineyard and Cellars Okanagan Valley Gold Label Brut (NV; 12% ABV; $$)

Just north of the central Washington State border, a vertical line of lakes, sheltered by the Cascade Mountains, delineates the Okanagan Valley. Due to a diversity of soil types and microclimates, many grape varieties can grow here, despite fiercely cold winters. For its part, sparkling-wine pioneer Blue Mountain has found success with the Pinot Noir, Chardonnay, and Pinot Gris for this blend. "This is their entry-level cuvée, but it really sets a gold standard," say the Winos. "It's rich and complex, with an interesting marzipan character, which we find common in a lot of BC sparkling."

NIAGARA PENINSULA

Niagara Falls isn't the only spectacular thing about Ontario's Niagara Peninsula. Squashed between Lake Ontario and Lake Erie, this oeno-production zone is famous for its sinfully sweet ice wines.

Henry of Pelham "Cuvée Catharine" Niagara Peninsula Méthode Traditionnelle Brut Rosé (NV; 12% ABV; $$)

The grapes that went into this rosé didn't freeze, but it's a given that temperatures were cool during the growing season. "With notes of fresh pastry and Ontario summer strawberries, this wine is a 'go-to' for us," say the Sparkling Winos.

Cave Spring "CSV" Niagara Peninsula Ontario Blanc de Blancs (V; 12% ABV; $$$)

Riesling pioneers Cave Spring are "quietly making some of Niagara's best bubbles," says Master Sommelier John Szabo, whom you'll meet in a sec. His pick from the winery's high-end "CSV" line is sourced from Chardonnay vines in the Beamsville Bench subappellation under the Niagara Escarpment. This rare release gets seventy-two months of bottle age prior to disgorgement.

Hidden Bench Niagara Peninsula Ontario Zero Dosage Blanc de Blanc[12] (V; 12% ABV; $$$)

Vinified only from organic and biodynamic estate-grown Chardonnay in the Beamsville Bench subappellation of the Niagara Peninsula, this wine spends seven months in barrel, then forty-seven months on the lees, as is fitting for a house known for its "meticulous attention to detail" as well as a non-dosé (fully dry) style, according to Szabo.

Trius Méthode Classique Niagara Peninsula Brut Rosé (NV; 12.5% ABV; $$)

The Winos also rave about this bubbly brut, describing it as "solid," not to mention a "fraction of the price of Champagne" at around $25 USD. It "expresses the elegance and fruit-forward character of Ontario Pinot Noir," say the two experts.

[12]   *This winery goes with the singular "Blanc" rather than the more commonly used plural "Blancs." See footnote on page 275, for more on this.*

John Szabo on the
New Crop of Canadian Bubblies

John Szabo is a Master Sommelier, beverage consultant, wine columnist, and partner and principal critic at winealign.com, an invaluable resource for Canadians struggling to know which wines to buy through their rather unhelpful state liquor board systems.

According to Szabo, Canada, like the US, went through a dark period of mediocre sparkling wine production in the 1970s, but thankfully, "Canada has evolved into a serious source of bubbles that stand with the best from around the world," he tells me. In fact, he adds, "Sparkling wine is the hottest and fastest growing category in the Canadian wine industry." So I asked Szabo to share his insider's picks.

Lightfoot & Wolfville Nova Scotia Brut Nature Blanc de Blancs (V; 12% ABV; $$$)

Two neighboring organic- and biodynamic-certified vineyards overlook the Bay of Fundy in Nova Scotia's Annapolis Valley, making for a never-ending dramatic show; the bay's tides rise and drop a full 50 vertical feet (15 m) daily, revealing the seafloor and towering spires of rock that turn into water and islands just a few hours later. According to Szabo, the standout structure, acidity, and flavor in this sparkling Chardonnay from a couple of eighth-generation farmers can be attributed to a rare soil type, called Wolfville.

Hinterland "Les Etoiles" Prince Edward County Ontario Traditional Method Sparkling Wine (V; 12% ABV; $$$)

Prince Edward County[13] is a headland on the north shore of Lake Ontario that's endangered by deep freezes almost every winter, which makes vinetending interesting. The payoff is a summer moderated by the lake effect and shallow, stony limestone soils that favor viticulture. This family-run sparkling-wine specialist makes a range that Szabo admires, and he describes "Les Etoiles" ("the stars") as the winery's most serious cuvée, with more than five years spent on the lees. The blend is Pinot Noir and Chardonnay, with a small addition of Pinot Gris.

Tantalus Vineyards Okanagan Valley Blanc de Blancs
(V; 13.3% ABV; $$)

Its vineyards first planted in 1927, Tantalus is today considered one of Canada's top wineries. This "superb" bubbly is sourced from a single block of Chardonnay vines. The winery's striking labels are designed by renowned Tahltan and Tlingit First Nations artist Dempsey Bob.

Fitzpatrick "Fitz Brut" Okanagan Valley Sparkling Wine (V; 11.6% ABV; $$)

Now-retired Canadian senator Ross Fitzpatrick and his family built their winegrowing reputation at the pioneering CedarCreek Estate Winery in British Columbia. Fitzpatrick, at Greata Ranch, a former fruit orchard on the west side of Lake Okanagan, was designed specifically for premium bubble production, according to Szabo, and "the intention shows in the quality."

---

[13] *Not to be confused with Prince Edward Island, near New Brunswick and Nova Scotia on the east coast of Canada.*

New Zealand

In the Southern Hemisphere, Christmas and New Year's Eve happen when the sun is shining bright and everyone's lying on the beach in a bikini. Which means that bubbly is the beverage to have in hand. Who needs rich red wine under such conditions?

Fortunately the Kiwis are located relatively close to Antarctica, as the globe rolls, and thus blessed with a cool maritime climate, where high-acid fruit is a given, and Pinot Noir and Chardonnay, the two big guns in the world of bubbly, thrive.

The cuisine couldn't be better for sparkling wine: Seafood reigns supreme, fish-and-chips are a staple, the local cheeses are superb, and the national dessert is the weightless, meringuey Pavlova, often with kiwi slices adorning the top. With apologies to Sauv Blanc, I am not sure why anyone would drink anything other than fine locally produced fizz.

MARLBOROUGH

Although Sauvignon Blanc accounts for more than 60 percent of the region's vineyard land, Marlborough's new guard of sparkling wines come firmly from the Chardonnay–Pinot Noir camp. The same strong maritime winds, hillside sites, and incessant sunshine that makes the Sauv Blancs from the South Island smell and taste so zippy and zesty might just be the ideal formula for brisk, racy sparkling-wine fruit.

As if we needed further evidence that New Zealand is in the midst of a golden age of effervescence, behold Méthode Marlborough, a group of winemakers who have created a society to support sparkling-wine production and set baseline quality standards. Any "Méthode Marlborough"–labeled wine is made via the traditional secondary bottle fermentation and aged for a minimum of eighteen months prior to disgorgement.

No. 1 Family Estate Rosé
(NV; 12.5% ABV; $$$)

Its title might be somewhat ridiculous and reductionist, but this really *is* New Zealand's most iconic sparkling wine house, and it was founded by Daniel Le Brun, whose family has been making Champagne since 1750, and who started an eponymous sparkling-wine brand that's today a

Touring New Zealand with Rebecca Gibb

Award-winning journalist Rebecca Gibb is one of only 380 Masters of Wine (MWs) in the world; she's also the author of *The Wines of New Zealand*. "Traditional-method sparkling wine remains a splash in the Sauvignon Blanc sea," Gibb laments. "The country has a climate that is well-suited to making refined traditional-method sparkling wines, but it requires expensive specialist equipment and an understanding bank manager happy to let wine sit on lees for several years before release," she confides. Thus, much of the fizz down here is simple, early-release, drink-now plonk, made via the Charmat method or carbonated, often from Pinot Gris or New Zealand's top grape, Sauvignon Blanc. However, there are a few gems:

Quartz Reef Méthode Traditionnelle Central Otago Blanc de Blancs (V; 12.5% ABV; $$$–$$$$)

"Central," as the locals call it, is a study in extremes. The winters are frigid, the summers are hot, and the arid, tanned landscape looks like it was scratched from the earth by an oversize Otago skink. Welcome to the world's southernmost wine region, in which Austrian-born winemaker Rudi Bauer has planted a biodynamic garden of Eden. "This vintage cuvée is a Chardonnay-dominant sparkling wine that is refined and linear, with almost four years on lees bringing rich autolysis-derived savory characters," says Gibb.

Cloudy Bay "Pelorus" Marlborough Brut (V; 12.8% ABV; $$)

In addition to Sauvignon Blanc, Cloudy Bay turns out delicious Pinot Noir and Chardonnay, and a 1987 collaboration with Schramsberg (California) winemaker Harold Osborne led to its acquisition three years later by Champagne house Veuve Clicquot. If you get to New Zealand, advises Gibb, it's worthwhile to seek out the vintage version of the Pelorus, which "reveals the estate's sparkling credentials." She adds, "A blend of approximately 60 percent Pinot Noir and 40 percent Chardonnay, picked from select low-yielding sites within the Wairau Valley, it spends between four and seven years *en tirage*, depending on the vintage, producing a richer, complex style."

household name in New Zealand. By the time they sold that business, the Le Bruns were New Zealand wine royalty. According to our expert Rebecca Gibb, a large proportion of Marlborough's best sparkling wines undergo their *tirage* and *dosage* at No. 1 Family Estate.

The house wines tend to be rich and sumptuous, and this pale-peach 100 percent Pinot Noir rosé has enough ripe fruit flavor of its own that it required no dosage. It has elegant aromatics of rose petal and lavender, a soft texture with fine-beaded bubbles, and a lemony finish.

Australia

In Australia—and New Zealand, it should be added, which is culturally similar in this regard—it is generally agreed that everyone deserves to party, and thus everyone should have access to good sparkling wine.

In addition to some lovely traditionally French-styled bubblies and lots of cheap slush, Australia has something special to offer, and that's Shiraz. No, not Blanc de Noirs, but red Shiraz that's fizzy. This is not light like a Lambrusco. This is an inky-dark, full-throttle red wine with notes of black currant and black pepper. The best examples are bottle-fermented according to the traditional method, and you will either love them or hate them. There's no in between, and there are very few exported. Our expert Tyson Stelzer will recommend the best of these in the box on the opposite page. But first . . .

TASMANIA

When one considers that Champagne is located at a latitude of approximately 49 degrees North, one can see why Australia is a bit too equatorially inclined to give proper bubbly a decent shot. Even the Mornington Peninsula, a Chardonnay-growing region at the southernmost coast of the mainland, can't quite hit the necessary acidity levels, what with its location at 38 degrees South.

Tasmania to the rescue. This wild, mountainous island, 271 miles (436 km) south of Melbourne, is prone to rainstorms and jaunty maritime gales, as well as home to the Tasmanian devil, the wombat, and the platypus. Summer temperatures are mild, and there are four true seasons—as opposed to many parts of Australia, where it's either "wet" or "dry," in true tropical style.

....

Jansz "Premium Cuvée" Pipers River Tasmania Brut
(NV; 12% ABV; $$)

Jansz debuted in 1986 as an experimental partnership between the Grande Marque maison Louis Roederer and a Tasmanian winery. This "méthode Tasmanoise" wine hits all the marks, with creamy aromatics that develop notes of honey, strawberry, and balsamic in the glass. The bubbles are more sturdy than elegant, but heck, this is a reasonably priced bottle from one of the world's most remote wine regions.

Tyson Stelzer on Australia's Vinous Seltzer

Award-winning wine writer and television personality Tyson Stelzer is the author of the annually updated *The Champagne Guide*. His home base is Brisbane, so he gets to taste a lot of Aussie bubblies.

According to Stelzer, Australian sparkling-wine consumption has increased threefold over the past decade, placing Aussies as the highest per-capita fizz consumers outside of Europe. Here are his must-try recommendations:

Seppelt "Show Sparkling" Limited-Release Great Western Shiraz (V; 13.5% ABV; $$$$)

"Seppelt made its first sparkling Shiraz in the Great Western region of Victoria in 1893 and its flagship 'Show Sparkling' remains the pinnacle of Australian sparkling wines," says Stelzer. (The name refers to the fact that the wine has won countless awards at wine shows.) "Its powder-fine tannin profile elevates it to astonishing longevity. Lobbed into the market at a decade of age, it is glorious on release and will unravel magnificently in time," avers Stelzer.

House of Arras Tasmania "Grand Vintage" Méthode Traditionnelle (V; 12.5% ABV; $$$$)

"Tasmania's entire sparkling production would fit into Champagne ninety times—and most of it is consumed in Australia—but it is worth hunting down," says Stelzer. House of Arras is Australia's most-awarded sparkling-wine house, he adds, thanks to "Grand Vintage," which he describes as "the ultimate blend." This extended-tirage Chardonnay-Pinot blend ages on the lees for a minimum of seven years.

Bellebonne Tasmania Vintage Rosé (V; 12% ABV; $$$)

Natalie Fryar, the former winemaker at Jansz (see previous page), works on a number of projects, including an artisan gin partnership with Kim Seagram (yes, *that* Seagram). But as far as Stelzer is concerned, Fryar's small personal wine label, Bellebonne, is her most exciting production. He describes this wine as balancing an "airy freedom, somehow lighter and more delicate than any before it, with the deep, resonant presence of red fruits."

South Africa

The southern tip of South Africa is possibly the most heart-poundingly stunning spot on the planet, what with the Atlantic and Indian Oceans meeting, waves crashing against rocky outcroppings, cliffs rising above colorful blankets of flowering *fynbos* (shrubs), sandstone mountains towering over towns, and penguins and ostriches wandering around like it's not weird at all that they should live in the same place. The human landscape is a bit more complicated, what with society still physically segregated by neighborhood and township, and eleven official languages spoken.

South Africans have a real thirst for light, frisky wines, producing almost twice as much white as they do red. Chenin Blanc, best-known for making floral Loire Valley whites from villages such as Vouvray, is the most prolific variety here, accounting for nearly 20 percent of plantings. Once upon a time, it was called "Steen" locally, and it was overcropped and made some seriously uninspiring wines, but times have changed and the Chenin is getting better and better.

Chardonnay accounts for just 7 percent of production, and Pinot Noir barely registers (a hybrid with Cinsault, called Pinotage, grows much better here), but there are enough windblown, high-elevation, south-and-east-facing vineyard sites for this Mediterranean climate to support some halfway-decent traditional-method wines, which are referred to as *méthode cap classique* (MCC) on labels, because the South Africans are not like the lazy Americans who still insist on using *"méthode Champenoise"* for no good reason.

might be tempted to smooth over any imperfections in the fruit with the distraction of a *dosage*. This blend of 77 percent Pinot Noir, 23 percent Chardonnay—with the disgorgement date on the back—sticks the landing. Appealing initial aromatic hits of apple, peach, citrus, pear, and bread dough move into more savory, toasty territory as the wine warms up. Owner Antony Beck clearly has a nose for bubbly, and as we went to press, he had recently launched a sparkling-wine-focused venture, Lytle-Barnett, in Oregon.

M·A·N Family Wines South Africa Sparkling Brut Chenin Blanc (NV; 12% ABV; $–$$)

Sometimes, a carbonated quaffer is just the right thing. This fizzy Chenin is a powder-puff of a wine, all simple notes of fresh flowers, white peaches, vanilla bean, and mandarin orange, appropriate for brunch on the beach.

Graham Beck "Premier Cuvée" South Africa Méthode Cap Classique Brut Zero (V; 12% ABV; $$$)

A Brut Zero is a bold move, in that it can be so difficult to grow Pinot Noir in South Africa that one

Simonsig "Kaapse Vonkel" South Africa Méthode Cap Classique Brut (V; 12% ABV; $$)

In the 1960s, Simonsig introduced European grape varieties such as Chardonnay to the nation, and was the first to make bottle-fermented sparkling wine. This blend of nearly half-and-half Pinot Noir and Chardonnay, rounded out with Pinot Meunier, has some odd aromatics: oysters, mussels, Brie, seaweed, musk. I'll give my assistant, Zoe, the last (positive) word: "It's like walking on a South African beach in a brand-new leather jacket!"

And cut. Who's up for a glass of bubbly?

$$$$$

England
Nyetimber

$$$

England
Ridgeview

$$$

England
Gusbourne

$$$

England
Hambledon

$$$

Cornwall
Camel Valley

$$

Nova Scotia
Benjamin Bridge

$$

Okanagan Valley
Blue Mountain

$$

Niagara Peninsula
Henry of Pelham

$$$

Niagara Peninsula
Cave Spring

$$$

Niagara Peninsula
Hidden Bench

$$

Niagara Peninsula
Trius

$$$

Nova Scotia
Lightfoot & Wolfville

$$

Ontario

Hinterland

$$

Okanagan Valley

Tantalus

$$

Okanagan Valley

Fitzpatrick

$$$

Marlborough

No. 1 Family Estate

$$$-$$$$

Central Otago

Quartz Reef

$$

Marlborough

Cloudy Bay

$$

Tasmania

Jansz

$$$$

Great Western

Seppelt

$$$

Tasmania

Bellebonne

$-$$

South Africa

M·A·N

$$$

South Africa

Graham Beck

$$

South Africa

Simonsig

Glossary

additions: There are a lot of things that can be thrown in the pot, so to speak, during the winemaking process. Sulfur dioxide (SO_2) is often used as a preservative. Carboxymethylcellulose (say that three times fast, or just say "CMC") can be used to discourage tartrate crystals from forming, negating the need for cold stabilization. Enzymes may be added to aid in clarification, enhance aromatics, and encourage foaming. Nutrient supplements may be used to speed along fermentation. None of these additions will be obvious in the finished wine, but consumers who prefer a more "natural" wine try to avoid wineries that use a lot of additives.

assemblage: The process of blending various lots of wines to make a base wine. It's pronounced in the French manner: *AH-sem-BLAHJ.*

atmospheric pressure: The force that CO_2 exerts on the inside of a sparkling-wine bottle. Champagne and other traditional-method wines are entombed in their glass prisons at about 6 atmospheres of pressure. Semi-sparkling wines, known as *pétillant* or *frizzante* (a category that includes Pét-Nats and Moscato d'Asti) are closer to 3 atmospheres.

autolytic: Spent yeast cells, aka lees, more or less self-destruct after the second fermentation, and this process is nearly as important as the fermentation itself. It's called autolysis, and it imparts a creamy texture and nutty, briochey aromatics to the wine. Because Champagne tends to age *sur lie* (definition on page 279) in the bottle for longer than any other sparkling wine, it wins the gold medal for autolytic characteristics.

base wine: Standard sparkling wine starts out as a still wine that's high in acid and fairly low in alcohol (approximately 10% ABV). This is called the base wine or *vin clair.* Tasted on its own, a base wine tends to be quite acidic, pungent, and vibrant; the second fermentation softens its sharp edges.

bead: The thread of bubbles that floats up in a sparkling-wine glass, most noticeable in a flute.

biodynamic: This holistic, homeopathic style of farming, drawn from the wisdom of traditional farming cultures, is even more difficult to pull off than organic agriculture. There's a spiritual aspect to biodynamics, as well, which accounts for its new-agey reputation. Many wine enthusiasts believe that biodynamically farmed vineyards are the purest translators of *terroir*.

Blanc de Blancs/Noirs: Literally, "white of whites" or "white of blacks," these terms refer to white Champagnes made either entirely of white grapes (typically Chardonnay)[1] or entirely of black grapes (typically Pinot Noir and Pinot Meunier). I think of Blanc de Blancs as akin to a chamomile-chrysanthemum tea, while Blanc de Noirs is maybe more like hibiscus–red currant tea. Both are delicious, but the first gives me more of a mellow, toasty, hay-and-sunflowers impression, while the second is more earthy, with tart red fruit notes.

bubblemaker:[2] A sparkling winemaker, who may or may not be a troublemaker.

cage: The corks on most sparkling-wine bottles are straining under a tremendous amount of atmospheric pressure. As your grandmother used to say, "You could put someone's eye out with that thing!" The cage is the twisted wire contraption that holds the cork in place; it's also called a *muselet*, from the French word for "muzzle." A "staple," or *agrafe*, is an alternative to a cage. It's a thicker metal bar that looks like a belt buckle and is more or less stapled over the cork.

cépage: Grape variety or varieties in a bottling. The *cépage* of most Blanc de Blancs Champagnes, for example, is Chardonnay.

Champagne: I know *you* know this, but your friends might not know this, so it's worth reviewing: Champagne is the name of a region in France. Thus, as is the case with most European wine designations, it is also the name of a wine. Because for the Europeans, wines are expressions of the places where the grapes are grown. So don't be calling anything other than Champagne from Champagne "Champagne," OK?

chaptalize: It used to be that the base wines in Champagne were *chaptalized*—that is, sugar was added—to make them palatable. These days, thanks to global warming, the practice is less prevalent.

---

[1] *I get why Blanc de Blancs or Noirs makes sense when the wine is made from two white or black grapes, like Chardonnay and Pinot Blanc or Pinot Noir and Pinot Meunier. But why use the plural* Blancs *and* Noirs *on the label when the wine is made from just one grape variety? Hugh Davies, president and head bubblemaker at Schramsberg, in California, explained it to me this way: "For us, the plural* Blancs *refers to the fact that we source the fruit from multiple vineyards, not the inclusion of another white grape variety like Pinot Blanc."*

[2] *I am not sure if this is actually a term, but I have been using it because one can only type "winemaker" so many times.*

coupage: A blend of wines from different origins or grape varieties. An *assemblage*, by contrast, is a blend of wines of the same origin or the same vintage.

Crémant: A term for sparkling wine in France and Luxembourg.

Cru: In Champagne, this term is used to refer to the villages where the vineyards have been highly rated by the French authorities. Grand Cru vineyard sites are generally accepted to be the best, and Premier Cru the second-best.

cuvée: This term typically means a blend of grapes, but in Champagne, it is also used to describe the first juice to come out of the press. A little context is all that's needed to discern which meaning is implied.

disgorgement/release date: More and more high-end traditional-method sparkling wine labels (and some corks) these days are printed with a series of small numerals, usually on the back label, but sometimes the front. These indicate the date when the wine was disgorged, and it is helpful if you're wondering how long a non-vintage cuvée has been sitting around or if a vintage wine has aged long enough. It's particularly useful for sommeliers who must manage large restaurant cellars. But for novice enthusiasts, it can assist in developing one's own personal sense of how much bottle age you like on a Champagne after disgorgement. In the case of Italian Prosecco or Lambrusco, the little numbers on the label indicate when the wine was bottled. The finest producers keep their juice in hermetically sealed tanks, then bottle their wines throughout the year to ensure that they are constantly releasing a fresh product. In this case, it's generally a good idea to drink the wine as soon after the date stamp as possible, so put Prosecco in your fridge rather than your cellar.

dosage (doh-SAHJ): The final, optional addition of *liqueur d'expédition* (wine-sugar solution) to sparkling Champagne, not to be confused with the practice of chaptalizing the base wine. (No-*dosage* wine is called "Brut Nature," or "Brut Zero.") The goal of this step isn't sweetness, but balance. Champagne expert Peter Liem has pointed out that some wines taste more bitter *with* a *dosage* than without it, and I agree: I find that an overgenerous *dosage* can result in a slightly metallic flavor, more like aspartame than sugar. Oregon sommelier David Speer, who founded the Champagne bar Ambonnay, describes this as the "orange juice-and-toothpaste effect," in which "the sugar brings out such a contrast with the acid that both become noticeable." If you want to really get into the weeds on this topic, ask a winemaker whether she prefers to sweeten her *dosage* with MCR (*moût concentré rectifié*— basically, concentrated grape juice), cane sugar, or something else entirely.

frizzante: See <u>atmospheric pres-sure</u>, page 274.

Grandes Marques: A term used for the most prestigious of the large Champagne houses.

grower: See <u>RM</u>, page 278.

late disgorged (LD): A traditional-method wine that has aged *en tirage* (in the bottle, on the lees) for a surplus number of years, well past the release date of the rest of the vintage. LD wines, also referred to as *récemment dégorgé* (RD) and *dégorgement tardif* (DT), tend to be pricey, because by holding on to their own inventory, the wineries are losing out on potential sales. Because the lees suppress oxygen, LD wines are surprisingly fresh given their age, while at the same time, they're more complex—in short, a rare treat.

lieu-dit: A significant single vine-yard that's not an officially recog-nized Cru, but is still named on the label of a "vineyard-designate" (as we say in winespeak) bottling.

maison: French for "house," used to refer to wineries in the Cham-pagne region.

mousse: French for "foam."

mousseux: French for "sparkling," sometimes used on wine labels to refer to wines that are neither Champagnes nor Crémants.

négociant: A wine-production firm that purchases grapes, juice, wine, or all three from an array of small grower-producers and blends the wines together to make a pleasing cuvée.

NM: Most of the wine from Champagne comes from the large houses, or *négociants manipu-lants*. They buy grapes, juice, or wine from smaller growers, before blending it together and marketing it under their own label.

NV: Sparkling wine is an oddity (along with fortified wine) in that much of it tends to be non-vintage, or NV for short. MV, or multi-vintage, would be the better term, since winemakers blend base wines from multiple vintages in order to maintain a recognizable house style year after year. Cham-pagne houses have been sharing more information as of late about their mysterious NV bottlings.

perlage: Effervescence in wines. The bubbles streaming upward in the glass can be said to resemble a string of pearls. Critics will often evaluate a sparkling wine based on how fine, abundant, or consistent the *perlage* is.

perpetual cuvée: A method of fractionally blending base wines from previous vintages to make a non-vintage cuvée that's similar to a solera (see page 278)—a term you might know if you are keen on Sherry. Each year, the vintner bottles a portion of the perpetual cuvée, aka perpetual reserve, for the secondary fermentation, then adds the current year's base wine to top the barrels off. Over time, as the number of wines in the cuvée increases, it grows more and more complex.

Prestige Cuvée: A very special, very expensive blend, from a top Champagne house. Also called a Tête de Cuvée.

prise de mousse: This term translates as "foam creation" and refers to the second fermentation.

RM: A *récoltant manipulant* (literally "grower maker," but referred to simply as a "grower") is a small family operation that grows and vinifies its own grapes under its own label. A similar term, "Pro-priétaires de Vignes," is another indicator that the winery owns and farms its own vines.

spumante: A term used to describe fully sparkling wines in Italy, in contrast to the more lightly sparkling varieties known as *frizzante*. See atmospheric pressure, page 274.

solera: This term is often thrown around by sparkling winemakers who are actually working with perpetual cuvées (see page 277). Purists demur at this loose usage, saying that the barrels found in the soleras of Spanish Sherry country typically have layers of *flor*, or yeast, growing in them. That said,

With My Apologies to Japan

One must draw the line somewhere, and for this book, the line was a row of grapevines. So I didn't write about all the other delicious sparkling beverages that are in their prime right now: the glorious new wave of dry foamy ciders made from heirloom apples, for example. Or, sadly, fizzy sake.

The Japanese term for "sparkling" is the impossibly charming onomatopoeic "shuwa shuwa," for the sound of fizz. As of 2017, the island nation ranked third in the world for Champagne imports, just after the US and the UK. And, in 2016, the Japan Awasake Association was founded to promote high-quality rice wines made sparkling by secondary fermentation.

Even the simplest carbonated sake can be a delight. Take, for example, Hideyoshi's "LaChamte," a charming semisweet soda pop of a rice wine. I dare you not to smile after taking a sip. Bubbles just do that to a person.

there are a few sparkling wine-makers who do embrace *flor*. (See page 65 for more on this.)

sur lattes: This means "on the slats," referring to the thin layers of wood that separate the bottles when they are resting on their sides, *en tirage* (see below).

sur lie: Traditional-method sparkling wines can spend time *sur lie*, or "on the lees," twice: First, as with many still wines, if the winemaker chooses not to "rack off," or remove, the lees, the base wine gleans richness from the spent yeast cells at the bottom of the barrel or tank. (Stirring the lees amplifies the effect.) Second, there is the all-important aging *sur lie en tirage*, or in the bottle, where the development of flavor, texture, and *mousse* has to do with the time the wine spends bottle-aging on the lees.

terroir: How are wine pros able to blind-identify bottles, going on sniff and sip alone? They will tell you it's the *terroir*, or sense of place, that a wine transmits. It can be difficult to pinpoint *terroir* in sparkling wines because the bubbles can be distracting, but if you taste numerous single-vineyard bottlings from a single producer, you'll notice that one might be earthier, another fruitier, another more minerally. These differences can be attributed to each plot of land's particular soil type, micro-climate, surrounding ecosystem, and more, all of which add up to *terroir*.

Tête de Cuvée: A Champagne house's top-of-the-line blend, also known as a Prestige Cuvée (see previous page). Famous examples include Moët & Chandon's Dom Pérignon, Louis Roederer's Cristal, Pol Roger's Sir Winston Churchill, and Taittinger's Comtes de Champagne.

tirage **(tee-RAHJ):** This literally translates as "pulling," and refers to the act of bottling, when the wine is pulled from the barrel into the bottle. In Champagne, the term "aging *en tirage*" refers to aging in the bottle, specifically on the lees after the *liqueur de tirage* has been added.

vintage: In Champagne, most wines are NV blends. Only the best wines from the best vintages are bottled on their own. That said, farming methods have advanced to the point where, for most *maisons*, every year is a "vintage" year.

Online Shopping Guide

(HOW TO GET THE GOOD STUFF AT YOUR DOORSTEP)

ASTOR WINES & SPIRITS

astorwines.com

New York, NY

This capacious Greenwich Village retail store has an easy-to-navigate site offering a broad selection ranging from bargain Lambrusco to high-end Champagne.

CAVEAU SELECTIONS

caveauselections.com

Portland, OR

A direct importer of artisan wines from Champagne and Burgundy. Join the Champagne wine club to receive regular shipments, or download the inventory spreadsheet to see what's currently in stock.

FAT CORK

fatcork.com

Seattle, WA

An online wine shop devoted entirely to direct imports of Champagnes from under-the-radar family growers, offering quarterly club memberships. The Seattle studio opens once a month for tastings.

HELEN'S WINES

helenswines.com

Los Angeles, CA (two locations)

An LA-based natural-wine trendsetter that curates rare finds from Europe and the US. The Champagne selection is small but superb.

K&L WINE MERCHANTS

klwines.com

Redwood City, San Francisco, and Hollywood, CA

Nearly five hundred sparkling selections and multiple retail-store locations make this a major player in fine wine. Online customers can join a Champagne club for regular shipments.

THE RARE WINE CO.

rarewineco.com

Brisbane, CA

One of the country's finest importers also sells wine retail through its website. A source for reliably aged vintage Champagne.

VINLEY MARKET

vinleymarket.com

Los Angeles, CA

An online monthly wine subscription service known for its affordable Rosé & Bubbles box and elegant gift presentations. Chic and millennial-focused, the site reflects owner Erin Vaughen Hlynsky's savvy.

WINE.COM

wine.com

Nationwide

With warehouses located all over the US, this online retailer offers an unparalleled selection and ships quickly. Wine experts are available via chat windows for instantaneous advice.

Bibliography

(JUST IN CASE YOU WANT TO BUBBLE-CHECK)

Boucoiran, Louis. Dictionnaire Analogique et Étymologique des Idiomes Méridionaux. Vol. 3. Leipzig and Paris: Welter, 1898.

Buchanan, Robert, and Nicholas Longworth. The Culture of the Grape, and Wine-Making. Cincinnati: Moore, Wilstach, Keys & Co., 1861.

Carosso, Vincent P. The California Wine Industry, 1830–1895: A Study of the Formative Years. Berkeley: University of California Press, 1951.

Cole, Katherine. "A New Wave of Umami Wines Blooms Under Flor." SevenFifty Daily, October 19, 2018. https://daily.sevenfifty.com/a-new-wave -of-umami-wines-blooms-under-flor.

Cole, Katherine, "Moscato May Be Out, But Saracco is Still In." SevenFifty Daily, June 12, 2018. https://daily.sevenfifty. com/moscato-may-be-out-but-saracco -is-still-in.

Cole, Katherine. "Why Portland Is Amer- ica's Champagne Capital." SevenFifty Daily, December 19, 2018. https://daily.sevenfifty.com/why-portland -is-americas-champagne-capital.

Columbus, Courtney. "Meet the Indiana Jones of Ancient Ales and Extreme Beverages." The Salt, June 30, 2017. https://www.npr.org/sections/thesalt /2017/06/30/532959384/meet-the -indiana-jones-of-ancient-ales-and -extreme-beverages.

D'Agata, Ian. Native Wine Grapes of Italy. Berkeley: University of California Press, 2014.

de Catel, Guillaume. Memoires de L'histoire du Languedoc: Curieusement et Fidelement Recueillis. Toulouse: Arnaud Colomiez, 1633.

Ferriter, Diarmaid. "Inglorious Empire: What the British Did to India." Irish Times, March 4, 2017.

Figiel, Richard. Circle of Vines: The Story of New York Wine. Albany: Excelsior Editions/State University of New York Press, 2014.

Franciacorta. "Origins and History." http://www.franciacorta.net/en /viticulture/origin.

Gabay, Elizabeth. "Clairette de Die— The Importance of Direction." Elizabeth Gabay MW. September 26, 2014. https://elizabethgabay.com/2014/09/26 /visit-to-clairette-de-die-the-importance -of-direction.

Grandes Marques & Maisons de Cham- pagne. "The Making of Sparkling Wine." https://maisons-champagne.com/en /encyclopedias/champagne-guest-book /before-sparkling-champagne/the -nineteenth-century/article/the-making -of-sparkling-wine.

Guy, Kolleen M. When Champagne Became French: Wine and the Making of a National Identity. Baltimore: Johns Hopkins University Press, 2003.

Illson, Murray. "Count de Vogüé Dies: War Hero Ran Moët." New York Times, October 24, 1976.

International Wine Review. "Prosecco, Prosecco Superiore, & Cartizze: Incred- ible Values from the Best Producers." November 13, 2017. http://i-winereview .com/blog/index.php/2017/11/13 /prosecco-prosecco-superiore-cartizze -incredible-values-from-the-best-producers.

Jefford, Andrew. "Jefford on Monday: Enigma Variations" Decanter, February 20, 2017. www.decanter.com/wine-news/opinion /jefford-on-monday/355237-355237.

Junyent, Francesc Valls. "Compitiendo con el Champagne: La industria española de los vinos espumosos antes de la Guerra Civil." Comunicación presentada al VIII Congreso de la Asociación Española de Historia Económica. Departament d'Història i Institucions Econòmiques, Universitat de Barcelona, 2005. www.usc.es/estaticos/congresos/histec05/b4_valls_junyent.pdf.

Kladstrup, Don, and Petie Kladstrup, Wine & War: The French, the Nazis, and the Battle for France's Greatest Treasure. New York: Broadway Books, 2002.

Liger-Belair, Gérard. Uncorked: The Science of Champagne. Princeton: Princeton University Press, 2004.

Lucan. Civil War. Translated by Brian Walters. Indianapolis: Hackett Publishing Company, 2015.

Lukacs, Paul. Inventing Wine: A New History of One of the World's Most Ancient Pleasures. New York: Norton, 2012.

Lynch, Kermit. Adventures on the Wine Route: A Wine Buyer's Tour of France. New York: Farrar, Strauss and Giroux, 2013.

Mazzeo, Tilar J. The Widow Clicquot: The Story of a Champagne Empire and the Woman Who Ruled It. New York: HarperCollins, 2008.

McGinty, Brian. A Toast to Eclipse: Arpad Haraszthy and the Sparkling Wine of Old San Francisco. Norman: University of Oklahoma Press, 2012.

McGovern, Patrick. Uncorking the Past: The Quest for Wine, Beer, and Other Alcoholic Beverages. Berkeley: University of California Press, 2009.

Miller, Montserrat. Feeding Barcelona, 1714–1975: Public Market Halls, Social Networks, and Consumer Culture. Baton Rouge: Louisiana State University Press, 2015.

Mount, Ian. The Vineyard at the End of the World: Maverick Winemakers and the Rebirth of Malbec. New York: W. W. Norton, 2012.

Napjus, Alison. "Revealing Champagne's Secrets." Wine Spectator, December 31, 2018–January 15, 2019.

Osservatorio Economico Vini. "Caesar and Cleopatra: The Irrefutable Evidence of Latin Texts." https://www.ovse.org/homepage.cfm?idContent=63.

Phillips, Rod. French Wine: A History. Berkeley: University of California Press, 2017.

Pinney, Thomas. The Makers of American Wine: A Record of Two Hundred Years. Berkeley: University of California Press, 2012.

Pliny the Elder. Delphi Classics Complete Works of Pliny the Elder. Hastings, UK: Delphi Classics, 2015.

Ragusa News. "Prosecco in Sicilia? Ma anche no!" February 10, 2016. https://www.ragusanews.com/2016/02/10/attualita/prosecco-in-sicilia-ma-anche-no/62352.

Razzo, Natalia. "Exclusive: Sparkling Wine Driving Industry Growth in 2017." Shanken News Daily, October 18, 2017. http://www.shankennewsdaily.com/index.php/2017/10/18/19400/exclusive-sparkling-wine-driving-industry-growth-2017.

Redding, Cyrus. A History and Description of Modern Wines. London: Henry G. Bohn, 1851.

Simon, André Louis. History of the Champagne Trade in England. London: Wyman and Sons, Ltd., 1905.

Stevenson, Tom. Did the Italians Invent Sparkling Wine? An Analysis of the Evidence of Chapter 21 of De Salubri Potu Dissertatio. Gloucester, UK: Berkeley House, 2014.

Stevenson, Tom, and Essi Avellan. Christie's World Encyclopedia of Champagne & Sparkling Wine. New York: Sterling Epicure, 2014.

Torelló Mata, Agustí, as told to Josep Forns Varias. Cava, Where Are You Headed? The Legacy of Agustí Torelló Mata. Vilafranca del Penedès: Edicions i Propostes Culturals Andana, 2015.

Varro, Marcus Terentius. The Three Books of M. Terentius Varro Concerning Agriculture. Translated by Reverend T. Owen. Oxford: Oxford University Press, 1800.

Vinitaly Wine Club. "Guide to Lambrusco." https://www.vinitalyclub.com/en/explore/blog/guide-lambrusco-brief-history-long-past.

Virgil. Aeneid. Translated by Frederick Ahl. Oxford: Oxford University Press, 2007.

Whitehouse, David. Glass: A Short History. Washington, DC: Smithsonian Books, 2012.

Wondrich, David. Imbibe! From Absinthe Cocktail to Whiskey Smash, a Salute in Stories and Drinks to "Professor" Jerry Thomas, Pioneer of the American Bar. New York: Perigree, 2015.

Work, Henry H. The Shape of Wine: Its Packaging Revolution. New York: Routledge, 2019.

Acknowledgments

The author would like to thank her enablers: the many sparkling wine importers, collectors, and producers who opened their doors and their cellars to her. Many of those doors were cracked open by editorial assistant Zoe Davis, who hunted down bottle images, set up appointments, checked prices and alcohol levels, and helped the author to understand the perplexing Pét-Nat palates of kids these days.

The author is also most grateful to editor Laura Dozier, designer Sebit Min, publisher Michael Jacobs, and the rest of the talented team at Abrams. Illustrator Mercedes Leon deserves a special round of applause for having a zanier sense of humor than the author and being game to draw *anything*.

She isn't sure why her family cheered her on when it felt like lunacy to write another book, but she could not have done it without their support. Her children are angels and her parents are her saving grace. Her employers, too, must be thanked for their understanding when she disappeared for weeks at a time and returned complaining of being "tired" of "too much Champagne."

Finally, she would like to thank her dentist for getting her through a year of high-acid assaults on her teeth and gums. And her accountant for helping her to write off all of that "research."

Photo Credit

Profound thanks to Outshinery, a miraculous service that generates picture-perfect bottle photography from label art alone. Outshinery stepped in during the design phase to ensure that our "Bottle Shop" spreads looked sharp. Check out their bottle image-generation software at outshinery.com.

Index

Editor: Laura Dozier
Designer: Sebit Min
Production Manager: Rachael Marks

Library of Congress Control Number: 2020931260

ISBN: 978-1-4197-47557
eISBN: 978-1-64700-178-0

Text copyright © 2021 Katherine Cole
Illustrations copyright © 2021 Mercedes Leon

Cover © 2021 Abrams

Published in 2021 by Abrams Image, an imprint of ABRAMS. All
rights reserved. No portion of this book may be reproduced, stored
in a retrieval system, or transmitted in any form or by any means,
mechanical, electronic, photocopying, recording, or otherwise,
without written permission from the publisher.

Printed and bound in China
10 9 8 7 6 5 4 3 2 1

Abrams Image books are available at special discounts when purchased in quantity for premiums and promotions as well as fund-
raising or educational use. Special editions can also be created to
specification. For details, contact specialsales@abramsbooks.com
or the address below.

Abrams Image® is a registered trademark of Harry N. Abrams, Inc.

ABRAMS The Art of Books
195 Broadway, New York, NY 10007
abramsbooks.com